HAMMERHEAD SIX

HAMMERHEAD SIX

HOW GREEN BERETS WAGED AN UNCONVENTIONAL
WAR AGAINST THE TALIBAN TO WIN IN AFGHANISTAN'S
DEADLY PECH VALLEY

RONALD FRY
Captain, U.S. Special Forces

WITH TAD TULEJA

NEW YORK   BOSTON

Hachette Books
Hachette Book Group
1290 Avenue of the Americas
New York, NY 10104

www.HachetteBookGroup.com

Printed in the United States of America

RRD-H

First edition: January 2016
10 9 8 7 6 5 4 3 2 1

Hachette Books is a division of Hachette Book Group, Inc.

The publisher is not responsible for websites (or their content)
that are not owned by the publisher.

Library of Congress Cataloging-in-Publication Data has been applied for.

Contents

PART III
Spring 2004

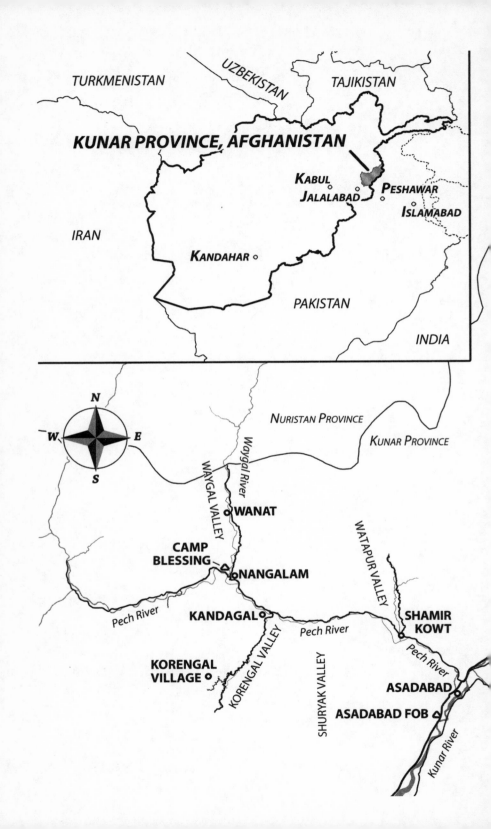

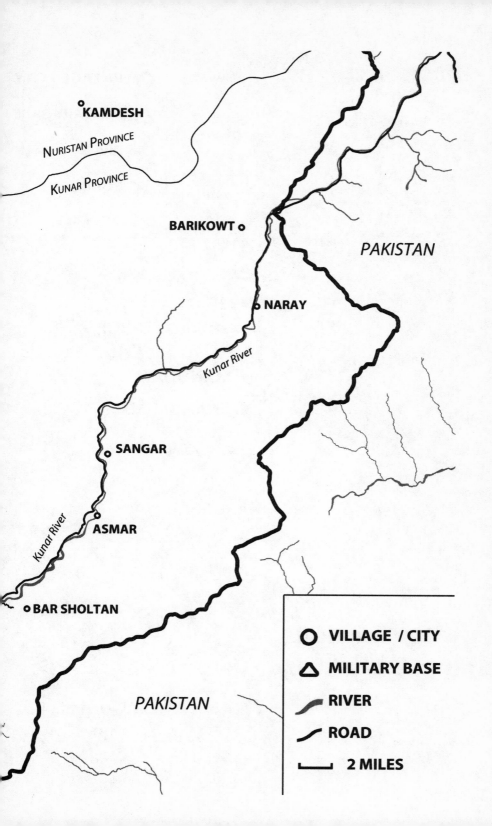

KAMDESH

NURISTAN PROVINCE

KUNAR PROVINCE

BARIKOWT

PAKISTAN

NARAY

Kunar River

SANGAR

Kunar River

ASMAR

BAR SHOLTAN

PAKISTAN

VILLAGE / CITY

MILITARY BASE

RIVER

ROAD

2 MILES

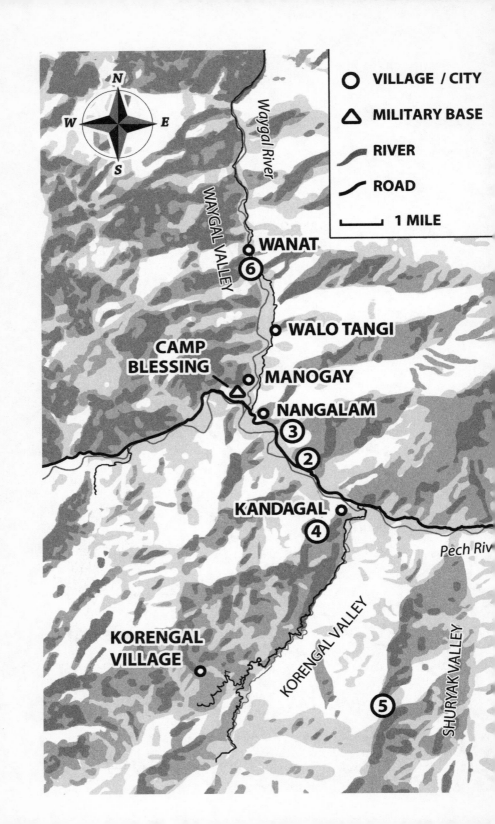

1. Ambush Nov. 2003
2. IED Attack Dec. 2003
3. Vehicle Checkpoint shooting Mar. 2004
4. Vicinity of enemy rocket launch sites
5. Vicinity of Operation Red Wings events 2005
6. Site of Wanat attack, 9 Americans KIA, 2008

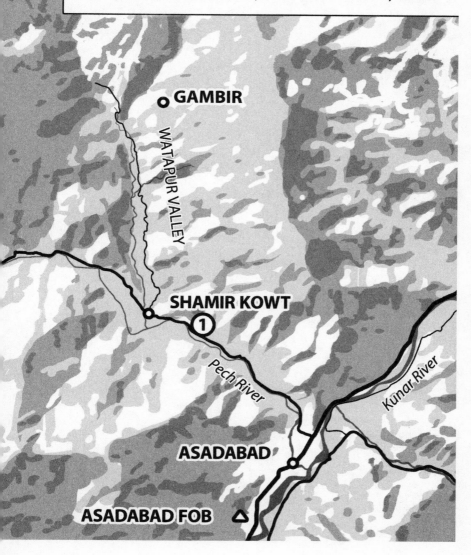

Author's Note

Green Berets don't generally chronicle their adventures, as that goes against our "quiet professional" ethos. For more than a decade, despite urging by journalists, friends, and veterans, I refused to put the story of the Camp Blessing experiment to paper, as the events we lived through seemed too personal. Eventually, though, out of a responsibility to share the valuable lessons we learned with the next generation of unconventional warriors, and also in deference to that part of my soul that has never left an obscure village in the Pech Valley, I decided to write this memoir about what our time in Afghanistan had taught me.

Some of the chapters were written with ease, recounting memories of a modern-day warrior-king and commander in a foreign land. Several chapters were written painfully, reluctantly, and with trembling hands. For the reader who has never been to the Pech Valley, it may be hard to believe that such a place, with such people, really exists. The veteran reader who has had the privilege of placing his boots on that bloody soil will know that it can sometimes feel all too real.

In a country whose past has earned it the sobriquet "Graveyard of Empires," the Pech Valley, in Afghanistan's northeastern Kunar Province, stands out as a particularly brutal killing ground. Here, huddled in the shadow of the Hindu Kush mountains, fiercely independent Pashtun tribesmen have for centuries resisted intrusion in their turbulent affairs. Twice in the nineteenth century they humbled British troops attempting to introduce them to the blessings of Empire. In the 1980s, as the freedom-loving mujahideen, they did the same to an invading Red Army. The Taliban itself was unable to conquer this region. The valley's tribes and clans, engaged endlessly in internecine fighting, unite only to expel foreign invaders. Once that is accomplished, they quickly return to their ancient internal struggles.

The American experience with the Pashtuns of the Pech has not been much different. In 2001, a U.S.-led coalition invaded Afghanistan in the campaign known as Operation Enduring Freedom (OEF). Even though it drove the Taliban government from power, it left the Pech Valley a sanctuary for Taliban, Al Qaeda, and other fighters who united to resist the American invaders and the new Afghan government. For the following decade it remained a hotbed of tribal animosities and insurgent brutality, as well as a death trap for U.S. troops. If you drew a circle on a map around the places in northeastern Afghanistan that have been particularly deadly for Americans—places like Wanat, Korengal, Ganjgal, and Kamdesh—the Pech River would run through the center of that circle. Ten of the twelve Congressional Medals of Honor that have been earned in Afghanistan were awarded for actions conducted on this violent terrain.

A rare exception to this pattern of bloodshed occurred as OEF was entering its third year. In the fall of 2003, a team of U.S. Special Forces (Green Berets) entered the Pech Valley, established the first "A" Camp to be set up since Vietnam, and undertook a struggle against Al Qaeda and Taliban forces for the hearts and minds of the people. These soldiers brought firepower into play when necessary. But as specialists in unconventional warfare (UW), they also repaired schools and clinics, cooperated with village councils in settling disputes, trained local security forces, and created an atmosphere of trust that made them more successful in bringing security to the valley than any outside force had been before. Before this team left the Pech in 2004, hundreds of locals who had fled to Pakistan during the previous decades of conflict were coming home, having heard that the valley was at peace—and that the Americans who had made this possible should be viewed as friends.

This was a dramatic break in a pattern that had lasted for centuries, and at the time this was duly noted by the press and military leaders. *Time, U.S. News and World Report,* and *60 Minutes II* all profiled the Green Berets' success, and senior officers visited their camp hoping to take home replicable lessons from their achievement.

Sadly, once this team of Green Berets left the valley and were replaced, the lessons their unit had learned about cultural sensitivity and mutual respect were forgotten; a more conventional search-and-destroy strategy took over; and very shortly, things reverted to form.

By 2005, the same region that had welcomed the Special Forces troops as peacemakers was the site of the *Lone Survivor* disaster; two years after that, the Korengal Valley, which runs into the Pech, became known as the deadliest place in Afghanistan. Eventually, more than one hundred Americans lost their lives in the greater Pech Valley. In 2011, after years of effort, it was abandoned by U.S. forces to an uncertain future. As pundits draw lessons from all that went wrong in the Pech and Afghanistan, it may be helpful to remember what, briefly, went right.

The official name of the uniquely successful Special Forces unit was Operational Detachment Alpha 936 (ODA 936). Its code name was Hammerhead Six. It was my privilege to have been their field commander. This is our story, and the story of the Afghan people whom we did our best to serve.

In this account of our time in the Pech Valley, I have tried to be as honest as security concerns would allow, highlighting our mistakes as well as our successes, as mistakes were often the most instructive events. This is not a hero story but a human story of camaraderie, loyalty, sacrifice, risk, and hope. I hope that it will aid both the military student and the civilian interested in understanding the nuances of UW to appreciate the depth and difficulty of this type of warfare.

A U.S. Army field manual defines unconventional warfare as

"operations conducted by, with, or through irregular forces in support of a resistance movement, an insurgency, or conventional military operations." In order to be successful at UW, Green Berets work shoulder to shoulder with local soldiers, mercenaries, militiamen, and other indigenous forces. We serve our own country's interests, but to do so effectively our focus, as suggested by our motto *De Oppresso Liber* ("To Free the Oppressed"), is to improve the lives of locals by freeing them from tyranny. We build tight bonds with our indigenous ("indig") allies— bonds that cannot be feigned or developed with an intent to manipulate. This makes UW an emotional as well as a military investment. In this book, I try to convey what that investment meant to one team operating in the gray zone of northeastern Afghanistan.

The book does not have a political agenda. I do not claim to be an expert in international affairs, U.S. foreign policy, or Afghan demographics. I confine myself to what I witnessed, over several months, in one troubled corner of the War on Terror. I do not describe every operation that ODA 936 conducted in the Pech Valley but rather some key events and topics that I feel best illustrate the story I want to tell.

Because of the sensitive nature of some of our operations, the manuscript was reviewed and edited where appropriate to protect operational security. Narrative details and conversations have been reconstructed from my own memories, those of my team members, and a journal that I kept while in-country. The names of local Afghans have been changed to protect our allies and friends who are still living there.

I dedicate this book to the many patriots—Americans, coalition allies, and Afghans—who have given their lives to end oppression in Afghanistan. We owe it to them to pursue knowledge and improvement so that we can focus on winning the unconventional wars that we fight. I hope this work will honor the sacrifices both of the fallen and of those who struggled against terror in that fabled land and came home carrying the ghosts of Afghanistan with them.

I destroy my enemy by making him my friend.

—Afghan proverb

When ye are in the service of your fellow beings ye are only in the service of your God.

—Mosiah 2:17

No matter how powerful one's armies, in order to enter a country one needs the goodwill of the inhabitants.

—Niccolo Machiavelli

Preface

Kunar Province,
November 2003

Along the ridge the column of men moved eastward. Walking single file, they dodged branches and skipped from boulder to boulder with the hardy grace of people at home in the mountains. From a distance, they might have been mistaken for carefree hikers, braving the half-light chill of the Afghan morning. Up close it was clear that their mission was not recreational.

The leader, tall and nimble, wore the black turban that signified his loyalty to the Taliban, the brutal fundamentalist government that a Western coalition had recently driven from power. A few others were similarly dressed, although most wore floppy *pakols*—the traditional woolen caps of Afghan males. All sported trim beards, and all but one carried firearms.

Someone with an eye for weapons would have seen in these arms the traces of Afghanistan's troubled history. Most of the band carried the Kalashnikov rifles—the jihadi-favored AK-47s—that the Soviets had used in vain against Afghanistan's celebrated "fighters for God," the mujahideen. Hundreds, perhaps thousands, of these rifles had been taken from slain Russian soldiers in the 1980s, and several of the young men walking along the ridge this morning had inherited their arms from their mujahideen fathers or uncles.

One of the band carried a British-made Lee-Enfield, a bolt-action relic that the CIA had provided the mujahideen for their fight against the Russians. On another's shoulder, resting as casually as a fishing pole, was the thick, deadly tube of a rocket launcher. Two men carried between them a DShK machine gun, while their comrades shared the burden of its ammunition, wearing belts of linked 12.7mm rounds across their chests like lost Mexican revolutionaries.

The one unarmed figure was a youngster—his faint beard betraying his youth—who was last in the line. The knife at his belt suggested that his elders would not outdo him in fierceness, but that was his only weapon. His right hand held a video camera. Every few minutes he would flick it on to film his comrades and then, panning to the right, the scrubby incline that led to the valley below.

Two or three hundred yards down the slope a dirt road ran alongside the Pech River, linking the village of Shamir Kowt, where the men's day had begun, to the American military base at Asadabad, seven miles away. It was on that road, the boy knew, that if Allah willed they would soon shed infidel blood. He was proud of his nation's fighting heritage and he was eager—they were all eager—to be counted among the faithful in this latest war against the West.

That war had been going on for two years, and for these guerrillas it had just taken an ominous turn. Ever since the Americans had driven the Taliban underground, the people of the Pech had resisted the new invaders and sided with the insurgency, just as a generation earlier they had resisted the Russians and sided with the mujahideen. The lifeblood of the insurgency was popular support. But now new players on the scene were disrupting that support.

They were Americans, these new players, but they did not behave like the typical "helmeted ones." They wore full beards, even as the Prophet had demanded, and their dress was like that of any Afghan villager. They were well-trained fighters, but it was not only their fighting skills that made them dangerous. It was that, in their daily patrols up and down the mountain valleys, they were spreading lies among the villagers and the *shuras*, claiming that they were friends of the Afghan people and only wished to help them build a "new Afghanistan."

Many of the valley's people believed these lies. From the Waygal district in the north to the Korengal in the west, people were welcoming and befriending the bearded infidels. Young villagers were even working with the American soldiers and turning against the insurgency. To the young men on that ridge this morning, this could not be allowed to stand. The bearded Americans must be driven out. A statement must be made: a statement in fire.

The band's leader had cause to be pleased with how the morning had gone so far. His guerrillas, combat ready before dawn, had started the day with prayer, then converged on the Shamir Kowt district house at first light. Peppering it with rocket-propelled grenades (RPGs) and AK-47s, they had dragged the district governor and his staff out of bed, chastised them for befriending the bearded ones, and reminded them of the perils that awaited those who insulted the Prophet or his teachings. Taliban founder Mullah Omar would be pleased, the leader thought, at how fervently he had defended the faith.

But there was more on his agenda than berating weak believers. He knew that the Asadabad base would have learned of the attack within minutes after they had left Shamir Kowt. The Americans would even now be donning their battle armor and rushing recklessly to the aid of their lackeys. They would be driving their vehicles breakneck along the valley road, anticipating a firefight seven miles to the west.

Insh'Allah, they would never get there. Here, two miles east of

Shamir Kowt, he would spring his trap, and his men would mete out the Prophet's justice.

Coming to a level patch of ground, the leader stopped. He looked down the rocky slope to the road and smiled. His view of the route the Americans would take began at a bend in the road to the east, toward Asadabad. It ended at a mud hut to the west, toward Shamir Kowt. Between the bend and the hut lay half a mile of open ground. Improvised explosive devices (IEDs) had already been placed in the road to immobilize the American vehicles directly in front of their fighting positions. When they arrived, not a tree, not a house, nothing would block his marksmen's view of the would-be rescuers. They would be like rabbits before the pitiless eye of a falcon.

This is the place, he said. Move quickly now.

At his command rifles were unslung, grenade launchers loaded, and the DShK settled in a cleft between two boulders. The ammo belts came off and hundreds of rounds of 12.7mm shells—shells that could pierce all but the heaviest armor—were laid out in readiness for the gunner and his assistant. As the men checked their weapons and loaded fresh magazines, the youngster with the videocam recorded their activity, as if framing instructional shots for a training film.

For a long time since the arrival of the Americans, this band had been hunted. Now, flush from the morning's success, they were feeling lighthearted, hopeful. For the first time in months, they were the hunters. And their quarry, this latest incarnation of unbeliever interference, was about to come into view.

With the trap set, the men waited. Five minutes, ten, fifteen. After twenty minutes, the Taliban leader had a flash of uncertainty: Had he miscalculated the driving time from the base? Or the eagerness of the Americans to demonstrate their prowess? No matter, he told himself. He remembered the saying.

You have the clocks. We have the time.

And then it was time. Dust rising just beyond the bend in the road told him that the rescue party was coming to his guns. He raised his arm, cocking the signal to fire.

Five seconds, six, seven. The front grille of a U.S. Army Humvee rounded the bend, then another, and a third. They were moving fast. In seconds they covered a third of the distance to the hut. They were rattling blindly to the heart of the baited kill zone.

Two dozen Kalashnikovs, a DshK, RPGs, one old Enfield, and a videocam pointed in deadly silence at the open stretch of road. A man with an RPG launcher adjusted his aim. The machine gunner tightened his trigger finger. No one looked at the leader.

They sensed rather than saw it when he dropped his arm.

PART I

Fall 2003

1

Into the Gray

To know that we know what we know, and that we do not
know what we do not know, that is true knowledge.

—Attributed to Confucius

September 2003

In the half-light of the C-17 cargo plane's cavernous hold, I could
make out the nodding figures of my recently assigned Special Forces
A-Team. Dressed in fatigues but unencumbered by battle gear, they
were trying to catch some Ambien-induced shut-eye while strapped
into the cotton webbing harnesses that served paratroops as bunks.
They were tough, well-disciplined soldiers, used to privation.
After the tortures that Special Forces training and numerous overseas deployments had put them (and me) through, a twelve-hour
plane ride was no big deal. I didn't expect complaints, and I didn't
hear any.

We had taken off from North Carolina's Pope Air Force Base
adjacent to Fort Bragg at 1700 and been in the air for six or seven
hours. Where did that put us? Over the Azores, maybe. Or
approaching the African coast. At that moment it didn't matter.
Soon there would be ample opportunity—maybe ample need—for

dead-on calculations of our position. For now I was willing to leave that up to the flight deck.

But if that particular item of uncertainty wasn't on my mind, others were. In warfare, as Secretary of Defense Donald Rumsfeld had famously observed the previous year, you had known knowns, known unknowns, and unknown unknowns. He had gotten flak for that comment. Some thought he was dodging responsibility for sending us to war in Iraq based on flawed intelligence about weapons of mass destruction (WMDs). Maybe. But whatever his motivation, the observation was accurate, and that September night I was giving it some thought.

When it came to known knowns, I could start with myself: Whatever this deployment brought us, I was up for the challenge. In a sense I had been preparing for it most of my life.

The son of a Vietnam vet and the grandson of a World War II vet, I had grown up in California in a patriotic family, with my older brother Rich named for President Richard Nixon and me named for Governor Ronald Reagan. Scouting taught me an appreciation both for Teddy Roosevelt's "strenuous life" and for our country's flag, and I earned the Eagle Scout badge at the age of fifteen. About that same time our family took an educational vacation to the East Coast, touring historical sites in Philadelphia, Boston, New York, and DC. One of my most vivid memories of that trip was walking with my father along the Vietnam Veterans Memorial, watching him pause and touch reverently the names of his friends, and then breaking down in sobs before the name of a buddy who was killed next to him in a Vietnam rice paddy. I felt at that moment not just pride but almost a kind of jealousy—a desire to experience that deep sense of connection, of military brotherhood, that meant so much to him.

At eighteen, I entered Brigham Young University on an ROTC scholarship and a year later, like many other Latter-Day Saints nineteen-year olds, took two years off to do missionary service—an experience that opened my eyes both to cultural differences and to our common humanity. At the end of my mission, I toured France and Switzerland with my parents and sister, and was lucky enough to find myself in Normandy during the fiftieth anniversary of the D-Day landings. Visiting Sainte-Mère-Église, a French town liberated by the 82nd Airborne Division; seeing the cliffs that Army Rangers scaled at Pointe du Hoc; touring the American cemetery and the Omaha Beach memorial—these were emotional experiences that reinforced my commitment to serve in uniform.

At BYU I became my ROTC class's battalion commander, and when I completed my business degree in 1996, I was commissioned into the Army as an infantry lieutenant. After nine months of intensive training, including Ranger School, I reported to the 82nd Airborne Division as a platoon leader and later as a company executive officer to a peace-keeping deployment in war-torn Kosovo. Kosovo was my first taste of the gray zone of war.

In 2001 I began Special Forces training. It was in a windowless room at the John F. Kennedy Special Warfare Center and School—the place we call "the schoolhouse"—that I learned of the 9/11 attacks: We thought it was an instructor's trick to have us take the day's lesson about terrorist cells seriously—until we saw the Twin Towers burning on TV. That had been two years ago. I hadn't yet been tested as a combat commander. But there was a job to be done, and I knew I was ready.

My other known knowns were also easy to identify. I knew that, in the wake of the attacks, my country was at war with a formidable adversary—a jihadi network that had mounted a devastating attack on the American homeland. As I watched the towers fall from that Fort Bragg classroom, I knew that the world had changed forever. President George W. Bush soon committed the nation to a Global

War on Terror. I knew that one theater of this new war was the ungoverned terrain of Afghanistan's northeast, which had become a haven for Al Qaeda operatives and where the mastermind of the 9/11 attacks, Osama bin Laden, was believed to be hiding.

I knew that, in boarding that C-17, I was leaving behind my wife, Becky, our two young sons, Tanner and Owen, our new daughter, Bailey (born just two days before my deployment), and the small, everyday joys of a husband and father. There was a sad irony in this. Shortly after my Kosovo tour, Becky and I had decided that I would transition from the regular Army to the National Guard, because we wanted to have more children and I wanted to be around for them. As I sat on the plane, realizing that the transfer had had exactly the opposite effect, I thought maybe it was my destiny to fight in this war, no matter what uniform I might be wearing.

Becky took the about-face with good grace. She felt cheated at first, as I left her in Washington State with three young children. But she understood and accepted the call of duty, including her own. In the English poet John Milton's words, "They also serve who only stand and wait." In some ways spouses like Becky, who sacrifice so much, deserve the title of "patriot" just as much as the loved ones they see off to war. I began missing her even before the C-17 was airborne. But I knew what I had to do, and so did she.

What else did I know?

I knew I was flying into a hot zone with seven good men who, like me, had survived a rigorous selection to become Green Berets. We were the nucleus of a Special Forces unit with the official title Operational Detachment Alpha (ODA) 936. The code name for our deployment was Hammerhead Six; as team leader, I was Hammerhead Six Alpha. Our assignment, in rough terms, was to enter wild Kunar Province, on the Pakistan border, and attempt to "eliminate, neutralize, and reduce" terrorist forces.

I knew that the legendary Pech Valley was in Kunar and was not under government control; much of it was in the hands of Taliban insurgents—the zealots who had ruled Afghanistan from 1996 to 2001, who had offered Al Qaeda safe haven after 9/11, who had been driven from power by U.S. forces, and who were fiercely committed to overthrowing Afghanistan's new American-backed government. Although on the plane that night I had not yet received our specific area of operation, something told me that the Pech Valley would be in our future.

As far as known knowns went, that was it. When it came to particulars, things got fuzzy. And the fuzziness began with the men themselves. As members of the 19th Special Forces Group, a National Guard unit out of Utah, they were more mature and varied in their skill sets than most regular Army troops. Like me, most were married with children. Most had been previously deployed on SF missions. Beyond that, though, how much did I really know about them? About their personalities, quirks, special skills, weaknesses? Not a lot.

With one exception, I had known these guys for only about six weeks. We had met in July at Utah's Camp Williams, where they had reported for combat training and where, for a year, they had been waiting for their newly appointed commander. The team leader slot had been open for a while, awaiting a candidate who, like the rest of the ODA, had passed the Army's Combat Diver course. Only the Army knew why our dive team had been assigned to arid Afghanistan. While the men waited, I had been finishing up at the Army's language school in Monterey, California, studying Mandarin. (My team was focused on the Asian theater but, like many others, was deployed to the Middle East after 9/11.) When I finally arrived I was met with good-natured expressions of amazement and jokes about being a real person, not just a figment of the Army's imagination.

At Camp Williams, we trained together for another month, focusing on marksmanship and room clearing in a Close Quarters Battle (CQB) training course. We had another few weeks at Bragg for briefings and additional mission prep. When we learned that we would be deploying to Afghanistan, every one of these guys had reacted professionally: they were serious, committed, and ready for the mission. Still, six weeks isn't much time. As I scanned their faces that night in the cargo hold, I realized that they formed part of my known unknowns.

The one guy I knew reasonably well was Jason Mackay, an engineer whom everyone called Junior and whom I had met in Key West, at the Combat Diver course. He was a funny, knowledgeable guy, easy to like. Jason did demolition work for construction companies, and he tended to assess all large, immovable objects as potential explodables. If you wanted something blown up, Junior was your man.

Our second engineer was Jimi Rymut. I knew he was twenty years my senior, that he had been fighting insurgents when I was in middle school, and that by reputation he was a walking encyclopedia of Special Forces lore. But in the C-17 that night I hadn't yet heard that lore, or any of his personal stories. I didn't yet know, for example, that in the 1980s, he had trained and been given the on-call order to carry a backpack nuke into Siberia, to destroy the Siberian Railroad tunnel should the Cold War turn hot. That night, what Jimi was capable of doing was still an unknown.

The same was true of Dave Moon, our senior weapons sergeant. Ranger and Special Forces qualified, he would prove to be a great asset. A miner from Montana, he loved big-game hunting and on first impression seemed hard of hearing. We had been in training some weeks before I caught him laughing at a joke that should have been out of his earshot and discovered that he was only deaf when it served his purpose. This was an interrogator-busting trick he had picked up in the Special Forces SERE course, which teaches Survival, Evasion, Resistance, and Escape while in hostile territory.

Mike Montoya, who had degrees in pharmacy and economics, was our senior medic. Mike had spent the last two years instructing other would-be Special Forces medics at Fort Bragg. He had a big smile and a bigger noggin, topped by a thatch of dark, restless hair. I didn't know yet what a gifted medic he would prove to be, but the team had already recognized his quiet intelligence: "You need that head," Junior would joke, "to hold your eighty-pound brain."

Sitting next to Mike was Ben Guile, another medic, who as far as I could tell from our few weeks' acquaintance, had little guile to match his name: I wondered if his hot temper would get us into trouble. He was obviously smart. Smart enough, I later learned, to earn an Ivy League degree and to make a living for a while selling precious stones in Southeast Asia. I didn't know that yet, and I didn't know either that Ben was as good at improvisation as anyone alive.

Roger Wilcox was our one communications expert—the commo guy. A-Teams typically have two of these, and an additional unknown was whether we'd get a second one after arrival. Roger was young and relatively new to Special Forces, but he seemed to know everything there was to know about his specialty, from the charmingly anachronistic Morse Code to the programming of military-specific applications. His surname had given him the easy nickname "Roger Wilco."

The team sergeant, soon to be a member of my leadership circle, or "head shed," was Randy Derr, our third medic. I felt surer of Randy than I did of anyone else. As an ICU nurse in civilian life, he obviously had the right stuff to handle critical care situations. At Camp Williams we had taken to each other immediately, and by the time we boarded that C-17, we had begun to see each other as friends. Randy would become the guy that everybody else went to for advice. He was as close to being a known known as anyone on the team.

An eighth member of the team, our intel sergeant Scott Jennings, was not with us on the C-17. Happily delayed in North Carolina for the birth of his daughter, he would rejoin the team in-country a few days later. Scott was a serious guy who didn't waste words, and in those few weeks at Camp Williams I had come to understand that when he did utter a sentence it was usually one you needed to listen to. He thrived in the water environment, and as an extra duty ran our battalion's dive locker. Smart and steady, Scott would be the third member of ODA 936's head shed.

Also absent from the transatlantic flight were some additional team members I hadn't even met yet. A Special Forces ODA consists of twelve men, each of whom has a special skill or team function. Typically, you have a team captain or detachment commander (18A), a chief warrant officer (18OA), a team sergeant (18Z), an intel sergeant (18F), two weapons sergeants (18B), two engineer sergeants (18C), two medics (18D), and two communications sergeants (18E). We still needed a chief warrant officer, a second weapons sergeant, and a second commo noncom. These slots were supposed to be filled in-country. That was another known unknown that was on my mind.

But it wasn't my team members that most concerned me. A greater point of concern was the mission itself. In fact, I was asking myself, what *is* our mission?

Our orders were to land in Kunar Province and ferret out bad guys. Kunar was a common entry point into Afghanistan for jihadi fighters from Pakistan, and the CIA had intelligence that several high-value targets (HVTs) were active there. But we hadn't been given pictures, or even names, of these targets. Senior-level briefings at Fort Bragg had provided only minimal information on their identities, the groups and villages loyal to them, and the tribal cultures where we would be serving. Tracking these men down would be a needle-in-a-haystack affair in some of the most forbidding terrain on the planet.

On a well-defined mission, you've got a reasonably solid handle on five bits of knowledge. You know (1) where you're going, (2) what you're expected to accomplish, (3) how you're supposed to accomplish it, (4) what success will look like, and (5) how to get out of there once the job is done. As I drifted in and out of slumber on that cross-Atlantic flight, it became clear that on this mission, the only thing I had down (in very general terms) was where we were going. No one above my pay grade had yet laid out—or, I imagined, figured out—what specifically we were being asked to do in this troubled part of Afghanistan.

"Getting the bad guys" (or, in Pentagonese, "neutralizing enemy personnel") was hardly a specific objective. You could say that about anything from a house search to a bombing run. Besides, as we already knew from countless news reports back home, the bad guys in this arena were as definable as smoke. "Terrorist insurgents" and Anti-Coalition Militia (ACM) were really just code names for a motley crew of Taliban, Al Qaeda operatives, mercenaries, local strongmen fighting for power or respect, and Islamic sympathizers united by nothing more substantial than a hatred of the West. And even if we were successful in killing these adversaries—in "stepping on cockroaches," as the jargon had it—it wasn't at all clear how that would fit into the bigger, strategic picture of winning a war.

Add the fact that the line between combatants and civilians—including kids—was notoriously indistinct and the fact that the deadliest threats to our troops were improvised explosive devices

(IEDs), and you get the picture. We were about to enter a zone where the enemy wore no uniforms, held no fixed position, and had only contempt for the Geneva Conventions. They also had relatives, friends, and neighbors among the local villagers. They shared religion, culture, and language with the people we were going to need to assist our efforts. Go get the bad guys? Sure. Which ones? Where? How?

To make matters worse, the new Afghan government—our alleged allies—seemed almost as hazy as the insurgents they were fighting. The country's titular leader, Hamid Karzai, shared his authority with warlords whose loyalty was questionable. Cronyism and corruption were rife. The Northern Alliance, the main coalition of anti-Taliban Afghans, had been in disarray since September 2001, when Al Qaeda assassinated its charismatic chief, Ahmad Massoud; in the region where we were going, they had never had enduring success or influence. In fact, nobody had. No foreign army from Alexander the Great to the Russians had been able to decisively conquer the Kunar and Nuristan regions of Afghanistan. We weren't likely to be met with welcome wagons.

In short, we weren't any surer of our friends than we were of our enemies. Not a situation designed to inspire confidence.

But hey, I thought to myself, we're Special Forces. Since their inception in the 1950s, the American military's Special Forces—popularly known as the Green Berets—had been trained to enter zones of uncertainty, to assess complex situations on the fly, and—first, last, and always—to *improvise*. If we encountered an obstacle that wasn't covered in the field manual or previous training, we'd find a way around it and then rewrite the manual. For Special Forces soldiers, being able to operate in the gray zone was a job requirement.

Special Forces training is notorious for its difficulty and depth, with only a small percentage of candidates making it through the training pipeline. After becoming an expert in his primary Military Occupational Specialty, an SF candidate goes through a selection process. If selected, he is off to qualification training (the arduous Q-Course), where he masters small unit tactics and refines his individual and specialty skills. The Q-Course culminates in the "Robin Sage" exercise, an elaborate month-long simulation of guerrilla warfare designed to teach thinking outside the box. After further training that includes survival school, airborne school, language training, and training in specialties such as underwater operations, the Special Forces soldier emerges with skills both physical and mental that make him second to none as an unconventional warrior.[1]

That being said, however, the "Special" in Special Forces refers less to the complex and trying nature of our training than to the missions we are tasked to conduct. We are expected to negotiate better than the State Department, gather intel as well as the CIA, outdo the Peace Corps in building alliances and running civil affairs programs, operate as surgical commandos when appropriate, and recruit, train, and lead indigenous soldiers with the charismatic skill of a Lawrence of Arabia. By 2003, our predecessors had been doing these things for sixty years, in some of the most inhospitable places on earth. I was looking forward to doing it in Kunar too.

I was looking forward especially to the "going native" aspect of Special Forces operations: the formation, training, and leading of "indig" troops. More than anything, that is what distinguishes Green Berets from other elite fighters like Rangers and SEALs. Even at his lethal best, a Ranger or SEAL is still an individual soldier with an individual rifle. A Green Beret is trained to turn one man, himself, into one hundred rifles—and to turn those rifles efficiently against the wiliest of foes. I like to think of us as "exponential commandos" or "force multipliers" for oppressed populations.

By 2003, the effectiveness of the Green Beret model for Afghanistan had already been demonstrated. When the Twin Towers fell, the Joint Chiefs had originally predicted that sixty thousand conventional troops would be required to defeat the Taliban. Instead of going that route, the Pentagon first tried an unconventional approach. In less than a month, 150 Green Berets, plus a handful of CIA paramilitary officers, were in-country, coordinating U.S. air power and working by, with, and through the Northern Alliance. This handful of soldiers, some on horseback, ousted the Taliban in less than three months—150 men, working with local fighters, defeating an army that controlled a country nearly the size of Texas. It was an awesome accomplishment, and I was confident that my team would follow honorably in their footsteps.

That was what I told myself, anyway, in the dim metallic cave of the C-17. I looked at the faces of the men that I was leading into a place where people wanted us dead, and I told myself we would do fine. I had good reason to believe it. I was leading the best of the best, and they deserved that confidence. The thought was temporarily comforting, and it made me relax.

But one thing continued to bug me as I closed my eyes. I had labeled some demons, the known unknowns that might give us trouble. The very act of naming them had deprived them of power. But what of the ones I couldn't name? What of the unknown unknowns? I was certain they were out there, too. What I didn't know was where they would come from, and when, as we went into the gray.

2

The Fort

An Outpost of Progress

—Joseph Conrad

October 2003

After a brief layover in Uzbekistan—a common insertion point for Afghanistan-bound troops—the C-17 set us down at Bagram Air Base, the large military installation in Parwan Province that housed the Combined Joint Special Operations Task Force (CJSOTF) for Operation Enduring Freedom. There, at the base's operational headquarters, Camp Vance, we were put through the expected routine of reporting, briefing, processing, and prepping for our upcoming infil.

I disliked the paperwork, but the briefings did give me a clearer sense of where we were headed. The capital of Kunar Province is the small city of Asadabad, which sits at the junction of the Kunar and Pech Rivers, about six miles from the Pakistan border. On its outskirts lay a military base known variously as the Puchi Ghar Army Fire Support Base, Forward Operating Base (FOB) Asadabad, and simply "Abad." It was at this FOB that we were to be stationed.

By all accounts, Abad was a well-run military establishment, and well defended by a combination of regular infantry, Special Forces teams, CIA guys, and Afghan irregulars whom the CIA had trained. Nobody suggested, however, that it was an unthreatened site.

A Russian post during the Soviet occupation, it had been overrun in the 1980s by a mujahideen force that had slaughtered the entire garrison rather than taking prisoners.[1] In its new incarnation, the post had been coming under attack from insurgents—in some cases, no doubt, the mujahideens' children. In mid-July, three coalition soldiers were wounded by an IED just south of the base. Later that month a B-52 had to respond to rocket attacks on the compound itself, and additional rocket attacks had occurred in August. As we boarded a Chinook for transport to Asadabad, we were well aware that we were entering a war zone.

The helo flight took about an hour. There were nine of us on this hop: the eight who had come from Bragg plus an Air Force air support specialist, Courtney Hinson, who had joined us at Camp Vance in Bagram. Courtney was a young stud who was likable the minute you met him. He liked us, too. Coming from a large Texas family, he had asked to be assigned to us because of our positive work ethic, which recalled one of his father's favorite sayings: "Many hands make light work." Still in his twenties, Courtney was already a seasoned combat veteran, having seen action in both Iraq and Afghanistan. As our unit's dedicated TAC-P, Tactical Air Control Party specialist, he would prove to be an invaluable asset.

Randy Derr, our team sergeant, had gone a few days ahead of us to prepare the transition with ODA 361, the Special Forces team we were replacing. He was responsible for recording the lessons they had learned and passing them on to me and the rest of the team. I knew Randy would do a solid job, but I was disappointed that I couldn't get a few days myself with the outgoing captain. Hammerhead Six was taking over a strategically important area in the War on Terror, and the handoff of the baton seemed limp at best.

As we headed east toward the Hindu Kush, the terrain seemed like a drier version of our own rugged West—the deep clefts and soaring ridges of classic ski country. I smiled to myself, thinking that we were probably better prepped than most teams on their initial deployment to Afghanistan. As part of the 19th Special Forces Group, we had prepared not at North Carolina's Fort Bragg or Kentucky's Fort Campbell but at Utah's Camp Williams, where the land more resembles the terrain where we would be fighting.

We were a mile or two away when I first saw the fort. And *fort* was the word. I had imagined the chain-link fences, sandbagged walls, and concertina wire that are typical of Army bases in this region. From a distance, the FOB didn't look like that. Its high walls were dun and gray, a mixture of adobe and stone, and they looked like they had been built a thousand years ago. I found out later that they preceded the Russian period by many, many years. Aside from some metal guard towers that the Soviets had added, the enclosure looked like it belonged in an old Hollywood movie: a remote British outpost as imagined by Warner Bros. As the Chinook approached a landing zone just outside the walls, I allowed myself a quick mental picture of regimental banners and pith helmets. But then the LZ came into view and I got serious.

The CH-47D is a two-rotor, twin-engine cargo helicopter that can carry more than thirty pax (passengers) or twenty-six thousand pounds of cargo. Two door gunners sit just behind the pilots, and there is sometimes an extra gunner on the rear ramp. Passengers exit the aircraft from the ramp, and this rear-door exit is a little slower and more cumbersome than just hopping out of the open sides of a Blackhawk. If you're dropping into a hot landing zone, you have to do it seamlessly to clear the bird and quickly set up a defensive perimeter.

Every member of the team understood how to execute that move, so I knew that once the helo touched down, everybody would be doing exactly what he was supposed to be doing. I wasn't mistaken. At touchdown, as the propwash flew away from the bird, the eight of us were down the ramp at a snap. In seconds we dumped our bags and cargo clear and formed a 360-degree security position around the aircraft. Our objective was to secure the LZ and the aircraft and to be in a defendable position once it lifted off and the operation began. Textbook stuff, really.

On this particular LZ, though, once the Chinook lifted off and the dust settled, we saw that the landing area had already been secured. It was being overwatched by the post's guard towers and by a couple of gun trucks just off the LZ. Before I could stand up I heard a familiar voice laughing at us for having successfully secured an already secure landing zone. "Looks super, guys. If you're done practicing infil techniques we can unload the gear."

Wearing a T-shirt, jeans, and the first hints of the beard that SF guys are obliged to grow in-country, there was our team sergeant, Randy Derr, raising a hand in greeting. "Good to see you," he said. "Welcome to Abad."

Up close, the exterior of the FOB continued to resemble the mud fortresses that the British had occupied in India. Inside, though, it looked much like any other Army base. Covering an area equivalent to three or four football fields, it contained enough low buildings— some wooden, some adobe—to house, feed, provision, and train a garrison of two hundred men. About 120 of these, we learned, were regular Army, plus another twenty-five Afghan irregulars; aside from a few CIA guys, the rest were Special Forces ODAs like ours. A few ODAs had been in Afghanistan since 2001.[2] We were replacing one of these early arrivals, ODA 361. When they left, we would be one of three Green Beret units based at the post.

The garrison also included six Afghan soldiers who had once been anti-Taliban militiamen and had recently been reconstituted as procoalition mercenaries. Randy explained that we were inheriting them from the outgoing ODA, and that the inheritance was sanctioned by ties of blood. The six were the nephews of a local warlord, a former mujahid named Malik Zarin, who was devoted to the Americans for reasons that probably had as much to do with self-interest as with love of country. According to Randy, when he agreed to loan the young men to us, he had first gathered them together in their village and said, "If anything happens to the Americans, don't come home." Talk about incentives.

I wasn't entirely convinced of the nephews' devotion. I had heard enough about tribal allegiances to suspect that loyalty to Americans was a fungible commodity. But I was willing to wait and see. I put Randy in charge of their training and supervision, and hoped that, in developing a bond with him, they could become our ears and eyes as we worked with other indigenous troops in the future and interacted with local villages.

We also inherited an interpreter. Mashal was an educated man from Jalalabad, and his fiancée was a teacher there. Randy said that ODA 361 had given him a glowing report, and in our first meeting I understood why. He had a perfect beard, wore American-style battle dress, and had a chipper, contagious attitude. Working first with the CIA in 2001 and since 2002 with the ODAs, he was devoted to his country and loyal to the Afghan-American cause. After a successful operation, he would often thank us for leaving our families behind to help his country. He was a bright, hardworking ally, and immensely likable.

We were also joined at Asadabad by an additional weapons sergeant, Ian Waters. Ian was originally attached to the 20th Special Forces Group, but he was reassigned to us for the Hammerhead Six deployment. That brought the number of our Green Berets up to ten—just two men short of a traditional A-Team complement.

Once we settled in, we also met up with the members of the Special Forces B-Team that had deployed with us. This term might call for a word of explanation. In civilian usage, A is seen as "better" than B, but that's not what it means in Special Forces. Among Green Berets, twelve-man A-Teams are the front-line ground troops, engaging the enemy head-on and executing the ground mission. They can't do this without expert supply and logistical support, and that support is provided by a B-Team.

In a typical SF company, you have six Operational Detachment Alphas (ODAs), each commanded by a captain like me, and one Operational Detachment Bravo (the B-Team), with the B-Team and the company itself commanded by a major—in our case a Maj. Kimball Hewitt, who was also the Abad commandant and my immediate superior in the chain of command. Three companies comprise an SF battalion, commanded by a lieutenant colonel. Our battalion, headquartered at Bagram's Camp Vance, was led by Lt. Col. Marcus Custer, Hewitt's immediate superior. Along with the other A-Team leaders, I was going to be given a wide scope of responsibility for our team's operations. But all of us knew that we couldn't get anything done without B-Team's assistance.

That broad responsibility had a big impact on how I saw our mission, and on how my perspective sometimes meshed with, and sometimes diverged from, that of the higher-up command. That complicated picture was the result of a Special Forces tradition in which A-Team leaders are far more responsible for setting their own agendas than are company commanders and even battalion commanders in the regular Army.

I had been in the regular Army in Kosovo, so I knew that, operationally speaking, it was a top-down organization. Generals set the big picture strategy; colonels, lieutenant colonels, and majors devise plans to implement pieces of that strategy; and captains and lieutenants (often leading companies and platoons) come up with tactics to move those pieces into place. These junior officers have no strategic responsibility and therefore no way to influence decisions made sometimes thousands of miles away at the top of the chain. They must carry out operation orders someone else has devised.

Special Forces do things differently. Because we operate in remote areas about which military planners know relatively little, it's rarely feasible for a senior officer working out of Fort Bragg to devise anything but a very general strategy. When Patton was pushing across Europe in the last days of World War II, he knew the terrain, he had good communications structures in place, and he was fighting a well-trained but entirely conventional army. With those operational advantages, he could confidently make pronouncements like, "We will reach the Rhine by Friday." Such confidence would be laughable in places with impenetrable terrain, lousy communications, and an enemy that blends in with the civilian population. In places like Vietnam and Afghanistan, a rigid top-down command structure won't work. To help you set and execute a strategy, you need eyes and ears on the ground to understand the human terrain upon which these wars are fought. Green Beret A-Teams provide those eyes and ears.

I knew all this before we arrived in Asadabad. I knew that a plan to "neutralize" the area's bad guys wasn't going to be spelled out in a memo from the U.S. Central Command (CENTCOM). I embraced that knowledge. It was a matter of pride for me, and for the rest of the team, that we were going to be entrusted with making our own war plans and be held accountable for their success or failure.

What I didn't know was the extent of the territory for which we were going to be responsible.

Once the team had moved all our gear into our "team house"—a couple of rooms of plywood and mud in the corner of the FOB— Randy gave us the lowdown on our situation. On his advance hop, he had been accompanied by the team sergeant of ODA 935, one of our sister teams also assigned to Abad. Both sergeants wanted the best housing and the best mission for their teams, and it was our good fortune that Randy opted for action rather than comfort. He conceded the comfortable housing to ODA 935 in exchange for getting what he suspected would be the more interesting area of operations (AO)—the Wild West country north of Asadabad. Thanks to his negotiation, we ended up with spartan digs but a target-rich, challenging environment.

"The horse trading wasn't that tricky," Randy explained with his characteristic wry humor. "There are a lot more possibilities for unconventional warfare north of the base, and it turned out that the guys in 935 really liked where they slept."

Our new AO was confirmed in a meeting with Major Hewitt, the quiet, reserved senior SF officer at Abad and the de facto base commander. We met him in the map room, a large planning area whose walls were lined with military charts. After he welcomed the team, he called our attention to a huge map of northeastern Afghanistan. A blue pin in the middle of it indicated our position. Pins of other colors dotted the rest of the map, indicating suspected nests of Al Qaeda or Taliban activity. The operable term was *suspected*. The pins showed locations about which the Army had bits of intel, but they didn't tell us anything about which bits were reliable. Lots of pins, but more questions than answers.

With a pointer, the major outlined what he identified as our AO: Kunar Province and adjoining Nuristan Province. We watched as he dragged the pointer north from the blue pin up to the Tajikistan border, then made a long semicircle east and south along the Pakistan border, and finally closed the circle west and north back to its origin. We were responsible for everything between Asadabad and the Tajikistan border. That included the huge, mountainous province of Badakshan, one finger of which (the Wakhan Corridor) touched the Chinese border. But intel hadn't detected much activity in that inhospitable area, so it was likely we'd be focusing our operations on Nuristan and Kunar.

Looking at the map, I started doing some rough geometry in my head. Scott Jennings, sitting next to me, was scratching figures on a piece of paper. He looked up, showed me the paper, and smiled. Scott was a man of few words, but his expression said it clearly: Is this guy kidding?

"Major," I said, "our math whiz intel sergeant here estimates that the area of operations you have outlined covers five thousand square miles. Give or take."

Hewitt chuckled. "Pretty close," he said to Scott. "Kunar's just shy of 5,000 square kilometers, Nuristan just under twice that, so your new backyard is 14,167 square kilometers. Give or take. That's 5,468 square miles. About fifteen of you, right? Counting the Afghans. That's 364 square miles per man."

I had to hand it to Hewitt. He made an obviously ridiculous proposition sound intriguing and maybe even doable.

It wasn't as if he had much choice. In 2003, there were only ten thousand coalition troops in Afghanistan. The Pentagon was concentrating on a new war in Iraq, which had begun in March, leaving commanders in Afghanistan with limited resources. As the majority of supplies and personnel were still being airlifted into the country, the challenge of managing supply, medical personnel, and maintenance was staggering. About eight thousand of the troops in-country were support personnel based in Bagram and Kandahar. That left only about two thousand men in the field to fight a very widespread insurgency, and many of those troops were occupied more in defending FOBs than in patrolling and gathering intel. Most field missions, therefore, were far wider than an armchair strategist might desire. In 2003, Major Hewitt didn't have twenty teams to distribute around all that sprawling real estate. He was dealing with the resources he had, and what he had was us.

Judging from the grins on my team's faces, they were taking it all in stride. I'm sure some of them were thinking, Major, you're nuts, but nobody said it. Somewhere in the back of my mind I was hearing the motto of the Navy Seabees: "The difficult we do at once. The impossible takes a little longer."

So we were to be the frontier guard for an area roughly the size of Connecticut. After I got over the initial jolt, I found myself pleased at the prospect. It was a huge responsibility, and I appreciated the trust. But it did raise questions about feasibility. Surely SF command, in giving us that massive area, didn't expect the fifteen of us to cleanse the entire area of hostile influence. Surely there had been some thought given to where we might most effectively focus our attention.

When I asked Major Hewitt this question, he just said, "It's your show. The teams before you have been chasing Taliban and Al Qaeda around these hills for the past two years. We've crushed a lot of them, driven others into Pakistan, but the stragglers are a bitch. I wish we had some addresses, but we don't. That's for you to find out. When you do, tell us what you need. Any assets, anytime. Understood?"

I understood all right. I understood that the SF tradition of letting the ODAs define the mission had its downside. Before that meeting, I was pumped to be given the authority to develop my own strategy and write my own orders. Once I discovered that this meant driving all the snakes from Connecticut with fifteen men, I was momentarily daunted by the task before us.

The situation made me think of the old Wild West story about a town in the midst of a riot that calls the Texas Rangers for help. An hour later one Ranger saunters into town, Colts on his hips and a glint in his eye. "Where's the trouble?" he asks.

"They only sent one Ranger?" asks a bewildered citizen.

"There's only one riot, ain't there?" the Ranger replies.

Like the Ranger, we'd figure it out, just as special operators from Robert Rogers on down had figured it out. But 360 square miles a man. Why not a thousand?

Implementing a strategy under the conditions described by Major Hewitt would obviously entail leaving the confines of the fort. Asadabad was a landing zone, a get-your-crap-together preparation place. If we were going to scour Connecticut for bad guys, we were going to have to get mobile, and to do it fast. This dictated much of our activity for the next couple of weeks.

For starters, we were going to have to get used to the terrain. In *War*, a record of his year in Afghanistan's Korengal Valley (an offshoot of the Pech Valley), journalist Sebastian Junger observes that, given the tactical importance of holding high ground, "an enormous amount of war-fighting simply consists of carrying heavy loads uphill."[3] Nowhere is that comment more apt than in Kunar Province. Asadabad itself is only 2,700 feet above sea level, but that figure is misleading, since the city sits in a mountain valley, and the walls of that valley rise in jagged creases to several times that height; within a couple of hours' walk from the FOB, you could be in windswept passes a mile and a half high. Since we would likely be carrying heavy loads up such inclines, we had to get our lungs and our legs in shape.

We started the conditioning immediately, by taking daily hikes from the FOB to one of the observation posts (OPs) that formed the compound's outer perimeter. Manned by squads of infantry, the OPs were half a mile away from the base and about another half mile up. Afghans do hikes like this without breaking a sweat. For us, the first climb brought back fond memories of being pushed beyond your limits in Special Forces and Ranger training. "It's just like Mountain Phase of Ranger School," our senior weapons sergeant, Dave Moon, joked, "except without the blueberry pancakes."

After a week, with our muscles adapting to the strain, we were clamoring up the slopes almost like goatherds. But that first trek? When we reached the OP, the young, already acclimated infantry on duty looked at us with eyes of self-satisfied pity. I don't mind admitting that we were smoked.

We also had to get used to being off-road rally racers. ODAs aren't typically armored units, but this was Afghanistan, where villages were miles apart and where IEDs were almost as plentiful as poppies. When we left the relative safety of Abad, we might have to drive at breakneck speed from one hot spot to another, and we might easily become the targets of random bomb planters, not to mention more organized groups of attackers. We would have to become adept at driving the vehicles that, like the Afghan irregulars, we were inheriting from ODA 361.

There were four of these: three armored Humvees and a Toyota pickup. The Toyota, which we were told was the Taliban's vehicle of choice, was no problem, but the Humvees required a learning curve.

The High Mobility Multipurpose Wheeled Vehicle (Humvee) is a U.S. government vehicle whose armored version in 2003 cost a quarter of a million dollars. Small change by Pentagon standards, but when you put three of them together and threw in a pickup, it added up to real money. For us that represented a huge fiduciary responsibility. Not to mention the fact that when we were on the move, the trucks would serve as motorized fortresses, our only protection against rockets and IEDs. We had good reason to give special handling to Uncle Sam's rides.

Asadabad had a motor pool that handled the Humvees' mechanical upkeep. Driving the things was another matter—a challenge which this handful of American males took to quickly. As teenagers, we had all done our share of pretending to be Dale Earnhardt, so the prospect of taking the corners too fast in a three-ton minitank was a little bit like getting extra ice cream. We all took turns at this, on the flats beyond the fort, as I assessed which of us would probably handle the rigs best if we were dodging enemy fire. Everybody was competent at the wheel, but Jason Mackay, Roger Wilcox, and Mike Montoya seemed to have an edge on the rest of us, so I decided that unless circumstances dictated otherwise, they would be our designated drivers.

That done, we turned to figuring out our moves on a routine patrol (if there was such a thing) and how we would respond to Kunar's surprises. For the next week, when we weren't in the sack or at chow, we divided our time between workouts in the base gym, firing practice on its range with our Afghans, and practice drills with the vehicles. I wanted to refine a standard procedure for any and all emergencies. What would we do if we lost a tire? Hit an IED? What if someone got shot? How would we approach a suspected target? In any given scenario, who would stand where with what weapon and be responsible for what job?

Like most Green Berets, I'm a believer in the adage "The more you sweat in peace, the less you bleed in war." Practicing with our guns and vehicles was a way of maximizing the chances that if there was going to be blood spilled, it wouldn't be ours.

But it's also possible to overthink. By the second week in October, with our practicing becoming almost automatic, I was starting to think we were caught in the snare of preparation. It was time to switch from drills to live ammo missions.

We were ready to check out the hunting in the wilds of Connecticut.

3

A War of All Against All

During the time men live without a common power to keep them all in awe, they are in that condition which is called war, and such a war as is of every man against every man.
—Thomas Hobbes

In Afghanistan there were more fingers than pie.
—John C. Griffiths

Afghanistan was a country seething with enemies. Not just Al Qaeda and the Taliban, but loads of ambitious warlords, commanding their own militias, who hated both the "infidel Crusaders" and each other. In 2003, with these multiple antagonisms unresolved, Afghanistan was perilously close to becoming a failed state. Given its long history of ethnic factionalism, corruption, and blood feuds, you could argue that this condition—a version of Hobbes's famous "war of all against all"—had been chronic for centuries. The more immediate origins of the current mess, though, could be found in the Soviet intervention of the 1980s.[1]

In 1979, as part of the cold war's new Great Game, the U.S.S.R. sent troops to Afghanistan at the request of its Marxist government, which was under attack from landowners and conservative Muslims. Beginning with a trickle of advisors, the Soviet support grew to more than a hundred thousand troops, of whom nearly fifteen thousand died either on the battlefield or later of their wounds.

Antigovernment Afghan fighters lost several times that many, and civilian deaths may have topped a million—many of the victims killed by Russian mines.[2]

While resistance to the invasion came from many quarters, its public face was that of the mujahideen. These "fighters for God" were composed not just of native Afghans but also of volunteers from around the Muslim world, sworn to wage holy war (jihad) against the Soviets. Their guerrilla commanders attained legendary status, and one of them, a wealthy Saudi named Osama bin Laden, would become the world's most famous mujahid when he founded the terrorist network Al Qaeda. In fact many of the insurgents we faced in 2003 had drawn first blood as mujahideen—a grimly ironic fact given that their campaign had been heavily supported by our own CIA.[3]

One heartland of the resistance had been Kunar Province—our current area of operations. Since antiquity, Kunar had been a trap for foreign armies, both because its fighting men were famously fierce and because its mountains favored guerrilla warfare. In 1978, when the Kabul government attempted to introduce modern reforms, its tribesmen attacked police and army garrisons. The government's response was the infamous "Kerala massacre," the execution of hundreds of resisters and the forcing of their families into exile in Pakistan.[4] That started a regional rebellion which drew in the Soviet troops, created hundreds of thousands of refugees, and made Kunar a center of mujahideen activity.

When the Soviets left Afghanistan in 1989, they left behind a puppet government with limited popular support and a patchwork of competing troublemakers who wanted to remove it. The ensuing civil war raged until 1992, when a new regime came to power led by the warlord Gulbuddin Hekmatyar. He governed for only four years, when a new player came on the scene.[5] This was a group of bellicose fundamentalists with the seemingly innocuous title of *Taliban*, meaning "the Students." (Many were the former students of a religious hardliner named Mullah Omar.)

Under Taliban rule, which lasted until 2001, the country was wrenched rudely back into medieval "purity." The Students drove out Hekmatyar and his fellow warlords and replaced them with a dystopian paradise in which petty thieves had their arms cut off; music, dancing, and kite flying (a traditional Afghan pastime) were abolished; soccer matches featured mass executions at halftime; and women were obliged to cover themselves, head to toe, in pale blue tentlike garments known as burkas.

All of this nourished an American distaste for the Taliban. Their apparent shielding of Osama bin Laden after the 9/11 attacks turned that distaste into military action. When the Taliban refused to surrender him to U.S. justice, the Bush administration cobbled together a coalition that invaded Afghanistan, ousted the Taliban, and set about pacifying regions, such as Kunar, that had rarely in their history known a stable government. The U.S. mission, known as Operation Enduring Freedom, was entering its third year when our A-Team arrived in the troubled province.

And troubled it was. Despite two years of coalition presence, and despite the fact that the big-time mayhem-mongers like Hekmatyar seemed to have gone to ground, Kunar (and Afghanistan) were far from pacified. There was a nominal government in Kabul, headed by Hamid Karzai, who in 2002 had been chosen by a meeting of the *loya jirga* (grand assembly). Karzai was favored to win a national election set for the summer of 2004, but when we arrived in Asadabad, that was nine months away. A lot could happen in nine months. Officially the insurgent leaders had been driven into Pakistan, but judging from the extent of anticoalition and anti-Karzai activity, their banishment wasn't a done deal. In September, when we arrived, explosions and rocket attacks were a nearly daily occurrence. As part of the ongoing attempt to bring security to Afghanistan's volatile northeast, we had our work cut out for us.

If our aim in Kunar, broadly stated, was to hunt down bad guys, we also had more focused objectives—or at least aspirations. Although our target list could conceivably include anyone with Al Qaeda or Taliban connections, our government (and Karzai's people) would be especially pleased if we managed to bring to heel the antigovernment commanders known as high-value targets, or HVTs—our "most wanted" list. At a September briefing by CIA officials, I was given the identities of those topping the list.

Number one, obviously enough, was Osama bin Laden, who had planned and executed the attacks of September 11, 2001. That act had shocked the world and brought the might of American arms to Afghanistan, where, it was believed, bin Laden was hiding out under Taliban protection. But 9/11 was not the first of his terrorist acts, and not the first time he had come to international attention.

In the 1980s, he gained prominence as a young mujahid who helped to fund the anti-Soviet resistance. In 1988, one year before the Soviets departed, he founded the jihadist organization Al Qaeda ("the Base"), devoted to purging Islam of modern influences and driving unbelievers, such as American troops, from his native Saudi Arabia. For the next decade he used his family's wealth to support Islamic extremism around the world. In 1998, he engineered the bombings of the American embassies in Kenya and Tanzania—acts that killed two hundred people and that made him, in the words of historian Ahmed Rashid, "a household name in the Muslim world and the West."[6]

Well before 9/11, then, bin Laden had become a threat to U.S.

interests everywhere. When the Twin Towers fell, he was the obvious prime suspect, and even though it took him until 2004 to admit it, both U.S. and British intelligence were convinced that he had ordered the attacks. The United States put a $25 million bounty on his head and demanded that the Taliban hand him over. When they refused, the U.S. response was Operation Enduring Freedom.

That operation drove the Taliban from power and forced them and their Al Qaeda allies underground. In some places they went literally underground, into caves along the Pakistan border. In December 2001, American forces, assisted by Afghanistan's Northern Alliance, bombed a cave complex at Tora Bora, killing a couple of hundred fighters but failing to capture bin Laden; he was thought to have escaped into Pakistan.

The hunt for the mass murderer continued, but by the time we arrived in Kunar in 2003, reports of sightings remained spotty and inconclusive. But he had relatives in the area—so it was said, anyway—so even though we weren't betting any money on our chances of capturing the planet's most wanted criminal, we realized that it was at least a possibility—something we might dream about when we were feeling lucky.

After the 2003 U.S. invasion of Iraq, the military issued a deck of fifty-two playing cards, each one identifying a member of dictator Saddam Hussein's political entourage. The aces were assigned to Saddam, his two sons, and his personal secretary. We didn't have such a deck, but if we had, Osama bin Laden would have been the Ace of Spades.

The person who might have been the Ace of Clubs was not nearly as well-known globally, but he was infamous within Afghanistan itself. This was Gulbuddin Hekmatyar. A native Pashtun, Hekmatyar founded the radical Islamist group Hesb-e Islami as a student in the 1970s, befriended and then fought the Soviets, and earned a reputation as a brutal, opportunistic commander. In the turmoil following the Soviets' departure, he fought other Islamists for political position until becoming prime minister in 1992. He held that post for four years, proving to be anything but a benevolent despot.

Forced from power by the Taliban, Hekmatyar hid out in Iran and then, in 2002, issued a tape from an unknown location, calling for jihad against the United States. In February 2003 the U.S. government froze his American assets and declared him a global terrorist. This was an ironic honor for someone who in the fight against the Russians had probably received more CIA money than any other mujahideen commander.

Hekmatyar was known to operate often in Kunar, where military documents identified his followers as HIG, for Hesb-e Islami Gulbuddin. Our CIA briefers wouldn't guess at his current location. But taking him, should we be so lucky, would bring sighs of relief to thousands he had attacked or betrayed.

Next in our hypothetical deck of cards, the Ace of Hearts might have been the Taliban's shadowy leader, Mohammed Omar. Born into a poor Pashtun family, he too fought with the mujahideen, losing an eye in combat. After the war he taught in a Pakistani madrassa (religious school), acquiring the sobriquet *mullah* as respect for his learning. After the Soviet collapse, he returned to Afghanistan and pulled together some of his former students intent on ending the warlords' corruption. In 1994, according to a local story, a woman appeared to him in a dream, asking him to end the chaos with God's help.[7] In response, he founded an armed group known as "the Students."

The group started out as dispensers of rough justice, hanging a warlord who had kidnapped and raped two girls, then executing two others who were planning to sodomize a boy. In an era of widespread thuggery, these guys looked like an improvement. The

Taliban, its ranks swelled by madrassa recruits and its coffers filled with aid from Pakistan's intelligence service, the ISI, became a militia, then an army. While disorder continued to reign in much of the country, Omar's students captured the capital, Kabul. In 1997, with Omar as "commander of the faithful," they renamed the country the Islamic Emirate of Afghanistan.

As head of the nation, Omar preached moderation but set up a draconian legal system that made *Taliban* a byword for backwardness. The oppression of Afghan women in particular became a cause célèbre in the West, but it was Omar's foreign policy that put him on America's enemy list. After 9/11, when he refused to surrender bin Laden, American talk turned to action and the mullah, like his Al Qaeda guest, went into hiding. He was still in hiding when we got there in 2003. But hundreds of the students he had inspired were still taking his orders. Taking down Mullah Omar would have been a gold ring.

Even before we got to Afghanistan, we had heard the names of these three HVTs. A fourth leader—the one who might have been the final ace in our foursome—was an unknown quantity. His name, we learned in the CIA briefing, was Abu Ikhlas al-Masri. An Egyptian, he had been, like bin Laden, one of the many foreign nationals who had cut their teeth in the jihad against the Soviets. Little more was known about him. Like bin Laden he seemed to have relatives in the Kunar area, and from there was said to be running Al Qaeda cells and possibly a training camp. The CIA, which considered him the main Al Qaeda commander in the Pech Valley, had put a bounty on his head of $20,000. Not Osama bin Laden stakes, but in a dirt-poor country, not loose change, either.

In the briefing that day, I had a feeling that this Egyptian terrorist might become our main quarry. The other three HVTs were players on the global stage. Ikhlas was a regional commander, and the area that we were about to go hunting in was, in a sense, his backyard. If I had to bet on our best shot of bringing down an HVT, I would have put my money on Abu Ikhlas.

"Do we have a picture of this guy?" I asked the CIA briefer.

He shook his head no. "Everybody knows him," he said. "But nobody admits to knowing what he looks like. Your A-Team, Captain, will be hunting a ghost."

That was OK with me. I wasn't afraid of ghosts. And we were ready for the hunt.

4

———

Hunter's Moon

Reconnaissance patrols provide the commander with timely, accurate information of guerrillas and the terrain they control. This information is vital in making tactical decisions.
—U.S. Army Field Manual No. 90-8, *Counterguerrilla Operations*

Certainly there is no hunting like the hunting of man.
—Ernest Hemingway

In American folklore, October is the month of the Hunter's Moon. So it felt appropriate that we began to explore our huge new AO at the beginning of that month, searching for hostile forces and for information. By the end of the month, we had gone on a dozen of these hunting expeditions, some day trips and some overnighters, familiarizing ourselves with the mountainous roads, meeting village officials, and conducting armed reconnaissance patrols in response to tips about HVTs or hidden arms caches. The roads were lousy, the officials could be standoffish, and the hiding of arms was practically a national pastime, so it was an educational but sometimes frustrating experience.

I've mentioned that Special Forces ODAs have more tactical latitude than regular Army platoons and companies. We plan and execute our own missions. In Afghanistan, ODAs were constantly gathering intel on the ground and making adjustments to exploit developing opportunities. This didn't mean that we played things by ear. In fact, prior to initiating any operation an ODA commander submits for approval an outline of what it will entail and what it's expected to accomplish. When approved, these outlines give the team an operational game plan that spells out every individual's tasks for that mission and also what support assets might be required.

Devising such plans is a collaborative activity. I always drew heavily on my team's insights, particularly those of my go-to duo Scott Jennings and Randy Derr. Every team member was responsible for contributing to the overall execution of the plan, while each one individually owned the part of the plan that was specific to his area of expertise. In our case, Mike Montoya and Ben Guile would determine the medical support plan; Roger Wilcox took responsibility for our radios, batteries, and anything else relating to communication; Jason Mackay and Jimi Rymut owned any engineering requirements; and Dave Moon and Ian Waters coordinated our weapons.

The guys would sometimes razz me about our chain of command, with Mike imagining that if we were on the Planet of the Apes, the head shed would be orangutans and the rest of them gorillas. It became a standard joke, after everyone had cast his vote for this or that option, for Jason to ask me slyly, "OK, Ron, now what are we actually going to do?" I took the ribbing in stride. Jason was a seasoned soldier. He knew that, when it came to final decisions, the buck stopped with me.

At the beginning of our Hunter's Moon, I wrote quick-and-dirty versions of our game plans: 5Ws, which indicated briefly the Who, What, When, Where, and Why of the operation. By midmonth, as our forays became more complex and required more logistical support, the plans became more traditional CONOP documents, that is, memoranda for the team and for command that described the "Concept of the Operation" in minute detail.

On October 7, for example, we began an armed recon mission from Asadabad into the Helgal Valley to the north. Before one boot stepped out of the FOB, the team had war-gamed a plan, and everybody had contributed to and read my CONOP summary for the three-day mission. It began with the heading "Task Organization," under which each team member was assigned to a specific vehicle and a specific task within that vehicle. Then came a detailed Concept of the Operation; listing the order of twelve checkpoints (CPs) between Abad and the town of Helgal; setting out to-the-minute arrival and departure times for stops along the way; and defining commo recognition signals to be used within the team itself and between the team and Asadabad, a Quick Reaction Force if needed, and a medevac team if needed. That was a lot of data points established even before we began—and this was on a mission where we weren't even asking for air or other external support.

The aim of the mission was to "promote U.S. operations and deny sanctuary to AQ/TB/HIG elements operation in Kunar Province." Although we didn't have the names of any specific elements, we knew we were looking for those loyal to Al Qaeda (AQ), the Taliban (TB), and/or our Ace of Clubs, Gulbuddin Hekmatyar (HIG). We were also, as the "promote U.S. operations" implied, aiming to build relationships with local people who might be induced to prefer our friendship to that of our adversaries.

Our first stop on this journey, about three hours north of the FOB, was the village of Asmar. Our CIA and SF predecessors had done good work here, so the people were welcoming. We had lunch with village elders in the shadow of an ancient castle. The kids were especially friendly and eager to hang out with the American strangers. There were lots of waves as we rolled by, and smiles as we practiced "candy diplomacy."

Farther on up the river the road narrowed, becoming impassable for our Humvees as we approached the Helgal Valley. This forced us to go into split team operations: part of the team maintained the vehicles while the rest proceeded on foot to meet with villagers, gauge support, and gather intel. In 2003, the maps were sketchy and the condition of roads not always clearly indicated, which made ground reconnaissance all the more important.

The people we met too were often hard to read: seemingly welcoming but guarded. Many of them, speaking through our interpreter Mashal, thanked the United States for its help in expelling the Russians and thanked us for helping them fight the Taliban. They were happy to accept our funding to repair infrastructure. But their friendliness seemed provisional. Even in Asmar, you came across the occasional iron face, the furrowed brow that seemed to say, "We're glad to be helped right now, but when are you leaving?"

As would become increasingly evident during our time in Kunar, Afghans are among the most pragmatic game players on the planet. They were adept at working nongovernmental organizations (NGOs) and the U.S. military to get support for reconstruction projects, but their real allegiances were kept guarded, and these could change swiftly in the pursuit of self-interest. This may have reflected an ancient talent for negotiation or merely the instinct for survival among a people who had lived in turbulence for so many decades. Either way it was clear that earning and keeping villagers' trust was a process that would take both patience and diplomatic skills.

We spent the two Rest Over Nights (RONs) of this patrol on the outskirts of villages, setting up a perimeter with the trucks' gun lines pointing outward and the fire sectors overlapping, so that we had 360-degree coverage against possible attackers. Nobody from AQ, TB, or HIG attempted to breach this circling of the wagons, although we were aware that we weren't alone. In the hills flashlights blinked on and off throughout the night—an old mujahideen signaling method. We knew folks out there with whom we hadn't had lunch were keeping midnight watch on the strangers in the valley. But we had no run-ins.

We returned from the Helgal recon on October 9. After a few days at Abad, we were on the road again, with new CONOP plans, to the village of Marah Warah in the north and then to the district capital of Shamir Kowt in the Pech Valley, where we had a meet and greet with district officials. At midmonth, we hooked up with another ODA, twenty Afghan allies, and some CIA guys to try to corner an HVT who had reportedly been sighted just south of Shamir Kowt. When we got there, he wasn't, and an arms cache he was supposed to have been hiding turned out to be a "dry hole."

Ten days later, we conducted our farthest foray north, to the town of Kamdesh on the Nuristan-Pakistan border. In 2009, Kamdesh would be the site of a U.S. military disaster: the loss of Combat Outpost Keating and of eight American lives in the coalition's most costly firefight since the 2008 battle of Wanat. The COP defenders' valor is the subject of journalist Jake Tapper's book *The Outpost*.[1] In 2003, that tragedy was six years away, the outpost had not yet been established, and Kamdesh was peaceful. The residents' attitudes seemed similar to those we had encountered in other villages.

That wasn't the case in Bar Sholtan. On our way to Kamdesh, we had passed through this smaller village without incident, but coming through it again on our way back, we got a different reception. Scowls met us as we drove through, and several men pelted us with wads of paper. Unfolding them, we saw they were leaflets that had been air-dropped by a PSYOP (Psychological Operations) team based at Bagram, urging people not to cooperate with the Taliban and heaping insults on Osama bin Laden. Even in remote Kunar, none of this should have been either surprising or offensive. And Bar Sholtan's people had been reasonably friendly on our way up to

Kamdesh. So I couldn't figure out why this procoalition propaganda had upset them.

Then our interpreter Mashal pointed out a blunder. Two blunders, really.

One of the leaflets had a cartoon of American planes dropping bombs on Taliban forces—a scene the PSYOP folks evidently meant to indicate the invincibility of American power. But the "Taliban" depicted in the cartoon looked exactly like any other Afghan tribesmen. True, they were labeled as Taliban. But in a region where few people could read, that didn't matter. As Mashal pointed out, the cartoon looked like a threat: "Cooperate with the Americans or we will bomb *you*."

The other leaflet stumbled in a different direction. It had a Photoshopped picture of Osama bin Laden, clean-shaven, and standing on a New York City street. I'm not sure what this was meant to indicate. Maybe his callous pleasure at visiting the scene of his crime? Or his non-Islamic attraction to Western decadence?

Whatever the PSYOP's intended message was, it was undercut by the figure's Photoshopped shave. This was probably meant to condemn him as both impious and unmanly but, as Mashal explained, the people of Bar Sholtan didn't take it that way. They might have been illiterate, but they weren't so stupid as to believe that the leader of Al Qaeda had gone over to the infidels. Like him or not, they knew that bin Laden would consider a clean-shaven face an insult to Islam. Depicting him beardless was perceived as an attack not just on him, but on their shared faith.

The leaflet was a classic case of cultural insensitivity—a "comic" insult that may have gone over well on a U.S. talk show but that in rural Afghanistan came across as blasphemous. With Mashal's help, I tried to mollify the villagers' anger, explaining that (a) no, we weren't going to bomb them and that (b) we had meant no disrespect to Islam. We said that we were embarrassed by the pamphlets and would do our best to stop any other missteps of this kind. The fact that we were now on a few weeks' growth of beard ourselves didn't hurt matters, but it was a touchy few moments, nonetheless.

I couldn't help thinking, as we drove away, that closer attention to how the locals might read things could have altered the PSYOP plan and saved us embarrassment. The team gave Chris Aguirre, a PSYOPs attachment who was temporarily acting as one of our gunners, a ton of grief on the topic. He agreed the leaflets had been a mistake, and that evening he sent a cease-and-desist e-mail to his command at Bagram.

Toward the end of the month, having become better acquainted with our AO, we conducted what proved to be the most successful but in some ways most frustrating of our October missions. This was a Sensitive Site Exploitation (SSE), code in this case for a weapons raid, not far from Shamir Kowt, where Anti-Coalition Militias (ACMs) were said to be storing mortars and other munitions. A CIA contact who gave the intel on this arms cache claimed its owner had been responsible for several IED attacks.

This part of the Pech Valley was Hekmatyar's known stomping ground, so we anticipated that if we met resistance, it wouldn't be amateur. We therefore put together a decent-sized task force. It included seven vehicles, two assault teams, a detailed medevac plan, and a strike force that included our Afghans, some regular Army infantry, civil affairs guys, two interpreters, two bomb disposal experts—twenty-five of us in all.

The operation went smoothly. We rolled up close to the target compound, set up two security teams just off the road, and had Dave and a couple of infantry establish "eyes on" by setting up a sniper position on the hill adjacent to the compound. Then the assault force, with Afghans in the lead, entered the property and, as we had rehearsed, isolated the kids and women from the man of the house. The ODA and Afghans searched and cleared all the rooms and the search for weapons began.

Our intel stated that the arms were underneath a boulder in the backyard. We found over eighty mortar rounds sitting there, just as described. Anyone who has served in Afghanistan will attest that such perfect matches between intel and reality are not very common. We were pleased, and a little surprised, that this recovery was a fruitful one and not a dry hole.

So the recovery part of the Shamir Kowt op had gone off well. What remained was the truly sensitive element: the decision of what to do with the owner of the arms.

Like thousands of his countrymen, he stored weapons as a hedge against the chaos that always seemed around the next corner, so that wasn't in itself proof that he was a Hekmatyar disciple. The man's accuser had claimed that he had participated in a direct attack against Americans and had used mortar rounds in an IED application. There was no way to assess that charge short of interrogation, and the presence of that much explosive ordnance on the property convinced me that interrogation was in order. In addition, even though we had secured some rifles here and there, this was our first serious arms-retrieval rodeo, and I wanted to be safe rather than sorry. With the man's wife and children looking on woefully, and the man himself protesting his innocence of ACM affiliation, I was torn, practically and ethically, for several minutes.

In the end I decided that, rather than risk letting an insurgent sympathizer stay in business, we would send the guy for interrogation to the coalition detention center at Bagram HQ. Maybe he'd reveal some intel and lives would be saved. Maybe he'd prove to be innocent, and they'd send him home. That was my thinking, anyway.

We packed him into the back of a truck, a gunny sack over his head as a security precaution, and started moving out. As we pulled away, I saw his wife with her face in her hands and his kids crying. At that moment, even though I could justify my decision on military grounds, I felt less like an American protector than like the Gestapo, intent on disappearing troublesome civilians to parts unknown. Nobody in the unit liked the scene any better than I did. Drawing close to the end of our Hunter's Moon recons, it was disconcerting that the only quarry we had bagged left a bad taste in our mouths.

I wasn't a Pollyanna. I knew that, in combing the hills of the troubled Pech Valley, we would no doubt have some blunders along with successes. But as the SSE site retreated in our rearview mirrors, those crying kids stuck in my mind. I wondered if, down the road, this tactical gain might turn out to be a strategic loss.

It got worse. About a week after we had transferred the mortar owner to Bagram, local elders told us the tip that had led us to the cache came from a neighbor with whom he had long been involved in a blood feud. In our area, these were common, as the Pashtun code required that even minor transgressions be either forgiven (at a cost) or avenged by arms. The resulting feuds could last for generations. Our forces could be unwittingly drawn into them if a wily informant manipulated us into doing his dirty work by telling us that his neighbor was AQ or Taliban.

Once we learned that a blood feud was involved, the guilt of the Shamir Kowt mortar owner became questionable. The informer might have planted the mortars himself, but even if they belonged to the guy that we had sent away, his involvement with the insurgency was open to doubt. The upshot was that on this "successful"

SSE, in addition to breaking up a family, we had inadvertently thrown salt in a wound.

When we discovered the new information, I immediately got on the phone to Bagram, explained that we had arrested the prisoner on biased intel, and asked that they return him to his family. This turned out to be the first of several calls that were met with the official version of "no dice." The logic was that if there was evidence enough to detain and question the individual, he would remain in U.S. custody until things were sorted out. It didn't matter how he had gotten there or even if he was guilty. He was now a Person Under Control (PUC). End of story.

As I recall that incident today, it still saddens me. I was never able to get further information about the man. I don't know if he ever got back to his family, or if he's still alive. But I doubt the strategic outcome was positive. When he went to Bagram, he disappeared into a bureaucratic black hole, while in a tiny village south of Shamir Kowt, a gaggle of kids, now young men and women, remember that it was Americans who sent him away.

In that Hunter's Moon a decade ago, I was an on-the-ground field commander, trying to figure things out. Sometimes that didn't work out well and I had to reassess. Unfortunately, people higher up who weren't on the ground thought such reassessment was unnecessary. The view from where I stood was gray and complex. Apparently, from 106 miles away it was clear as a bell.

This was not a situation designed to inspire confidence. Especially since I knew that even though we had just spent a month trying to get bad guys in our gunsights, sooner or later we would be in theirs.

5

A Baited Ambush

Guerrilla war is far more intellectual than a bayonet charge.

—Col. T. E. Lawrence

On the morning of the attack, I was up early.

At Asadabad we used a large tent as an impromptu gym, and I was lifting weights there with Courtney Hinson, the airman attached to Hammerhead Six as air support specialist. We had been in-country for a month, and we had begun to appreciate the old cliché: warfare is mostly boredom, punctuated by occasional moments of terror.

In our case, "boredom" wasn't quite right, because we had been busy with daily firing practice, patrols into the Kunar and Pech Valleys, meetings with Afghan elders, and the training of the men we had on loan from their warlord uncle. Asadabad had also been hit by a couple of rocket attacks which put the entire base on high alert. But the relative quiet was frustrating. All of us were hungry for a little action.

On the first day of November 2003, we were about to get it. I had just finished a second set of pull-ups and was reaching for my water bottle when a young infantry corporal stepped into the tent and saluted briskly.

"Captain Fry, sir?"

I returned the salute. "That's me."

"You're needed ASAP, sir. Major Hewitt wants a meeting in the briefing room right now."

"What's up, Corporal?"

"Don't know, sir. Some trouble up the Pech is all I know."

I slugged down some water and grabbed my shirt. "Time for a shower?"

"Negative, sir. Double-time, they said."

I liked the young soldier's no-nonsense manner. Courtney and I followed him out of the "gym," and we jogged the couple of hundred yards to the camp's central building. When we reached it, I could see that, whatever had gone down in the Pech Valley, a Quick Reaction Force (QRF) was already on it. A platoon of regular Army cavalry from the 10th Mountain Division in full battle dress, about fifteen strong, was piling into Humvees loaded for bear. As we entered the building, they were tearing off north on the road to the valley, thick clouds of dust rising behind them.

The Humvees were light skinned, I noted with dismay—*light skinned* meaning "thinly armored." My Special Forces unit had been equipped with the heavily armored Humvees that the Defense Department, responding to reports of IED attacks, was just then beginning to distribute. But at that point in Operation Enduring Freedom, most regular Army units that had deployed with their own equipment and vehicles—including this quick-reaction platoon—were still making do with suboptimal sheeting. Some units, frustrated by bureaucratic delays, were armoring their own vehicles with junkyard scrap metal. People joked about the resulting "hillbilly armor," but there wasn't anything funny about it if you were taking rounds. The QRF lacked even this jury-rigged protection.

The camp commander was Maj. Kimball Hewitt, the officer who had introduced us to our sprawling AO. When we entered the room, he got right to the point.

"The district house at Shamir Kowt is under attack. Their

security is two or three minimally trained policemen. The district leader called the Asadabad police for reinforcements and Asadabad called us. They all sound rattled, so it's hard to tell what they mean by attack, but it sounds like RPGs and Kalashnikovs, I don't know what else. The QRF just left here for Shamir Kowt. Captain Fry, you and your men will follow immediately. Assess damage and coordinate with local Afghan forces to pursue the attackers. The Cav guys will be on-site and will secure the area awaiting your arrival. Any questions?"

Shamir Kowt was a cluster of mud houses that served as the administrative capital of the Watapur District. Its officials had become friendly with coalition forces, and doubtless that was why it had come under attack.

"Do we know the size of the attack force, sir?" I asked.

"Negative. Big enough that they want help, is all I know."

"Are they still firing? Any casualties?"

"Don't know."

"Any friendlies in the area?"

Hewitt shrugged. "Aside from the two cops, I don't know. I've given you everything I have, Captain. It's on you, now. Get there ASAP and if the fight's still on, let us know what you need. Understood?"

"Understood, sir."

"All right. Move out."

My team had already been alerted, and by the time the two-minute briefing was over, they were assembled and ready to roll, weapons double-checked and Humvees purring. I suited up, grabbed my M4 rifle, and did a quick head count and commo check. The lead vehicle held five of us: Roger Wilcox driving, Courtney behind him, our gunner Dave Moon on the .50-cal turret, me riding shotgun, and behind me our interpreter Mashal, who seemed less than thrilled to be invited. Greg Kindler, a soldier from another ODA at Abad, jumped in a truck to join the mission. Our convoy also included an explosive ordnance disposal (EOD) truck and its crew.

When we left the gate, the Cav dust was out of sight. We were fifteen minutes behind them.

The distance from the firebase to Shamir Kowt was just under twelve kilometers, or roughly seven miles. Going north, you first passed the Kunar provincial capital of Asadabad—forty thousand Allah-fearing Pashtuns—then a handful of mud-hut villages until you came to the mouth of the Pech Valley. You turned west into the valley and, keeping the river on your left, you passed more mud huts, more scraggly grass, more lunar landscape, until you hit the civic hub called Shamir Kowt. Hell-bent for leather on the lousy Afghan roads, you could make it in twenty minutes. In Asadabad we stopped to coordinate with Malik Zarin, our Afghan guys' uncle, to send some of his troops to Shamir Kowt to assist. We were back on the road in sixty seconds.

This was to be our first engagement in-country, and my guys, I wasn't surprised to see, looked calm and alert—exactly what you want from your team as you approach a firefight. No "Get some!" posturing, just professional, confident lucidity. The motto of the 19th Special Forces Group—of which ODA 936 was one unit—was "Anything, Any Place, Any Time." Well, this was Kunar Province, November 2003. Whatever "anything" was, we were ready.

You couldn't say the same for poor Mashal. He was a trusted aide, and he hated the Taliban, so when I told him he was needed, he didn't hesitate. But he wasn't happy. He held it together for the first few minutes, as we drove northeast along the Kunar River. But when we turned left onto the rougher road we called Route Blue, his face fell. I hadn't told him anything about what we were doing, but he knew that if we were heading up the Pech, it wouldn't be good. We weren't a mile past that left turn when he leaned out his window and vomited. I smiled to myself and Courtney tried, not very successfully, to suppress a laugh.

I checked my watch. Six minutes from Asadabad, fourteen to go to Shamir Kowt. The Cav unit should arrive at the district house in a couple minutes, give or take. Which meant that when I radioed them, what I ought to have heard was something like "We're almost there" or "ETA in five."

What I heard instead was machine gun fire—a lot of it—and a panicky voice yelling "Hammerhead Six, Hammerhead Six, this is QRF. We are pinned down, repeat we are pinned down. Taking heavy fire. Where are you!" It was the voice of a young soldier who had probably been in the Army less than a year. This may even have been the guy's first rodeo.

If the Cav unit was taking enemy fire several minutes before it could possibly have reached the district house, they had been jumped along the way. It looked like we were going to become, as our commo expert Roger joked, "a QRF for the QRF." There was no way of knowing how bad their situation was, whether we could pull them out of it ourselves, or whether we needed additional support. But there was no percentage in assuming the best. I nodded to Courtney.

One benefit of working with good people is that when things get hairy, you don't need to waste words. Courtney was still in his early twenties, but he was a combat veteran who had directed numerous air strikes in Iraq. He knew exactly what my nod meant. Without a word he jumped on his satellite radio, trying to locate available air support. While we waited for a response, I tried to form a mental picture of what we might find ahead.

We had been up and down Route Blue on routine patrols, so I knew it well. I thought I had a good idea of where the Cav guys—who didn't know the road—might have been surprised. During a recon the week before, we had set up an overnight base about a mile east of Shamir Kowt in a broad, flat plain up against the hills. It was the only spot near Shamir Kowt where our three vehicles could be sheltered from prying eyes and still have good visibility up and down the route. A smart guerrilla would set his trap in that area, where the only cover from an ambush was a single mud building at a bend in the road. At that point, there were low hills on either side of the road, set far enough back to give attackers cover and high enough to give them an elevation advantage. From three hundred meters away and one hundred meters up, they could throw whatever they wanted down at our troops.

Even better from a bushwacker's perspective, before reaching even the meager cover of the mud house, a convoy would have to pass through eight hundred yards of open ground—a classic kill zone. Imagine driving the length of eight football fields in light-skinned trucks while guys in the hills took potshots at you. I was visualizing that shooting gallery and hoping I was wrong.

Ten minutes from Shamir Kowt, maybe five from the suspected ambush site, and here, hurtling toward us, came one of the QRF Humvees. Screeching brakes. We were side to side for twenty seconds. There was fresh damage on the vehicle's side from small-arms fire. The driver was their supply sergeant.

"What's happening up there?"

"It's bad, sir." I could see the same panic in his face that I heard over the radio. Not the panic of a man afraid but of a professional not wanting to fail his troops. "There's tons of 'em, and we're running low. I'm going for ammo. We got hit by an IED and now we're in a crossfire. Machine guns and RPGs. You gotta get there!" And he was off. I didn't even have time to ask him where exactly his guys were pinned down. We revved the trucks back into motion.

Now we had three radio lines open. Courtney was talking to air support, and I had two handsets working. On one I was communicating with the QRF and Asadabad; on the other I was passing on info to the rest of my team. I could hear the Cav machine guns rattling and Asadabad telling me to be there yesterday. "You got to get there now, Hammerhead Six. Get there and take over. What's your ETA?"

"Four mikes."

That turned out to be close, but it was a long four minutes.

When we pulled into the east end of what I had supposed would be the kill zone, I saw that I had been right. About three hundred yards ahead of us, the four remaining Cav Humvees were stopped just short of the bend in the road. They hadn't even made it to the protection of the mud building. They were exchanging heavy fire with the hills to the north. I didn't see any sign of the crossfire the supply sergeant had mentioned. A plus, if it turned out to be true.

What we did next was dangerous but unavoidable. Normally you would take every precaution not to enter a kill zone. You would try to maneuver on foot, to flank the enemy. As the Army Rangers' founding father, Robert Rogers, had put it in his original standing orders, you would try to "ambush the folks that aim to ambush you."[1] But in this broad plain, that wasn't feasible. The terrain was too steep for a quick flanking operation, and with the Cav guys under fire, we didn't have the luxury of executing a slow one. We had to go in.

The supply sergeant had said that they had run into an IED. Racing toward the firefight, we narrowly missed another IED. This one had been placed unburied in the road, apparently as a marker to guide the attack. Swerving to avoid it put us into the open space off the road, and this unplanned maneuver had an unintended benefit: it drew some insurgent fire away from the Cav. As we were

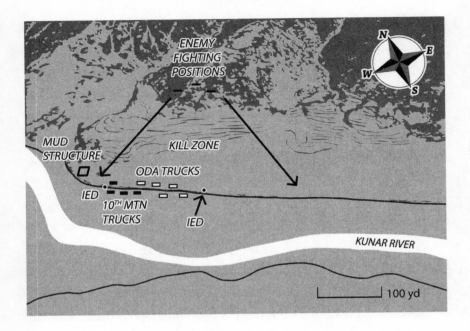

positioning our Humvees at angles that would further protect them, we could hear the pinging of 7.62mm rounds—standard for the Russian guns that the insurgents were using—bouncing off our steel hide. It's not a happy sound, but it beats the sound of those bullets piercing subgrade armor. Once we were in position—this whole thing took less than a minute—I yelled to our weapons sergeant.

"Take 'em, Dave!"

Like Courtney, Dave Moon didn't need much instruction when it came to a crisis. As I spoke, he was already rotating the turret of his .50-caliber machine gun toward the north and beginning to answer the muzzle flashes that were coming from the hills. Roger Wilcox was feeding him ammo with one hand and holding binoculars in the other, scanning the hills for targets. Our other trucks and the Cav guys were manning their turrets too, while Jason was working an extra M-240B 7.62mm machine gun that he had grabbed out of the trunk of his Humvee. So we had steady firepower answering the attack.

That wasn't optional. The enemy was throwing down an impressive display of lead. They had obviously come prepared for a sustained fight, and the hills were alive with muzzle flashes from several fighting positions. It was mostly small-arms fire, but punctuated with the occasional burst from a DShK machine gun. Intermittent bursts from our M4s—largely symbolic at this distance—added to the pandemonium, as did the rough blasts of our MK-19 grenade launcher. Mashal crouched behind a truck, hands over his ears. I noticed with satisfaction that Malik Zarin's six nephews had taken a position of rear security and were returning fire with the same vigor as the Americans.

With the air full of lead, our chief medic, Mike Montoya, cracked me up when he turned to me and shouted with mock surprise, "Those guys are trying to kill us!" Then, scanning the group to see that no one needed his medical skills, he pointed his gun at the hills and returned fire. Civilians sometimes think of an armed medic as a contradiction in terms, but that's not Special Forces logic. A dead medic doesn't do anybody any good, which is why, in a scrape, his first job is to keep himself, and those around him, alive. Or, as Mike liked to put it, "Sometimes firepower is the best medicine."

In the midst of the uproar, Courtney was working his satcom. He held the hand mike away from his ear and yelled to me, "A-10 available and en route!"

That was welcome news. In Afghanistan in 2003, there were one or two air support assets aloft at all times, ready to be directed where needed at a moment's notice. The asset of choice was the Air Force's celebrated A-10, a missile- and bomb-carrying behemoth that had been used extensively in Operation Desert Storm and also in Kosovo. The government calls it the Thunderbolt. Troops call it the Warthog, for its ponderous ugliness; and the Tankbuster, for its awesome payload. This included a 30mm Gatling-style cannon, missiles, cluster bombs, and—the kicker—a number of five-hundred-pound "general purpose" bombs. It was a five-hundred-pounder I wanted to order for our friends in the hills.

"When?" I yelled.

Courtney cupped his hand over the mouthpiece and yelled back. "ETA 10 mikes!"

The yelling wasn't optional. When a .50-cal machine gun is firing full tilt, the noise is roughly in the 165-decibel range. That's fifty decibels louder than a Chinook rotor blade or the percussive mayhem of your average death metal band. It's also forty decibels above the level where you start to feel pain. With our two .50 cal machine guns, an MK-19, and an M-240B firing next to me and four Cav guns going near by—not to mention the zinging coming out of the hills—we were feeling that pain bad. I thought at one point that my eardrums would burst. It was next to impossible to hear, and hard to think.

You didn't have to think much to realize that our position was sketchy. I detected no activity from the south, so there was no crossfire—good news there. But we were still in a kill zone—an exposed position from which the enemy can target you at will. The trucks afforded us some cover, but not enough for comfort. And ten minutes under fire is a very long time.

Our ammo might last that long, I thought, but I didn't know about the Cav's supply. I needed a situation report from their leader, a young, lanky lieutenant who towered over me. He was clearly relieved that we were there, but he was too wound up to give a good sitrep.

"What's your status?" I shouted.

"We're yellow on people, sir. And yellow on ammunition."

If I had ever learned the technical meaning of *yellow*, I had forgotten it. "What does that mean?" I said.

Bucking the *rat-tat-tat* all around us, he tried again. "Our status is 70 percent."

That wasn't any clearer than *yellow*. He was using terms from his unit's Standard Operating Procedures manual. I needed plain English.

I also needed him to know—I needed his platoon of teenagers being shot at to know—that we would be all right. This wasn't a day at the beach, but I knew enough about command to realize that if I didn't keep it together, nobody else would either. However I felt inside, I had to look like Mister Cool. I put my hand firmly on the young leader's shoulder.

"Look at me," I said calmly. "Forget the SOP. How many of your men are shot, what vehicles are damaged, and how many bullets do you have?"

That woke him up, and he gave a clear report. Nobody hit (thank God for that). A couple of vehicles shot up (light-skins suck). Four tires gone, lead vehicle disabled by an IED just before the mud structure. And down to a couple hundred rounds of .50-cal per vehicle. More on the way, if the supply sergeant returned.

It could have been worse. But since a .50-cal can spit out eight to ten rounds a second, the QRF firepower was fading fast, and in another few minutes, if we kept answering the attackers' barrage, we'd be low, too.

I wasn't sure pouring all that lead into the hills was doing much good, anyway. We had their muzzle flashes to sight on, but they had good cover, and as effective as a .50-cal is on personnel, it won't penetrate a boulder. Grenades from the MK-19 were potentially more effective, but that would take landing rounds behind dug-in positions. As for small arms: At that distance an M4 round loses most of its lethal punch, so our riflemen were using their scopes mostly to locate targets for the machine gunners. Unfortunately, the ambushers had set up so far away that they weren't in grave danger from our response. The constant dust kicked up from incoming rounds and the occasional tracer let us know they were still fully engaged in the fight.

As I was running to my truck to talk to Courtney a barrage of machine gun fire sprayed the ground between us and a round whistled by my head. Courtney got a grin from me with his wry reaction: "At least they've run out of RPGs!"

"Keep low," I shouted to the Cav troops and our gunners, "and sight on the flashes. A-10 on station in under ten."

The uproar continued as I counted down the minutes. Eight minutes. Six. Five. Then, humming up from the south, the aircraft's engines. The Warthog is not a quiet beast, and three or four minutes before Courtney's estimated ETA, we could already hear it rumbling in to our rescue.

The attackers could hear it, too, and they knew what it meant. Even before the plane came into view, the hillside muzzle flashes became less frequent; by the time the A-10 got close enough to do any damage, the firing had stopped. This, we would learn, was typical Taliban tactics. Practicing what the guerrilla leader Lawrence of Arabia called a war of detachment, they would attack small units from cover and then break contact before being decisively engaged. An A-10 engagement would definitely count as decisive, so when they heard the Tankbuster's engines, they split the scene.

With the enemy dispersed, there was no need to spend ordnance, so I called off the air strike and ordered our guys to cease fire. The A-10 pilot swung back toward home, but it took me another couple of tries before my team and the QRF guys got the message.

Coordinating a ceasefire when you've got ten people shooting isn't as easy as yelling "Hold your fire!" One person will stop but then hear somebody else still firing and start up again, and those mixed signals can stoke the action for some time. Plus, if you give an eighteen-year-old a machine gun, you induce euphoria. Two of the young Cav studs were so cranked at the prospect of mowing down the now-invisible bad guys that Dave had to grab one by the shoulder.

"It's over, dude! They're gone."

The kid looked like somebody had just pulled the plug on a video game. But he stopped firing, and so did his buddy. The last spurt of their guns ended a firefight that had lasted probably thirty minutes. The A-10 dipped below the hills. All was quiet.

The fight over, I gave the QRF lieutenant new instructions. Off-loading some extra spare tires to replace the ones that had been shot out, I told him that his team should stay in position, repair whatever damage they could, and guide in the other Americans and Afghans who would be following us into the valley. The EOD team would stay with the Cav to destroy the unexploded IED. The ODA would continue to Shamir Kowt.

In the frenzy of the firefight, it was easy to forget that we had driven out here in the first place not because of an ambush but because of an attack on a district house. For all we knew, it was still under attack. Now that the situation had been stabilized—happily, with no loss of life—it was time to return to our original mission.

As we piled back into our Humvees, Randy came up to me smiling.

"Look at this," he said, turning to Courtney. "Takes us through our first rodeo in a boonie cap."

For a second I didn't get it. Then I put my hand to my head. What I should have felt was the hard Kevlar shell of a combat helmet. What I felt instead was what U.S. troops since Vietnam have been calling a boonie cap—the cotton hat you wear on a long-range patrol or recon mission but not a good choice of headgear when you're being shot at. In all the excitement, I had forgotten to put on my helmet.

My team took it as an intentional gesture of bravado in the face of danger; the QRF soldiers saw it as proof that Special Forces are fearless and bulletproof. I was thankful that somebody was looking out for me that day, and I couldn't help but remember Union general John Sedgwick, killed at the Battle of Spotsylvania by a Confederate sniper. His last words were, "They couldn't hit an elephant at this distance."

The ambush earned us and the QRF guys the Combat Infantry Badge, the Army's official acknowledgment that you have been under fire. I was pleased with that and grateful that we had survived the fight without casualties. However well I had nailed the Mister Cool act, though, I told myself that this was the last time I would go into battle without my helmet.

As we drove into Shamir Kowt, we passed rows of villagers whose faces I couldn't read. Some seemed tense, others hostile, others indifferent. But nobody seemed terrified or apprehensive, and I took that to mean that the danger was gone. At the district house, that turned out to be true. The attackers had punched the structure hard with mortars and RPGs and smashed or burned some furniture and supplies. But no one had been killed or even physically harmed.

That was strange. Taliban fighters were not a merciful lot. They routinely punished thieves by cutting off their hands.[2] It was unlike them to be less brutal with district officials who had made the mistake of befriending Americans. Talking with those officials, though, soon made us understand why they had been spared. It took Mashal (visibly happy to have made it here alive) a few minutes to sort out multiple versions of the early-morning events. Then he gave us the gist of what had transpired.

Just after dawn, twenty or thirty Taliban fighters had attacked the house with Russian arms—AK-47s and RPGs. They had broken down the door and dragged the officials outside. Then the Taliban leader, waving a Koran in their faces, lectured them about how ashamed they should be at working with Americans. The Americans were evil men, he said, *kafirs* who wanted to defile our women and imprison our mullahs. Allah, blessed be his name, would punish them if they spoke to the evil men again.

"Then they went away," Mashal concluded. "They took their guns and their camera and they went back down the valley to fight the infidels."

We weren't surprised to hear that the raiders had been carrying Russian guns: RPGs and Kalashnikovs left over from the 1980s were their favorite weapons. And the badgering of the leaders sounded like the standard Taliban stump speech. But a camera? That was weird.

"They filmed you?" I had Mashal ask one of the officials. "When they were telling you how bad we were, they had a camera running?"

"Yes. When they left, too. Still the camera was running, as they went away."

"And they went away this way"—I pointed back down the way we had come—"back down the valley toward Asadabad?"

"Yes. To fight the infidels."

The story cleared up a lot about that difficult morning.

It told us, for starters, that the men who had attacked the QRF were the same ones who had attacked the house. In fact it looked like they had set up the aggressive but limited attack on the house with the express purpose of drawing us into a trap. Knowing that coalition forces would be obliged to come to the aid of the house, and knowing that we would pursue them into the hills west of Shamir Kowt (their logical escape route), they had set the ambush *east* of the town—at a place where common sense would tell you they were running away from. They had pulled off a clever "baited ambush."

The story also suggested why the district officials weren't killed. Why kill them when, by filming them being lectured and then spared, you could have video evidence of how merciful you were? By 2003 our adversaries' media savvy was already well-known, and listening to the report of the morning's events, I suspected that sooner or later a home movie about Taliban piety would show up on jihadi websites. When a few months later that turned out to be true, it didn't shock me. What did surprise me—what I never suspected that day in Shamir Kowt—was that the ambush itself would appear in that same video. How we turned that discovery to our advantage is a story I'll get to later in the book.

As a young commander, I learned a lot that morning.

I learned first that our adversaries were not the dumb-as-dirt ragheads of video game fame. They were seasoned fighters, some of them the mujahideen—or the sons of the mujahideen—who had humiliated the Red Army twenty years earlier. Their seasoning showed in the astuteness of their tactics. In the course of a single morning, they had created a convincing cry for help at the district house, planned and executed an ambush against U.S. professionals, evaded capture by a well-timed retreat, and gotten the whole thing on film for propaganda purposes.

These were clearly not a group of suicidal fanatics, eager to sacrifice themselves for a higher cause. Nor did they seem primarily interested in maximizing our pain. Setting up their positions so far from the road indicated that they were rational actors, committed both to their own survival and to maximizing the propaganda value of a well-planned operation. If all they had wanted to do was to wipe out *kafirs*, they could have set up closer to the road, or even in the mud building. But that would have meant dead Taliban—and no home movie. So while I had contempt for their so-called morality, I had to give them credit for battlefield smarts.

In fact, the design of the ambush could have been lifted straight from our own Ranger Handbook. It states that you should initiate an ambush when "the majority of the enemy is in the kill zone"; that you should "[withdraw] all personnel and equipment...from observation and direct fire"; and that you should "not become decisively engaged by follow-on elements." I doubted that our antagonists had read the handbook, but they had followed its battle plan with eerie precision. Obviously, based on this day's baptism of fire, "neutralizing" the bad guys was not going to be easy.

I also learned something about working with Afghan allies.

I learned, for example, that our military's concept of chain of command had barely gotten a foothold in Kunar Province. Once the district leaders had finished their spiel, I looked around to see which indigenous forces had shown up to provide them—and us—armed assistance. There were three groups of about thirty men each, representing the militia loyal to Malik Zarin, a platoon-sized element from the Border Brigade, and a contingent from the Asadabad police. (In 2003, the Afghan National Army had not yet come together.) Each group had lined up in formation, trying to look like king of the hill, with each group's leader advancing a different plan of pursuit, and the whole scene accompanied by head shaking in the ranks.

Ninety generals, no privates. These were the guys that Major Hewitt had charged us to "coordinate" with, and you could see at a glance that doing so would be different from issuing orders you knew would be obeyed.

Choosing a plan of pursuit was pointless anyway, because the time for effective response was long gone. Last contact with the attackers had been half an hour ago and almost two miles away. They wouldn't now be hanging around the bend in the road, awaiting the arrival of a massive reaction force. Instead, to borrow a phrase from British strategist Sir Basil Liddell Hart, they would be flitting back into the mountains, nimble as mosquitoes.[3] It made no difference if we went with the militia plan or the Border Brigade plan or the police plan. There was no way we were going to catch the mosquitoes.

But our Afghan allies wanted to do something, to feel that they were contributing to the good fight, maybe to feel that their honor was not imperiled by inaction. After listening to them argue for ten minutes—more pursuit time lost—I decided why not? Let them contribute. Let them see that we valued that contribution. Let them go on their wild goose chase.

Since each of the three groups had its own idea of where the goose might be, I agreed to have them split up and follow their own game plans. I took note of which sector each group would be searching, and I asked that when they overtook the attackers or discovered their whereabouts, they report back to me on their handheld FM radios. This afforded each of them the sense of responsibility they were obviously seeking, and it meant that if and when they reported back, they might bring us some intel we could use. This wasn't what Major Hewitt had meant by coordinating, but at this early stage of our alliance with that gaggle of generals, it seemed the wisest option. Diplomatically, at least, it was a fruitful one: the Afghans, whose cooperation we were going to need, seemed flattered that we were entrusting them with the chase.

It had been an instructive morning. I had learned that our fiendish enemy was also fiendishly clever. I had learned that working with Afghans was going to require diplomacy. And as we left Shamir Kowt to return to base, I learned one other thing—something that went to the heart of unconventional warfare and that let me know our work here would not be simple.

We were headed back down the valley and I was thinking about the rows of unreadable faces we had seen upon arriving. I had seen Mashal talking to some of them, and I asked him about it. What were they thinking? What did they think of the attack, the morning's events? What did they think of us?

"They are very happy, *Commandon*," he said, using the Pashto term of address for "commander." "They did not think you would come to their village to help them. They are surprised and grateful."

The answer should have pleased me, but it did not. I could understand why the villagers would be grateful. But surprised? The last thing they should have been was surprised.

The whole point of a Special Forces mission was to help indigenous populations resist their oppressors. *De Oppresso Liber*, that was our motto. We took it seriously, and we were acutely aware that to fulfill that charge, it was essential to win the support—the hearts and minds, as the expression went—of the local people. If the people of this one village were surprised by our coming to their assistance—if they didn't understand that we were there on their behalf—we obviously had work to do in the communications department.

6

Hammer and Anvil

Unless you know the mountains and the forests...you cannot maneuver effectively with an armed force.

—Sun Tzu, *The Art of War*

November 2003

We had been at Asadabad FOB for a month when Bagram finalized plans to take the fight more aggressively to the enemy. The traditional fighting season in Afghanistan was the spring and summer. As the weather turned colder, many jihadists who had come to Afghanistan in the spring would be returning for the winter to their homes in Pakistan. In an attempt to capture or kill them before they escaped over the border, senior command planned an elaborate search-and-destroy mission known as Mountain Resolve.

We knew something was up when a group of SEALs showed up at Abad from Task Force 121. These men were older than the average SEAL, and their short-barreled rifles indicated they were not looking for fights in the mountains but were set up for close quarters combat. Unlike Green Berets, SEALs aren't much interested in winning hearts and minds; their focus is to get in and out of hostile territory quickly and eliminate or capture HVTs. These particular SEALs were part of the group usually referred to as Seal Team

6—the Special Ops guys who eventually killed bin Laden in 2011. While they were at Abad, I spent some time with their unit commander, a Navy lieutenant named Rich. We got on well, discussing the area and anticipating the challenges of the upcoming operation.

If you ask a Mountain Resolve veteran to describe that operation, he'll tell you that it was spearheaded by the 10th Mountain Division of light infantry, in cooperation with Army Rangers and Navy SEALs; that it began at Zero Dark Thirty on November 7, when Chinooks dropped several hundred troops of the division's famed Warrior Brigade into Nuristan Province; and that its mission was to cleanse the area of Anti-Coalition Militias (ACMs). He might remember that Mountain Resolve was a "hammer and anvil" operation, designed to crush the ACMs between the hammer of 10th Mountain, advancing north up the Waygal Valley, and the anvil of coalition forces waiting upstream.

If the vet was there, he'll remember that snow made the already rugged terrain nearly impassable, that the troops had to hire local donkeys to haul their equipment, and that in trudging uphill and down through the tortuous Hindu Kush, they lived up to their reputation as mountain professionals. He might also remember that the operation secured a few small arms caches and the death of a midlevel Hekmatyar commander named Ghulam Sakhee.

All this is part of the public record. What's not part of that record is the more complicated story of what Mountain Resolve failed to bring to fruition. It's not taking anything away from the courage or tenacity of the regular Army soldiers to say that, from a Special Forces perspective, there was something sadly unresolved about Mountain Resolve.

I had my doubts about the operation even before it began. When I was briefed on it a few days before the initial air drop, I expressed surprise to Major Hewitt that a massive assault into our AO was going to be spearheaded by regular forces who—despite their expertise in mountain combat—knew next to nothing about the terrain. In addition, the villagers of these mountain reaches were often standoffish and sometimes hostile. They had been down this road before, with the "helmeted ones" of the Red Army, and they had not yet been given a reason to trust coalition troops more than they did the Soviets. To go into this area with no local knowledge seemed unwise.

The main CIA operative in Asadabad thought so, too. I once heard him refer to his tattered copy of *The Bear Went over the Mountain*, an account of the Russians' Afghanistan experience, as the Operations Order for Mountain Resolve. "We've just updated it," he joked, "with PowerPoint slides."

"The Pech and the Waygal, sir—that's our area," I told Major Hewitt. "We've been here a month and we have some contacts there, elders and local militia, who may be willing to give us information. Finding HVTs, that's a shot in the dark. With respect, I'd like to volunteer my team's services. Maybe we can narrow the search."

To me the offer seemed like common sense. The major didn't disagree. But he wasn't in charge of the operation.

"These plans have been in place for weeks, Captain," he said. "This is a major assault to deny the enemy sanctuary, and the conventional forces will be heading up the operation. They have the resources and manpower to execute. But your team—in fact, all of the ODAs—will be playing a critical role."

He explained that, while he fully expected the "hammer and anvil" strategy to be effective, it was possible that some HVT quarries would escape the crunch. If past experience was any indicator, these nimble few would attempt to flee Afghanistan for safe haven in Pakistan. To do so, they would have to cross the Kunar River.

"Your objective, Captain, is to prevent them from doing so."

So we were to be border guards. Not just us, but all of the ODAs operating in northeast Afghanistan. There were three of them tapped for the mission, and each of us would be assigned to a certain stretch of the river, tasked with blocking the escape into Pakistan of any insurgents who had slipped the Big Army net.

We were overqualified for the job, which irritated my team. Dave Moon spoke for all of us when he rolled his eyes and grumbled, "Three years Ranger and Special Forces training so I could be a border guard?"

On paper, though, it wasn't a totally bad plan. With 10th Mountain and coalition forces pinching respectively from the south and the north, and a string of ODAs guarding the river crossings, Taliban and Al Qaeda operatives—maybe even Hekmatyar or Abu Ikhlas—would be nearly surrounded. Assuming the militants chose to flee east instead of deeper into the western highlands to avoid our infantry, the scheme had a sort of geometrical elegance.

But the Pech and the Waygal and their peoples were not geometric. To anyone who had spent more than a few weeks in these mountains, it was evident that this neatly laid trap could easily go awry.

Along the river, one obvious problem was coverage. When the orders came down, our team was assigned to block the crossings along a twenty-kilometer stretch of the Kunar River. There were twelve of us, plus our six Afghan allies, so the math wasn't encouraging—less than one man per kilometer. Of course, if a fleeing ACM fighter decided to use one of the three bridges in that area, our job would be simplified. But based on what we had learned of our adversaries so far, they didn't seem the types who were afraid of getting their feet wet. We obviously needed a larger interception force.

We addressed this problem—I won't say we completely solved it—by enlisting the help of local Afghan fighters. In the riverfront village of Asmar, we met with an Afghan Militia Force (AMF) commander who had about forty soldiers at his disposal. The overall Special Ops commander in Afghanistan, Col. Walter Herd, was fond of saying that the default for any decision was to "get the Afghans to do it."[1] Jimi Rymut, who was proving to be an astute team member, echoed this view. "Why don't we use some of the local folks on this mission?" he asked. "It can only help us and it will give us some good experience in seeing how these people tick."

This made sense, so we provided the AMF with food, winter coats, sleeping bags, two-way radios, and a modest financial incentive, and asked them to help us cover the area's two bridges. I also promised a bonus for any militant they helped identify or capture. And I reminded them of the existing bounties on Abu Ikhlas, Hekmatyar, and other HVTs who might pass through the area. This was admittedly risky, since we might be asking them to turn in someone they admired, but we were banking on the fact that money talks and hoping that it might diminish the luster of any anti-Soviet heroes who were now fighting their own government.

Since our new allies were local guys who knew the language, enlisting them also addressed a second major problem: the inherent difficulty of telling friend from foe.

This was a problem throughout Afghanistan, and it was the main reason I was skeptical about Mountain Resolve. The infantry was trying to eradicate bad guys from a huge area with virtually no information about who they were looking for. In Kunar and Nuristan in 2003, every male between twelve and ninety carried a rifle. Owning a gun was no indication of ill intent, and as I've noted, there was no deck of cards of the most wanted HVTs. We didn't even know what Abu Ikhlas looked like. He could have waltzed up to a coalition checkpoint in broad daylight and been waved on across the river to "visit a cousin."

The situation was further complicated by the fact that, in a land where blood feuds could go on for generations, villagers were not above falsely identifying their enemies as Taliban as a way of calling in the big guns to do their dirty work for them. We had already run into this problem in Shamir Kowt, when on a false tip we had sent a probably innocent mortar owner off to Bagram.

The solution for this problem was to get local people to see us as friends, so they'd be willing to say honestly "This one's Taliban" or "There's the Egyptian." So incentivizing the folks in Asmar made good sense. As a way of managing what strategists called the human terrain, it tilted the odds in our favor. In an arena where the advantages of physical terrain were on the bad guys' side, maintaining that edge would be critical to our success.

We left our Afghan garrisons at Asmar and proceeded up the river to the village of Barikowt. There we arranged the same kind of protection for a third bridge. And there the importance of human terrain came further into focus.

On the second day in Barikowt, with the bridge covered, we took a walk around town. Given that we were in a war zone, it was a strangely placid experience—more like a tourist's walkabout than a military patrol. What we found was as unexpected as it was fortuitous. Like most Afghan towns, Barikowt was poor—so poor that it could not support a full-time physician. Its small clinic was abandoned, because the doctor who sometimes ran it was in Pakistan, and the shelves that should have held medicines were virtually empty. All ODAs have at least one medic, and we had three. Here was a golden opportunity for us to help folks in need, and in the process maybe pick up some points in the hearts-and-minds game.

Mike, Ben, and Randy began brainstorming how to organize a clinic, what supplies we already had, and what additional ones we needed. Ben, always resourceful and comfortable working in a foreign market, quickly identified a couple of pharmacies that carried drugs imported from Pakistan. They had limited stock, but as the local people had limited cash, it wasn't being rapidly depleted. So, thanks to Ben's Rx recon, we had located an available supplier for when our own stock ran out.

We reopened the abandoned clinic that afternoon, putting out the word that our medics would be seeing patients the following day. By early morning the waiting line was ten people long, and over the next two days our medical trio saw probably a hundred people, treating everything from broken bones to intestinal troubles to infected wounds. Simply as human outreach, this was a gratifying experience, but it also counted as a small victory in unconventional warfare. It was amazing to see how much goodwill—not to mention shared information—you could generate by giving antibiotics to a coughing six-year-old.

The military calls this kind of thing a medical civic affairs program, or MEDCAP. We just referred to it as sick call. By whatever name, it was obviously appreciated by the people we served, and the attitude of watchful waiting that had greeted us on our arrival was soon replaced by cordiality and gratitude. By the end of our second day in Barikowt, people were stopping us on the street to offer their thanks, to hand us flowers, and to invite us in for tea.

I'm not sure that the planners of Mountain Resolve would have considered this a tactical victory, but I certainly did. We ran similar MEDCAPs in several other villages, and each one reconfirmed a growing understanding that, in the fight for control that we were waging with Al Qaeda and the Taliban, not every effective weapon could be measured in calibers. Band-Aids and penicillin could also break down walls.

Mountain Resolve had been under way for a week when we entered a small town called Naray, just south of Barikowt. Its chief of police, a man named Wakdar, had earlier been befriended by CIA agents; he was more than usually welcoming to Americans and more than usually antagonistic to the Taliban. Tall and weathered looking, he cut an imposing figure in Army battle dress uniform pants, a traditional Afghan *pakol*, and a khaki vest that made him look oddly like a photojournalist. Hardworking and determined, he insisted that his officers always wear their uniforms—not a universal practice in these parts—so that we could identify them at a distance as fellow anti-Taliban.

Wakdar was eager to help us in capturing insurgents, and at one point his eagerness got the better of his judgment.

We had just finished morning chow when two Toyota pickups pulled up to the field where we parked our vehicles. The chief had captured a man who he said had been posting night letters on villagers' doors. Night letters were leaflets distributed, usually under cover of darkness, by Taliban sympathizers. Generally they railed against the influence of foreign devils. At this point in our deployment, many of them warned villagers not to vote in the national elections that were slated to take place just after the new year.

Accompanied by Roger and our interpreter Mashal, I approached the police chief. As we spoke, two of his men went to the back of one of the pickups and unloaded a man with his hands bound and a bag over his head. They placed him on his knees next to the Toyota. The two cops looked both pleased and pissed, and I noted as we approached them that Wakdar had his hand on his holstered sidearm. Roger posted himself behind the prisoner and kept a watch on all parties.

Wakdar started talking excitedly, gesturing toward the hooded figure with contempt and obviously wanting us to applaud their capture of this Taliban agent. Mashal's translation, following a couple of beats behind the chief's rant, revealed that he had arrested the culprit because his leaflets promised to kill anyone who voted. Then, with about a two-second interval between them, two things happened.

Wakdar pulled his pistol out of its holster and Mashal said, "So we will now execute this criminal."

Roger, with a look of surprise that mirrored my own, instinctively moved to the side to avoid getting splattered by pieces of the prisoner's skull. At the same time I heard myself saying, "Whoa! Hold on!" as my hands went up in protest.

"Let's talk to this man first," I said hurriedly. The chief looked puzzled but nodded agreement.

When we took the bag off the guy's head, it was obvious that he had been badly beaten. Through swollen lips he protested that he had threatened no one, that he was in fact a government worker, and that the "night letters" he had been carrying were flyers *urging* people to vote.

Mashal read one and confirmed that this was true. If the arresting officer had been literate, he would have known that. But neither he nor any of his colleagues—including our buddy the police chief—could read. At the time of his arrest, the prisoner's explanation had fallen on deaf ears: in the cops' view, it was patently ridiculous, and their rough "interrogation" had revealed the truth.

This put me in an uncomfortable situation.

Chief Wakdar had obviously screwed up, but I didn't want to embarrass him in front of his men; nor did I want to discourage government officials from capturing night-letter carriers. I thought about it for a moment and then decided to tread delicately over this rocky patch of the human terrain. First I thanked the chief and his men for their vigilance. Then I mildly upbraided the government worker, pointing out that had he notified the chief of his intentions before distributing the leaflets, this unfortunate misunderstanding—and his beating—could have been avoided.

"You were doing the village a service," I told him, "but you were acting in the dark. The police saw that you were acting suspiciously, and that is why they stopped you. They were doing the village a service as well."

I thought that threaded the needle between praise and correction pretty well. Wakdar seemed pleased that I had turned his blunder into an understandable mistake, and the government worker promised to be more careful. When the police returned to their station, I took the worker aside and apologized for the misunderstanding. Part of our job in Afghanistan, after all, was to help establish a stable post-Taliban government. I wanted this guy to know that we were on his side. I also gave him some money for medical supplies. I wasn't happy about Wakdar's interrogation methods, but it was a cultural custom that seemed beyond my ability to resolve.

The episode might have turned out much worse. It wasn't the first time justice was stymied by miscommunication. It wouldn't be the last.

The incident had an interesting long-term outcome. As Roger reflected on the scene that originally confronted us—a bagged and beaten prisoner about to be shot—he saw the makings of a teachable moment. Today, as an instructor of Special Forces in training, he uses it in a role-playing exercise to impart the need for Green Berets to think on their feet. In a training exercise, he has his students encounter exactly that scene, with fellow instructors playing the prisoner and the gun-waving chief.

"The cop is about to take this guy down," he says to his class. "What are you going to do?" When his students ask him how he came up with such a crazy scenario, they're sobered to hear that, in Afghanistan, it happened for real.

A day later, Wakdar brought us a second roughed-up prisoner. He had been found with notes and sketches that suggested he was "watching" the Americans. Denying charges that he was a Taliban informer, the man was laughing fitfully, mumbling, and staring off into space. Wakdar thought he was acting crazy as a ploy to escape detection. Chastened by his earlier mistake, though, he wanted our medics to check the man out to see if in fact he had mental problems.

This was another tricky situation, because none of our medics had the training to do a psychological workup. Neither did a battalion physician's assistant who helped in the MEDCAP for a couple of days; when we asked him about it, he simply laughed. So we were stuck. The prisoner looked mentally unsound, but what did we know? And I didn't want to return him to Wakdar's tender mercies, because I knew he would only beat a confession out of him. Randy and I talked and decided that rather than keep him in limbo in Naray, we should get one of the 10th Mountain noncommissioned officers who were resupplying us to bring him to Abad, where he could get his injuries treated and also undergo a proper mental health workup.

This worked out well. Within hours of arriving at the firebase, the guy realized the game was up, and he copped to the ruse. It turned out that he was an enemy intelligence officer—we never discovered whether he was Taliban or Pakistani—and that he had information about an ambush that had been planned on a Navy SEAL unit.

These were the SEALs we had met in Asadabad just before Mountain Resolve. They were part of a Joint Task Force known as TF-121, who had been involved in HVT captures in Iraq and were now attempting to do the same in Afghanistan. They had passed through Barikowt on their way to Kamdesh, to hand over to my command a unit of Mohawks—Afghan Special Forces—who were originally supposed to accompany them up the valley. Their commander, Rich, had told me that he was uncomfortable working with indigs, and would I take the Afghans off his hands?

"Ron, working with the local monkeys is not our gig," he told me. "That's a Green Beret thing. Can't you take them for a while and teach them how to eat snake or something?"

I gave him a hard time about this comment, arguing that the Mohawks could be a critical asset to his team as they went into an unknown area with no knowledge of the local language. He was unconvinced. No surprise, really. It wasn't SEAL philosophy, any more than it was 10th Mountain philosophy, to "let the Afghans do it." Rich and his guys were literally and figuratively SEALs out of water. So I took charge of the Mohawks (who proved a valuable addition to the Border Brigade), and the SEAL unit continued its trek alone.

Three days had passed. The SEALs were now on their way back from Kamdesh, unaware that they were driving into an ambush. Luckily, the intel provided to Asadabad by Wakdar's second prisoner averted a tragedy. AH-64 Apache helicopters were dispatched to the ambush site, and the insurgents were eliminated before the SEALs entered the kill zone. I was profoundly grateful to Wakdar, and I told him so. The SEALs only found out later that, with minutes to spare, they had dodged a fusillade of AK-47s.

I couldn't help but think that they might have dodged it earlier had they hung on to the Mohawks.

Wakdar was a cordial host. One of the most vivid memories I have of our time in his village was of a meal we had on the police station roof. From there we could see the valley, the river, and the village on the other side. We had spent the day doing MEDCAPs. Now, under a full moon, we were enjoying Wakdar's hospitality, sharing stories and dipping pieces of naan, the traditional Afghan bread, into bowls of meat and rice. Sitting in a large circle with the chief and some village elders were Roger, Scott, Dave, Courtney, Mike, myself, and a squad of soldiers from the 10th Mountain Cav that had come to Naray to assist us. One of them, licking juice from his fingers, said in an amazed whisper, "I've never done anything like this before."

"Like what?" asked Scott.

The young Cav soldier looked around the circle of old men and shrugged. "You know," he said hesitantly. "Native...kind of stuff."

The statement was revealing. Here was a young American soldier who had been in Afghanistan for months (he had landed at Bagram in June) and had never once had chai and naan with local people. That said a lot about our military posture here. ODAs might be out in the boonies talking to goatherds, but for the majority of coalition forces, the only Afghans they were likely to have any intimate contact with were enemy fighters trying to cut them to ribbons. For most troops, Direct Action, or offensive operations to seize, capture, or destroy targets (that is, "killing people and breaking things"), was the name of the game; meetings on the human terrain were not part of the job.

"I know what you mean," said Scott. "This Afghan chow ritual is new to me, too. But in some ways it's also very familiar."

Then he said something that really sparked my thinking about what we as a Special Forces unit were doing here.

"When I was in Poland on an LDS mission—this was in 1991—I really got into the culture. The food, the music, what people talked about. Not the vodka, of course," the good Mormon said with a laugh. "But the connection to a foreign culture, the idea of being in someone else's country and trying to understand their take on things, trying to build relationships at a time when the people were just transitioning away from the Cold War—all of that was amazing. I think that experience prepared me well for what we're trying to do here."

Hearing Scott's recollection, a light went on for me.

I had been an LDS missionary, too, in Switzerland, where I had interacted with people from almost every country in the United Nations. In some small way I had gone native in Geneva, and remembering that slightly scary but fascinating experience of being a stranger in a strange land, I saw that what we were doing in Afghanistan wasn't without a precedent. Not for me and Scott, anyway, or for the other ODA guys who had served as LDS missionaries in various parts of the world. Not for anyone who had visited a foreign country and done more there than check off tourist sights.

"Tashakur," I said to our host, thanking him for the meal. And silently I said a thank-you to the young Cav soldier. His comment had started me thinking.

In some ways we really were like missionaries. In fact, after Naray I felt that, aside from the fact that we were armed, we were more like missionaries than like Crusaders. Rather than spreading the Gospel, we were trying to spread a solution to the chaos that Afghans had experienced for the past thirty years. That entailed something more than neutralizing the enemy. I saw that our mission here also had to do with respecting the locals and doing sick calls and bringing a semblance of safety into troubled lives. And delivering the good news about democracy, that exotic concept that had yet to take a foothold here.

Of course there were differences between the LDS and Special Forces versions of missionary work. During my time in Switzerland, no one had lobbed a rocket in my direction. For a while, working the MEDCAPs and supervising the Mohawks and sharing naan with Wakdar under a full moon, it was tempting to forget that.

It wouldn't be long before we got a reminder.

7

Odysseus Redux

Sing now of the wooden horse, fashioned by Epeius with Athena's aid and brought by artful Odysseus to the city's gate, its belly filled with warriors who would lay Troy low.

—Homer, *Odyssey*

All warfare is based on deception.

—Sun Tzu, *The Art of War*

In mid-November, with Mountain Resolve in full swing, B-Team called us to Asmar, a small town an hour north of Abad, for a Direct Action planning session with Major Hewitt. The code name for the commo and logistics headquarters there, Castle, gave things a medieval feel despite the presence of twenty-first-century technology. When we arrived, we learned that a former Taliban commander, now a local thug, was thought to be hiding weapons in his compound at Sangar, a nearby village. Command wanted to secure the cache and its owner through a Sensitive Site Exploitation, or SSE—military jargon for a weapons raid. Leaving our Mohawks and AMF on bridge detail, we set about planning the operation.

We first sent a four-man recon team—Scott with an interpreter, an Afghan soldier, and the informant, all in Afghan garb—to drive by the village and identify the compound in question. Scott, with his thick, dark beard, could pass for an Afghan from a distance. He was perfect for this type of recon. When they reported back, it became evident that securing the weapons was going to be a delicate affair.

In this part of Kunar, there were tons of small valleys, rivers, and trails that ran from the mountains bordering Pakistan to the Kunar River. These were the escape routes that our manning of the bridges was designed to cut off. Sangar was nestled between the Kunar River to the west, an east-west tributary that bordered it to the north, and a dirt road that bordered it to the south. It was only twelve miles from Pakistan, with a clean river bed and dirt road that ran all the way to the border. A likely transit point for insurgent arms.

The village contained about thirty compounds. The largest one, our target's sanctuary, was set far back from the entry road, close to the natural perimeter of the Kunar River tributary. The river wasn't the site's only protection. The compound was encircled by high mud walls that gave it a fortresslike appearance. Our target, it seemed, had a castle, too.

Guarding the compound were two sentries cradling AK-47s, one at the compound itself and another on a wall next to the road. They could indicate a larger force in the compound or around the area. The sentry on the wall next to the road had me concerned. "He's got a clear sight line down the road," Scott said. "Two-fifty, maybe three hundred yards, until it bends on the way back to Asmar. That's the closest we're going to get before being spotted."

The layout put us at a disadvantage. Any military vehicle traversing that three hundred yards of open ground would alert the sentries and give them plenty of time to move or hide the weapons—or, worse, prepare us an automatic fire welcoming party. As was common in this region, the terrain was too steep to permit a flanking operation: that too would be detected before we could reach the target. We considered a night raid, but even then we might be spotted approaching the target. In addition, there was no moon that night, and our Afghans, who would support us, had no night-vision equipment. The thought of blind, adrenalin-filled trainees running around a dark village didn't make me optimistic about our chances of success. So it looked like the element of surprise was off the table.

That deficiency was not to be taken lightly. Ever since British colonel J. F. C. Fuller had laid out his "principles of war" just after World War I, students of military science had accepted surprise as a tactical plus.[1] In the U.S. Army Field Manual, it's one of the nine basic principles of effective operations. Here in Kunar, we were constantly reminded of its importance, because our fugitive enemy relied on it so extensively. That had been clear in the November 1 ambush of the QRF, and it was clear every time a patrol hit an IED. Surprise was the very lifeblood of the insurgents' toolkit. For this SSE, I wanted to turn the tables on them, but given Scott's recon report, that seemed unlikely.

But maybe not impossible. Sitting with the team around a planning table just outside of Asmar, I suddenly remembered Homer, and I had an idea.

"What about the Trojan horse routine?" I asked.

I was referring to the most celebrated example of surprise in the Western military tradition: the "wooden horse" stratagem used to vanquish Troy. Unable to take the city after a ten-year siege, the Greek army pretends to sail away during the night, leaving behind a huge wooden horse. The Trojans, delighted at the "gift," drag it into the city. That night, out of its side climb Greek warriors led by wily Odysseus, the inventor of the ruse. They overcome the Trojans and burn the city to the ground.

Every student of warfare knows the wooden horse story, so I knew it wouldn't take much explaining to the team.

"Go on," Scott said.

"They'll be on the alert for a Humvee or anything else looking like it's coalition. But what if we used a jingle truck, put our guys inside, and drove it up to the compound? Like any other delivery truck. They might figure out something was up, but by then ten or twelve of us, jumping out, could easily take down the guards, and we'd be in."

Jingle trucks were civilian vehicles that were heavily decorated with paintings, fabric, chains, and other metal adornments. The cost of the decoration gave their owners prestige, and the jingling of the hanging metal gave them a name.[2] There were jingle trucks in every village in Afghanistan, and we were on good enough terms with some of the local tradesmen that locating a suitable one wouldn't be a problem. In fact, during that planning session, one was parked in the street right in front of us, unloading supplies from Asadabad.

Working out the details was less complicated than fashioning a hollow horse.

First, we commandeered the truck. Acquiring local resources in this way has been a military prerogative for centuries, and it can be accomplished with greater or lesser finesse. The nadir of finesse would be, for example, General Sherman's devastation of the Southland during his March to the Sea. Such a snatch-and-grab policy would have backfired for us in Kunar. Any Afghan whose goods we appropriated needed to feel that we had engaged in a fair market transaction, not armed robbery with an M4. In borrowing the jingle truck, therefore, we paid its owner triple what he would have made driving it back and forth from Asadabad. He was more than happy. (We didn't dwell on the possibility that it might get shot to hell during the SSE.)

The truck was an old Russian supply truck, open-top design, so we had to rig a canvas tarp over it to conceal our "Greeks." On

Scott's suggestion, I decided the concealed attack force would be composed of Afghans rather than the ODA. Scott had been increasingly pleased with their willingness to take responsibility, so I figured this was as good a time as any to have them demonstrate their skills. After adding in the Afghan militia from ODA 934, we had twelve Afghan soldiers ready to go. In keeping with the mantra of "letting the Afghans do it," we would stay in reserve; the Afghans would be the face of the operation.

For it to succeed, they would have to rehearse, so we spent that afternoon going over the assault details. Beneath the tarp they would be unable to see where they were, so we agreed on a two-tap signal from the driver to let them know the truck had gotten as close to the compound as the narrow village streets would allow. They would then jump out, breach the gate, and secure the area. Scott, Randy, and Dave had been drilling them on the fine points of search and secure for weeks, so they knew the proper procedures for threat assessment and room clearance, and the difference between securing a suspect, beating the crap out of him, and just shooting everyone in the compound because they might be the enemy.

To many Afghans in 2003, the idea of Rules of Engagement was an abstraction. In perpetual conflict for generations, they had evolved their own, pragmatic version of ROE: when you have the upper hand, take it. That wouldn't do when we were storming a compound that might contain many more innocents than insurgents. To avoid civilian casualties, we had to teach them new rules, such as "Don't shoot immediately when you go in a door" and "Before questioning, be sure all rooms are cleared."

Using a compound next to the AMF headquarters in Asmar as a practice site, we ran the Afghans through multiple trials of this "secure the objective" phase, until we were satisfied they could follow the ROE with minimum risk to themselves and to bystanders. The

B-Team approved immediately and they sent the plan to Bagram for approval by the Combined Joint Special Operations Task Force (CJSOTF). As expected, CJSOTF approved the CONOP as we laid it out.

Having received the CJSOTF green light, we settled in for the night, the gurgling of the Kunar River easing us to sleep. For a few drifting moments I almost forgot we were at war.

Early on November 13 we put the SSE into gear, rolling a three-vehicle convoy north out of Asmar. In a lead Toyota were Jimi dressed as an Afghan and one AMF soldier. About a hundred yards behind came the motorized "horse," driven by our interpreter Mashal, with Scott riding shotgun. Taking up the rear at an additional three-hundred-yard distance was an armored Humvee, with Roger at the wheel, me next to him, Dave on the .50-cal, and two more of our guys riding inside. We would provide command and control, and the .50-cal would provide rear security and overwatch the SSE. From the turret, Dave would be the first to see the compound as we approached.

The gaps between the vehicles weren't arbitrary. The idea was that the Toyota would stop on higher ground about fifty yards past the target. It would provide security on the east-west road past the compound to prevent leakers from leaving the target area and to prevent anyone coming from the east to assist the target. I stayed way behind in the Humvee because we didn't want to be seen until our "Greeks" were overpowering the guards. If all went well, by the time the sentries spotted us, the guys in the jingle truck would already be in control.

That was pretty much how it went down.

As the Humvee rounded the bend, I could see, three football

fields ahead, that most of the Afghans were already on a fast clip toward the compound; the last two were just then jumping out of the truck that had stopped on the main road. Roger floored it: no need for holding back now that the game was on. In seconds we squealed to a stop behind the jingle truck, jumped out, and raced after our Afghan buddies.

It was quite a race. The Afghans may not have been through Special Forces training, but they were a fit crew, and they had the advantage over us of having grown up at this altitude. It was no piece of cake catching up to them. When we did so a couple of minutes later, we instantly appreciated the value of a rigorous rehearsal: they had secured the compound with impressive speed. All rooms had been cleared, and they had under close watch the compound owner as well as a sentry who, as the jingle truck approached, had been so startled that he fell off the wall. A second sentry, the owner's son, had been asleep in the compound.

Our trainees greeted our arrival with broad smiles. So far so good: guards disabled, rooms cleared, and the suspect ready for questioning. He was an old man who didn't look very much like a Taliban commander; but it would be reckless to take such appearances at face value. He was standing in the inner courtyard of the compound, his wife and two teenage sons behind him, with an expression that I couldn't decipher. Confusion? Outrage? Apprehension?

SSEs are a tricky dance at this point, because you've entered another man's house without an invitation, and you're about to subject him to questioning in front of his family. In a culture as patriarchal and shame averse as this one, that's risky business. If he turns out to be innocent of any wrongdoing, you've insulted him for no reason and opened the door to retaliation from his kinsmen. Even if he's guilty of something you don't like, such as abetting HIG or the

Taliban, you might earn his neighbors' enmity by taking him away. In the battle for the human terrain, the cost could be high.

Another complication was that, as we had learned in the October "Gestapo" incident, informants lied. For all we knew, the sentry might have been securing his family compound from a Taliban threat in the next village and we could be acting on a tip that was meant to hurt our allies. We had it on decent intel that this compound and this village elder were in some fashion in league with our enemies. But we had acted on "good" intel before and discovered too late that it was a trick to get revenge on a hated neighbor. I was still smarting over that early mistake as, talking through our interpreter Mashal, I asked the old man where he was hiding his weapons.

Predictably, he denied knowing anything about weapons. That, of course, was ridiculous, as there wasn't a house anywhere in Afghanistan that didn't have a rifle or pistol or old Soviet grenade stashed somewhere. I pursued the matter for a moment, the old man responding in wide-eyed protest. I was getting nowhere when a kid about ten, who had been watching from the sidelines, walked up to Mashal and murmured something to him. Mashal turned to me.

"In the creek," he said. "On the far side of the house."

Why the kid volunteered that information I don't know. Maybe his father had a beef with the old man. Maybe his brother had been tortured by the Taliban. Maybe he looked at our triumphant Afghans and thought, That's for me. Of course he also might have been lying, trying to throw us off the scent. Whatever the reason, it was worth following up on his tip. We gave him a Power Bar— candy diplomacy—and he ran off down the street grinning.

The creek he had mentioned was a stone's throw away. With a metal detector we swept the near bank, then the far one, with no hits. I was beginning to favor the "lying child" explanation when

I noticed a large boulder in the middle of the stream. On a hunch I walked over to it. I pointed the flashlight attached to my weapon into a recess that the water had carved in it long ago. There, stacked snugly in a hole protected from the stream, was a neat pile of 107mm rockets, 82mm mortars, and recoilless rifle rounds.

Finding the cache was a fluke, but our Afghan soldiers looked at me as if I had superhuman powers of detection. I did nothing to disabuse them of the delusion.

We removed the weapons from their lair, prepped and padded them for transport, and loaded them into the Toyota for shipment back to Asmar—the first stop on their eventual destination, Asadabad. Then I returned to the old man's compound to resume questioning. If the cache had contained just small arms, I might have let the whole thing go, but storing ordnance of this heft went beyond the traditional frontier norm of keeping a musket over your door against bandits and wolves. As we sat down to tea together, I had Mashal ask him why he had hidden the weapons and if he was my enemy.

Certainly not, I was assured. He had a thousand reasons for holding on to those old Russian arms. I listened politely but half-heartedly, knowing that for all his talk the real reasons were the ancient ones: arms were a protection against enemies—foreign and domestic—and they were also collateral in a resource-poor country. Indians stored silver bracelets, crash-averse Americans stored gold bars, Afghans stored guns. There was no particular reason to suppose that this man, just because he had concealed twenty-year-old ordnance, harbored ill will toward the coalition. And he said as much.

"No, no Taliban. I am a friend to the Americans."

OK, I thought. Prove it.

"You know," I had Mashal tell him, "that I could take you to Bagram." He stiffened at the word. "But when you say you are not my enemy, I want to believe you. I am not your enemy, either. I want to help your village and I would like your help. I would like to know about the men who are our enemies. Your enemies and mine. There are Taliban in this area. Where are they?"

He didn't know exactly. But he did share some information about insurgent activity in the Shigal Valley highlands west of Asmar. This wasn't breaking news, since the whole thrust of Mountain Resolve was to target that area. But the fact that he was willing to share it spoke well of his intentions. It let me know he was no friend to that area's warlord, Gulbuddin Hekmatyar. He might not have been as committed to destroying the insurgency as our Afghan soldiers were, but it didn't seem likely that he was a threat. I decided to leave him alone.

When he learned that he would not be taken away from his family, he thanked me profusely and gratefully accepted the Power Bars that we gave to his kids. Then, almost ceremoniously, I handed him an AK-47 and three magazines that we had taken in the search of his compound and let him know that, as he was our ally, we didn't want to leave his family unarmed. In the rough neighborhood of Kunar, we respected his right to protect them against our common enemy. As he took the weapon, I could see in his eyes that this simple demonstration of trust had gone some way to offsetting the disappointment he must have felt at having the larger arms confiscated.

In returning the AK-47, I was applying a lesson I had learned from my experience in Kosovo. In a country of perennial conflict, when you completely disarm a villager, you are inviting his enemies to take advantage of his vulnerability. Faced with that threat, he may feel forced to partner up with unsavory characters—like a Taliban insurgency—to protect himself and his family. When everyone has at least the equivalent of that musket over the door, it creates a certain sense of balance that tends to keep local troublemakers at bay.

As we drove away, the arms cache in tow, my guys were as thankful as I was at how this particular raid had panned out.

"This feels a lot better than the last time," Roger said.

I couldn't have agreed more. Drawing on the element of surprise to mount a simple but effective raid, we had ended the SSE with proud trainees, a solid arms cache, and a village that saw the Americans as judicious and merciful. I was glad we had followed Odysseus's lead. And that, unlike the Greeks, we had managed to take our objective without burning it down.

The completion of the SSE almost closed our involvement with Mountain Resolve. We returned the old man's arms cache to Asadabad, where it would be either destroyed, requisitioned back into coalition magazines, or distributed to friendly Afghan forces. Then we returned to the Kunar River crossings, where we divided our time between bridge detail, supervising AMF on bridge detail, and relaxing in the Border Brigade building. HBO's *The Sopranos* was a monster hit at that time, which meant that when we weren't keeping an eye out for our HVTs, we were watching Tony Soprano wreak havoc on his.

In the two plus weeks we had been away from Asadabad, combat was starting to look a little boring. The 10th Mountain guys were trudging up and down forty-five-degree inclines, but so far the bad guys they were supposed to be driving in our direction hadn't made an appearance. I kept my opinion to myself, but I couldn't say I was surprised. I was getting used to seeing the enemy as perpetual no-shows.

But that didn't last. On the morning of November 22, while patrolling the road along the river, the Humvee Randy was driving narrowly missed an IED, in an explosion that hurled rocks into the turret and nearly deafened Ben, who was manning the gun. If the bomb had gone off any closer, it might have disabled two-thirds of our MEDCAP team. Randy treated Ben on the spot and he returned to Asadabad, where he was diagnosed with a ruptured eardrum—an injury that got him a Purple Heart.

The following day, a Toyota driven by Green Berets from ODA 934, en route to link up with us, was rocked by another IED, severely injuring two soldiers and their interpreter. We heard the explosion, drove to their aid, and joined a firefight in progress, as the other ODA peppered the hills to the west, where they had seen some of the attackers disappear. They followed in pursuit and were understandably pissed when the search came up dry.

The two attacks occurred two and a half weeks into Mountain Resolve—just about the time that a 10th Mountain company commander was claiming on a DOD website, "We're showing the ACMs that there is no place that they can hide because we'll find them."[3] I don't know what map he was looking at, but apparently it didn't include Naray.

8

—

The Experiment

These facilities were designed to allow the U.S. military to establish a presence in a sometime hostile environment while offering some degree of protection to its inhabitants.

—*Special Forces "A" Camp Manual* (1994)

It's not all kicking in doors and chasing old men with Enfields.

—Jimi Rymut

In Mountain Resolve, a huge amount of manpower and operational expertise was employed for nearly a month in beating the bushes of a five-thousand-square mile landscape. U.S. forces engaged insurgents in a number of incidents and secured some weapons caches like the one we had taken near Asmar. In terms of flushing out bad guys, though, there wasn't much to show. The one notable loss on the insurgent side was the killing of a Hekmatyar commander named Ghulam Sakhee. All of the other High Value Targets, including our four bad aces, escaped the net.

This is not to impugn the dedication or professionalism of the troops involved. Without question, the soldiers of 10th Mountain, the Rangers, the SEALs, and the Green Berets who undertook the mission demonstrated extraordinary vigor and persistence in the harshest of conditions. That said, a fair verdict on the operation's strategic success would be "inconclusive." This realization was not lost on Special Forces command. When the operation wound down and we returned to Abad, we found there was already some high-level buzz about a shifting of gears. Coalition forces had spent nearly a month trying to clear a vast area of hostiles through conventional methods. Considering the results, the strategic consensus was starting to shift toward putting a greater emphasis on unconventional warfare.

Since UW was a Green Beret specialty, I was eager to find out what this meant for Hammerhead Six. I didn't have to wait long.

On November 25 I found myself in a meeting with Major Hewitt and our B-Team's senior noncom, Command Sgt. Maj. Allen Smithee. Smitty was a jovial, experienced soldier well liked by the troops because he understood the B-Team's role and didn't let ego get in the way of his duties. More than once, when a senior officer was explaining a support issue to the ODA, I saw my guys look respectfully toward Smitty, as if to say, What's the real story, Sergeant Major? That November day, the real story was that our role was going to expand. We were done being only cache busters and border guards. Senior command had decided to try an experiment.

ODA 936 was going into the bush to set up an "A" Camp in the Pech Valley.

This was exciting news. "A" Camps were remote bases manned by A-Teams like ours. They differed from large firebases like Abad and from combat outposts (COPs) not so much in size as in intention. Designed as strategic elements in the UW game, they served as outposts of counterinsurgency firepower, but also as hubs of health, safety, and welfare for threatened populations. In the words of an unofficial manual written by Special Forces veterans in the 1990s, the "A" Camp serves as "an operational base to carry the battle to the enemy," but also as "an administrative center which must maintain constant contact and services with the population base of the local area."[1]

The need for popular support makes running an effective "A" Camp more complicated than manning a machine gun emplacement. The Green Berets who had in the past operated "A" Camps were soldiers first, but they also functioned in their remote bailiwicks as medics, carpenters, teachers, diplomats, engineers—you name it. Whatever an indigenous population needed to protect itself from assailants and build a better life for its children, the Special Forces of an "A" Camp were there to provide it.

The "A" Camp model had been developed and used famously in Vietnam. In 1961 a Special Forces sergeant named Paul Campbell, accompanied by agricultural specialist David Nuttle, had walked into the highlands hamlet of Buon Enao, set up a clinic, and began working with local leaders to erect a perimeter, train a defense force, and foster agricultural development. Over the next few years, this experiment was copied throughout Vietnam, as Green Berets set up camps in dozens of other villages.[2]

These camps—called "A" camps after the A-Teams that built them—were at the front line of counterinsurgency operations, in a war where conventional front lines had little meaning. The Green Berets who manned them served as a strike force against Vietcong attacks, trained Civilian Irregular Defense Groups (CIDG, pronounced "sidge"), conducted civil affairs and community development projects, ran PSYOPs to offset enemy propaganda, and built intelligence systems that included recon patrols, observation posts, and agent networks. In all of this work, the involvement of locals—as fighters and laborers—was a key to success.[3]

Until it was replaced by a more conventional "sweep and destroy" approach, the Vietnam "A" Camp experiment netted some impressive results. Soldiers at these outposts constructed or repaired hundreds of schools; relocated, housed, and fed tens of thousands of refugees; distributed millions of pounds of food; renovated dozens of hospitals; and provided medical care to a million individuals. These were admirable results from a humanitarian perspective, but they also reduced the Vietcong's appeal to the affected villagers— a desirable outcome in a time when the conventional war was not going well.

On that November day in 2003, I knew some of this history, and I knew the pride that Special Forces took in their Vietnam-era elder brothers. To most American civilians, the term "Green Beret" probably summons up a picture of a silently lethal, Rambo-style "snake eater." There's something to that picture, but the image that Special Forces soldiers are more likely to have of themselves is that of "quiet professional," as much at home building a bridge as firing a rifle. That was the picture inherent in the "A" Camp tradition. So when I learned that Hammerhead Six was being tasked to revisit the Vietnam experiment, I was simultaneously humbled and thrilled. When Major Hewitt asked me what I thought about the idea, I didn't hesitate.

"Locked and loaded, sir. When do we leave?"

The answer to that question was ASAP. But ASAP wasn't the same thing as immediately. Like any other major strategic operation, setting up an "A" Camp would require logistical support, and this meant that, even before choosing a location for the camp, we would have to request what we needed—or thought we needed—to make it a reality. In Afghanistan in 2003, such requests were made to Camp Vance at Bagram in a formal document called a Statement of Requirements (SOR). As soon as the idea of the camp first came up, I sat down with my team to prepare this wish list.

Most of the items on the list were by-the-book choices. We knew we would need tents, generators, fuel, ammunition, food, .

vehicles—the essentials for a team about to go deeper in-country. But we also had some fun with the SOR. By the time we were ready to send it off to Bagram, it included Oakley sunglasses for everybody (the Afghan sun is fierce) and a flat-screen TV (to watch CNN—or *The Sopranos*). Jason, who had done underwater training with me, wanted to ask for a decompression chamber. When I pointed out that we were several thousand miles from a dive-worthy water source, he was unfazed. "It won't hurt to ask," he said. "Worth it just to imagine the look on the quartermaster's face."

With the SOR submitted, we next had to decide where to put the camp. We needed a site where an ODA would be best positioned to promote American military goals and the health, welfare, and military readiness of local villagers. ODA 936 had been assigned the Pech Valley, but other locations were being considered as well. The SF theater commander, Col. Walter Herd, thinking perhaps of how often insurgent ghosts disappeared across the Pakistan border, initially leaned toward sites near the Kunar River, at villages to the north like Barikowt and Naray. Others favored the village of Kantiwa, deep in the hills of Nuristan. Later in the war, most of these sites would have camps set up in their vicinity, and they would all be modeled on the one we built in the Pech.

The site I favored, about fifteen miles upriver from Abad, was on relatively high ground at the intersection of the Pech and Waygal Rivers. There was a small compound there, in the village of Manogay, that years ago had been partially built and then abandoned by an NGO. During Mountain Resolve, it had been serving as the field base and tactical operations center (TOC) for the 2nd Battalion, 87th Infantry from 10th Mountain. The battalion nickname was "Catamounts," and the camp itself had been referred to as Catamount. There were other possible locations farther up the Waygal

Valley, but as soon as I saw Catamount's advantages—relatively high ground, good sight lines along two valleys, and proximity to villagers under our protection—I started to think that this should be our new home.

I didn't have much time to second-guess myself. At the end of November we learned that 10th Mountain would be redeploying out of the Pech, and that if we were going to take their place at Catamount—and take advantage of their existing security as we moved in—we had to do it on the double. That was what we did. We had originally expected to be flown there in helos, but the birds fell through, so on the night of November 30 we found ourselves packed into our three Humvees, three jingle trucks, and one cargo Humvee, rattling into the valley along Route Blue.

That route had become one of the most dangerous roads in Afghanistan, and had recently seen attacks from snipers and IEDs, so I was happy that Bagram had seen fit to give us air cover: a B-1 bomber and two Warthogs were our moving-day escorts. Even so, I remained wary. As we approached Shamir Kowt and passed through the plain that had been the "kill zone" of the November 1 ambush, I scanned the hills on either side of the road, wondering if there would be a repeat performance. Not this night, luckily.

There was another reason that the transit to Catamount was such a rush job. The 10th Mountain commander there, a lieutenant colonel named David Paschal, intended to conduct a weapons raid on a nearby madrassa, and he wanted our help—actually, the help of the Afghan soldiers who were under my command. Paschal was a savvy and culturally sensitive individual. He knew that having Americans raid a religious school (even one harboring arms) might not be well received by pious locals, so when he found that we were coming to Catamount, he asked if he could use our indigs as a first-line strike force. In exchange, he would leave a platoon of his infantry behind as extra security for us once the main detachment left. This sounded like a good deal both ways, so I said sure.

We got to Catamount in the dead of night, took a quick briefing about the raid, and were on the move again within an hour. It was a hike up to the madrassa, but by dawn the SSE was in place. The folks who slept in the school woke up on the first day of December in the watchful company of fifty U.S. soldiers and six Afghans. The school was secured, its residents reassured by the presence of our indigs that this wasn't a "Crusader" operation, and a weapons search commenced. It came up dry, but that wasn't the case for a site a little farther up the hill.

Scouring the woods for anything suspicious, one of the Afghans came upon a 107mm rocket emplacement. It appeared abandoned at first, but a closer look revealed a remote firing mechanism. The rocket was hooked up to a motorcycle battery, which would provide the launching spark, and an alarm clock, which would activate the battery. The alarm was set for noon—just a few hours after our arrival—and the rocket was aimed at the Catamount compound.

The calibration mechanism wasn't high-tech—just a pile of rocks supporting the rocket housing to provide an Afghan version of "Kentucky windage." The guy who put it here wouldn't have earned any engineering awards. But I wouldn't have bet my life on his calculations being wrong. I had to admire his resourcefulness—and the instinct for self-preservation that would put him far from the site when the rocket was launched. Newcomers to Afghanistan might joke about raghead zealots, but if you were facing hajji as an enemy, you developed a respect for his ingenuity and survival skills.

Lieutenant Colonel Paschal and his staff were pleased by the success of the operation. He extended to me a level of respect that captains don't always get from career senior officers, and I appreciated what he was willing to do to help my team be successful in the transition. For personal reasons, he was also a vocal champion of using Catamount as the "A" Camp site. His soldiers had just spent three weeks there looking for the enemy. Although they had only caught a couple of small fish, Paschal felt that they had made some gains in terms of community rapport that he didn't want to see lost when 10th Mountain left.

"When we got here," he told me, "the local government was intimidated and basically out of the picture. They didn't even want to talk to us for fear of Taliban reprisals. We've gotten them a little ways past that. But if we leave now and nobody takes our place, it's back to square one. We'll have spent three weeks in the shit with nothing to show for it."

For a regular Army officer, Paschal had a well-developed sense of the SF approach. The infantry's job is to close with and destroy the enemy, which in simple terms means killing people and breaking things. In counterinsurgency you understand that winning and holding the human terrain is the true objective. Not all combat officers are hardwired to adjust to this important nuance. Paschal was. He knew that developing community trust was as important as neutralizing snipers. And he knew that when you had taken high ground—whether it was physical or human terrain—you had to work to hold on to it or you'd soon see it roll down past you like Sisyphus's stone. Actually, you'd see it *hurled* down past you with insurgent assistance.

Aside from the opportunity for sustaining rapport, there were also defensive reasons for favoring Catamount in an area that was so volatile with insurgent activity. Its location at the juncture of the Pech and Waygal Rivers made it an ideal spot from which to conduct operations along the two valleys. Set on relatively high ground, it offered a good overview both of Manogay and of a nearby sister village, the slightly larger Nangalam. From a "field of fire" perspective, it was favorably placed.

The compound itself, once 10th Mountain left, suited us well. Its concertina wire perimeter was rudimentary, but that could be fixed. So could the buildings. The dilapidated remnants of the old NGO installation included a half-built school, a stable, a former tuberculosis and HIV clinic, and a few other unsteady or abandoned structures. It wasn't much, but it was more than our Vietnam predecessors had started with.

Another attractive feature was the proximity of a government district house, with which the compound shared a fence. Since having the support of the local government would likely increase our chances of success, I thought that having the Manogay police chief and the district governor literally next door would be a valuable asset should we set up camp here.

Lieutenant Colonel Paschal agreed. He brought me over to the district house and introduced me to the district leader and the police chief as "the new U.S. commander." That was premature, since nobody had yet signed off on Catamount as the site of the "A" Camp, but it was all right with me. Compared to the shaky transition I had experienced upon our arrival in Abad, this was extremely helpful.

The madrassa raid had taken place on December 1. The same day, still at Catamount, we had a surprise visit from some heavy brass: Colonel Herd, accompanied by generals Stanley McChrystal and John Abizaid. The generals were respectively the heads of Joint Special Operations Command and U.S. Central Command (CENTCOM).

I had heard their names early in my career. I got my start in the same place they did: the 504th Parachute Infantry Regiment. McChrystal had served in the 82nd Airborne and the Ranger Regiment, and had been an ODA commander. A well-known figure in the Special Ops community, he was currently heading up the counterterrorism efforts of Joint Special Operations Command. In 2009 he would become the commanding general in Afghanistan. General Abizaid, also an 82nd Airborne and Ranger veteran, had seen combat several times in his career. As a young Ranger captain he had parachuted into Grenada and commanded an Airborne battalion during the first Iraq War. He had also served as assistant commander for the 1st Armored Division in Bosnia-Herzegovina, commandant of West Point, and commander of the 1st Infantry Division in Kosovo. In 2003 Abizaid had responsibility for all countries in the Middle East, North Africa, and Central Asia—most important, Afghanistan and Iraq.

These heavy hitters had come to be briefed on Mountain Resolve's success and to get a take on the transition that would happen when 10th Mountain left. I took the opportunity, supported by Lieutenant Colonel Paschal, to make the case for our ODA as the logical next stewards—and for Catamount itself as the perfect "A" Camp site. The generals liked that there was a transition plan but deferred to Colonel Herd for the discussion on location.

"I've met the local leadership, sir," I told Herd. "The police chief and the district leader. They know the commitment we made with Mountain Resolve, and I believe that we are well positioned here to sustain the political stability that 10th Mountain has fostered."

It was a bit of a selling job, since I had only met the local leadership that day. But despite his initial leaning toward other venues, Colonel Herd wasn't that hard to convince. He gave us his informal blessing on the spot. A day later, Lieutenant Colonel Paschal and I received an official "Assumption of Command" letter. The letter said that effective 4 December 2003, ODA 936, with Captain Ronald Fry in command, would assume control of U.S. forces in the Pech Valley. Catamount would become the site of our new "A" Camp.

It would be, I was told, the first Green Beret "A" Camp of its kind to be established anywhere since the end of the Vietnam War.

Then things moved fast. Within a day, Chinooks started to arrive every few hours, picking up 10th Mountain soldiers in groups of twenty to take them back to Abad and new assignments. About forty soldiers remained as a permanent security detail, but most of the 10th Mountain complement was gone by the fourth. The helos also picked up the 105mm howitzers—hefty artillery pieces—that had been positioned in the poppy fields to the east of the compound: they were a huge supporting complement to the infantry's footprint, but they wouldn't be conveying to our small group.

It was disconcerting to see those guns go, but we were glad to learn that, thanks to Lieutenant Colonel Paschal's intervention, two of his mortars and their crews *would* be staying. He was aware that with our smaller footprint, we would be at high risk, and he made the case to higher-ups and his staff for us keeping the mortars. I actually overhead that conversation as I was waiting in his outer office to speak with him. He was on the phone to somebody at Bagram, and he was pretty fired up.

"We've *got* to leave them the mortars," he said. "Without them, they're sitting ducks, no way to respond."

There was a pause as Paschal listened to the response, which I couldn't hear. Then he spoke again, very deliberately. "If I don't leave the mortars, these boys will be killed. That is my decision." Apparently that settled the issue, and Paschal hung up.

Overhearing that conversation made it crystal clear—just in case I had forgotten—that we were about to set up shop in a very rough neighborhood. The outgoing sheriff might have been on our side, but the vicinity was full of outlaws—some armed with a lot more than six-guns—who would be doing their damnedest to put us six feet under. I was glad that a good guy like Paschal had our backs. So was Dave Moon, our senior weapons sergeant: he knew what a major component of our defense the mortars could be.

As the helos took the infantry out, they also brought in the goods for our "A" Camp experiment. The first of the resupply flights arrived on the fifth. We were happy to see that our SOR had been duly noted, and that most of the things we'd requested were coming off the Chinooks. No decomp chamber for Jason, amazing to report. But we got our Oakleys and food, our ammo and fuel.

Later that day, with the troop transport completed, Paschal and I shook hands for the last time, as Catamount transferred formally from his command to mine. This entailed two solemn and humbling announcements.

One was the official transfer-of-operational-control message that came in over the radio: "Hammerhead Six now has operational control of U.S. forces in the Pech." It took a second for the gravity of the officialese to sink in. My team was now in charge of a vast, hostile territory, and as their commander I was accountable not just for their safety but for that of six Afghan mercenaries, dozens of infantrymen, and a wide array of Pashtun and other tribesmen, not all of whom were in my cheering section. I was thirty-one years old. I had led troops before, but this was the first time I think I truly appreciated the meaning of that old military phrase "the burden of command."

The second announcement was even more humbling. One of the things that transfers with command is the authority to grant permission to fire on a target. This is called clearance of fires, and in a way it's a license to kill—technically, to give artillery the clearance to kill. When I heard Lieutenant Colonel Paschal announce "Clearance of fires is handed over to Hammerhead Six," I knew that my team had assumed an awesome responsibility.

That realization was confirmed on December 6. This was the day after the Chinooks had resupplied Catamount and departed. I woke up that day eager to see what the new assignment might bring us, and I was surprised to be met by a smiling Colonel Herd. He wanted to wish us well on the "A" Camp experiment and to assure us that we would get the resources we needed. I gave him a brief sitrep and a sketch of what we hoped to accomplish with the indigenous forces (Randy and I had already worked out a rough training time line). I also gave him a tour of the camp. He seemed satisfied with all of this, and confident that his experiment was in good hands.

His satisfaction grew to visible pleasure when I asked him if he'd like to fire one of the Soviet mortars we had repaired and a 12.7mm DShK machine gun. Full bird officers don't often have the time or opportunity to get their hands dirty and fire enemy toys like that. Herd took to it like a kid fresh out of boot camp.

Before he left that day, the colonel also put a thought in my head that, even though I didn't realize it at the time, would grow to be a kind of touchstone for our activity in the Pech. He invited me first to smoke a cigar with him—a bonding ritual, I suppose—and was a bit surprised when I informed him that, as a Mormon, I didn't touch tobacco. But he took this in stride, lighting up a big stogie himself and puffing on it contemplatively. We chatted for a few moments about camp logistics, and then he turned to me with an avuncular smile.

"How does it feel, Captain Fry, to be a warrior king?"

I was still trying to get my head around being in charge of an "A" Camp. The question threw me. "Sir?" I said.

He explained that while I might see myself chiefly as a military commander, I was going to find, before long, that a person in my position had a job that tended to expand in all directions.

"You're a soldier first," he said. "But you're the law here, too.

Before the year's out, you're going to be judge, cop, mediator, nurse-maid, and wise man to people in these hills you haven't even met yet." He puffed on the cigar and blew out the smoke. "Something to think about, Captain."

"I'll do that, sir," I said.

I was thinking at the time, Nursemaid and wise man? I doubt that. On that crisp December morning in the upper Pech Valley, being an "A" Camp commander seemed like a full-time job. I had yet to discover just how accurate the colonel's prediction would prove to be.

PART II

Winter 2003–2004

9

The Neighborhood

If you don't visit the bad neighborhoods, the bad neighborhoods are going to visit you.

—Thomas Friedman

When restraint and courtesy are added to strength, the latter becomes irresistible.

—Mahatma Gandhi

Although the Catamount site had served well enough as a firebase during Mountain Resolve, turning it into a proper "A" Camp would require some home improvement. We set to that task almost before the helos flying 10th Mountain out had disappeared. There was a lot to do, from shoring up the concertina perimeter to digging sanitary latrines, from installing generators and outfitting sleeping quarters to test-firing and positioning our defensive weapons. In those first few days we were a dawn-to-dusk construction crew.

In this we had the assistance of Lieutenant Colonel Paschal's security platoon, our own Afghan mercenaries, and a curious and industrious cadre of local workmen. Hiring them was a tactical decision. Lieutenant Colonel Paschal's soldiers had kept pretty much to themselves. I didn't want us to do that. I wanted us to mix with the locals, to buy things in their shops, to leverage their skills. By having local workmen help us improve the camp, we would be giving them skin in the game, boosting the local economy, and giving our own presence a boost in their eyes. Following the SF mantra about doing everything by, with, and through the indigenous population, we aimed to be facilitators of the locals' success, not their bosses. Above all, we wanted to be good neighbors.

This was consistent with how an "A" Camp differs from a firebase. A firebase is set up to provide artillery support and a sanctuary from which special ops or infantry forces may conduct short missions. An "A" Camp is designed to secure long-term influence by earning the loyalty and friendship of a local population. Building relationships and thereby denying those relationships to the enemy—that in a nutshell *is* the mission of a Green Beret "A" Camp.

It was hard work in those first days, with much of it supervised by our tireless engineers, Jimi Rymut and Jason Mackay. Since he had run civilian blasting crews, I put Jason in charge of the local workers. He hired a couple dozen of them and put them to work on two security measures: closing off a road that ran through the compound and constructing a hard perimeter of Hesco baskets filled with rocks and dirt from a nearby poppy field.[1]

Electrical power was provided by a new thirty-kilowatt generator that Jason had his interpreter Sahim buy for us in Taliban-thick Pakistan. Sahim was a lively youngster with perfect American English. During Mountain Resolve, they had passed on the street in Barikowt one day and Jason had jokingly asked, "What's up, brother?" Sahim had responded, smiling, "Going good, brother, how you doing?" At that point Jason thought he might have found a good terp. Later, as a test of his trustworthiness, he gave Sahim thirty bucks to buy supplies in town and the kid returned with the supplies *and* change. Having Sahim secure a Pakistani generator was quicker than following the Army's sluggish procurement protocol, and the shopkeeper didn't mind the color of our money.

The run-down facility rapidly took on new life. By December 3, just two days after the madrassa raid, I was able to state in my nightly sitrep that we had sandbagged the living areas, dug the pits for mortar emplacements, fortified our fighting positions, and created a modicum of hygiene by installing numerous piss tubes and hand-washing stations. Roger and Courtney had wired our team house so that we had lights and power for our computers, radios, and TV. Ben had even managed to rig up a shower. No hot water yet, but we weren't complaining.

Our home improvement surprised the young soldiers on our security detachment. One day, when one of them was giving me and Randy a report, he looked at the flat-screen TV admiringly. "Wow, sir, I wasn't expecting that." Randy just grinned at him and said casually, "War doesn't have to suck, son." It was too early to tell how badly the Hammerhead Six deployment might end up sucking, but that comment became an instant hit with the guys. We still consider it one of Randy's best one-liners.

The morning of December 5, with Mashal by my side, I met with the police chiefs and elders of three towns near the camp, in order to assess the local situation and assure them that we were there to help. Such meet and greets would soon become a weekly, sometimes a daily, aspect of my responsibility as "warrior king." On this first go-around, I was happy to find that they seemed pleased to have us in their backyard. Time would tell whether that sentiment held.

December 5 also saw the arrival of our first Red Ring resupply flight. Military posts throughout the country were resupplied by helicopters along regularly scheduled, color-coded routes; Asadabad was on the Red Ring but Catamount was not, as it had been a temporary camp. We weren't in dire need of supplies, but being on the Red Ring would be evidence that the "A" Camp idea had gone live and was recognized by the Bagram logistics team. If they sent out extra supplies, they expected us to stay. If not, it would mean that somebody had pulled the plug on the experiment.

That morning, therefore, I was down at the helo LZ with Jason and Randy, weapons at the ready and dressed in T-shirts, Oakleys, and body armor. When the first resupply Chinook hove into view, we burst into laughter, high fives all around. Any doubts we had about the mission's sustainability flew away in a cloud of prop wash. We were on the Red Ring route. I wrote in my journal that evening, "We actually have an "A" Camp that is being resupplied and we are king out here. It's like a scene out of a Vietnam movie. We are living the SF dream."

That night, basking in the historical significance of our situation, we relaxed with a movie. Becky had sent me a DVD of the 1968 pro–Vietnam War epic *The Green Berets*, and although we had all seen it before, the time seemed ripe for a repeat screening. So, with the camp's perimeter secured by the Afghans and infantry, we gathered in the darkness of our new team house to watch John Wayne and his A-Team battle the Vietcong.

The movie was based on Robin Moore's book of the same name, which at the time was a huge hit.[2] Although the movie departed from the book, it did effectively describe the Green Berets' interaction with local people, their difficult relationship with local fighters, the tension between a corrupt host government and military officials, and the reality of a dedicated enemy outside the wire. These were good reminders of what lay ahead of us.

The screening gave us a couple of moments of levity. One of them came the first time the film showed Wayne, playing a Green Beret colonel, carrying his M-16 by the sight mount, as if it were a suitcase handle. Any drill instructor would have given him crap for that, and our weapons expert Dave Moon didn't let it pass. "Is that the new standard, Ron?" he asked me. "Do we get to carry our rifles like that?"

Another scene shows the "A" Camp's front gate—a huge wooden structure with a crossbar used as a lock. When we reached this point in the film, a light popped on behind me. I turned around to see Jason, a Surefire flashlight sticking out of his mouth and his hand scribbling something on a piece of paper.

"Brainstorm, Junior?" I asked.

"You bet," said Jason. "That gate. Got to have it." He was waving the paper in the air like a crazy man, with a smile brighter than the flashlight.

I paused the film and hit the overhead light that Roger had made functional the day before. Jason hopped up and passed the sketch around, like a first grader who had drawn his first house.

"Awesome!" said Roger.

The next day Jason took some measurements and made a blueprint. By the end of our first week there, with Hesco bastions in place, mortar pits dug, and gun emplacements meeting the most meticulous of specifications, ODA 936's "A" Camp boasted an "awesome" front gate copied from a thirty-five-year old Hollywood flick.

We had fun with John Wayne's foibles, but it was in a spirit of camaraderie, not disrespect. This was true as well of our interactions with each other. Small military units are known for verbal jousting, and ODA 936 was no exception.

I've mentioned that Mike would joke about my head shed—Scott and Randy—being orangutans lording it over the gorillas. But he got as good as he gave, mostly because of his massive, shaggy Afro. Some of us thought of him as the unit's resident mountain man, and Jason at one point nicknamed him Grizzly Adams. On the other hand, Courtney, my preferred weight-lifting partner, who was as muscular as anyone on the team, got endless grief because of a wispy beard that stood in contrast to his physique. Jimi's "advanced" age—he was close to fifty—gave him the obvious moniker Grandpa.

Jason, who was never short of a clever dig himself, got razzed by everybody because of a tattoo-in-progress. He had started getting inked back at Bragg, intending to have his left arm covered with a seascape and a hammerhead shark. It was such a complex job, though, that he had to leave the States before it was finished, and so he wore it, throughout our deployment, in outline form. This led to comments like "Couldn't stand the pain, could you, Junior?" and "Your arm is so damn big the guy ran out of ink." As anyone who has served in a war zone will tell you, such banter, taken in stride, alleviates tension and enriches rather than disrupts unit cohesion.

We wanted to be good neighbors. But neighborliness is a two-way street. It wasn't long before we got some reminders that, in this particular stretch of the Afghan hinterland, we couldn't count on our good intentions being reciprocated.

The first reminder came just after noon on December 7, in the form of two rockets. They came from a ridge to the south and overshot our new home by about two hundred yards. Whether this was Abu Ikhlas's calling card or an opening jab from the HIG or Taliban forces we couldn't tell, but the message was clear enough: you're not welcome here. We peppered the ridge with a few mortar rounds, but this was little more than an acknowledgment of message received. The ridge was too far away to get true eyes on, and I knew from our experience on the madrassa raid that whoever unleashed the rockets would probably be long gone.

Coming on Pearl Harbor Day, the attack had a certain poignancy, and despite its ineffectiveness it did bring our situation into focus. As the incoming tenants of the Catamount site, we might share laughs about hot showers and Hollywood gates, but when you came down to it, the Kunar hills were crawling with the worst kind of neighbors. The kind who would happily burn down your house and who would, if Mullah Omar hadn't outlawed dancing, do a jig in the ashes.

We had been enjoying our honeymoon period—a brief respite

from the valley's normal turmoil. The rockets changed that. If on the sixth we were in danger of relaxing our guard, on the seventh we were back on high alert. I was almost thankful that the attackers had snapped us back into gear. It was useful to have a reminder every now and then that in addition to building the camp and recruiting soldiers to add to our initial six nephews, we had an enemy that needed our help in getting to his version of heaven.

The next day, we got another reminder.

This one was closer to home. It came from a building about fifty feet from our new John Wayne gate. This was the district's main religious center, the Manogay mosque. I hadn't yet met its leader, a young mullah named Zawar who provided spiritual guidance to hundreds of families in the Pech district. Once we arrived at Catamount, he also became the "pastor" for the six Afghan soldiers we had on loan from Malik Zarin, as well as a handful of new recruits who, eager to align themselves with the valley's new warlord, had volunteered to join us. It was from these allies in training that we got our second heads-up about unfriendly neighbors.

I was sitting in the team house, drafting an e-mail to Bagram about our progress, when Randy approached looking concerned. I had put him in charge of the Afghans, and their trust in him was evident in the fact that they had come to him with disturbing news.

"Our next-door neighbor," Randy said, "has been preaching fire and brimstone against the infidels. He says we're Crusaders. We're here to insult their religion and defile their women. The Afghans are uncomfortable. They know he's wrong, but the guy's a mullah. They don't know what to do."

In traditional Muslim cultures, mullahs are like priests or ministers are to Christians. They are seen as holier, more learned—spiritually more *correct*—than the everyday worshipper. In Afghanistan in 2003, many of them had spent their boyhoods in madrassas memorizing the

Koran. So if you were a devout Muslim and a mullah spoke from the pulpit, even if you thought he was speaking nonsense you held your tongue. I understood our Afghans' feeling "uncomfortable." They were hearing what they knew to be false, but they could not correct their spiritual leader without being seen as infidels themselves.

Somebody had to set the record straight. Letting a "damn the infidel" sermon go unanswered would be tantamount to admitting that the mullah was right. If that idea got around, we would have much more trouble on our hands than some uncomfortable allies. I had to pay Mullah Zawar a visit.

I sent for Mashal, who had already heard about the dilemma from the soldiers, and sent him to the mosque to arrange a meeting. While he was gone, Randy and I drafted a sales pitch that we thought might swing the mullah to our side. When Mashal returned saying that the mullah agreed to meet me that afternoon, I ran the idea past him.

"As our forces here grow, the mosque will be serving dozens, maybe hundreds, of new worshippers. We would like to thank the mullah for giving our Afghan brothers a place to worship. And we would like to offer him a small gift to offset his additional costs. Do you think he would be offended by such an offer?"

Mashal looked at me with wide eyes. He was too courteous a man to laugh in my face, but I had the impression he was suppressing a guffaw.

"Offended? No, *Commandon*. He will not be offended. He will accept the gift."

With that assurance, Mashal and I set off to the mosque.

Mullah Zawar was a slight figure about my age—both younger and gentler looking than I had anticipated. He greeted us at the door, bowing slightly. We removed our shoes, entered a small office, and sat on cushions in a circle. An assistant brought tea. I commented on the physical beauty of the mosque. I might have downplayed this angle if I had known then that it had been built largely with Wahabi money—the same source that had bankrolled 9/11. The mullah acknowledged my good taste with another small bow. Then we got down to business.

I first assured him that all of my men—whether Muslim or not—had a profound respect for Islam, and that we had come here not to convert his flock but to provide security against those who would bring misery to his homeland. Then I acknowledged the obvious: because of our presence here, he would soon become the spiritual adviser for a large number of Afghan troops who would be working and fighting alongside the Americans.

"We are very grateful," I said, "that our Afghan soldiers will be able to worship and to learn from you in this holy place. I believe that a soldier who prays is a better soldier because he is doing God's work. I thank you for the support you are giving my Afghan soldiers. I hope that together we may, with God's help, bring prosperity and peace to this beautiful valley."

The mullah listened attentively to Mashal's translation. "Insh'Allah," he said, in a reverent whisper. "God willing." So far so good.

"But these new members of your community," I went on, "will be many, and Manogay is not Kabul, not a place of great wealth. We bring you our Afghan soldiers, but we also bring you more work. If it is acceptable to you, and if God wills, I would like to lighten the burden that these new worshippers will create. Would it be proper for you to accept a gift from the American forces to thank you for the care you provide for our Muslim brothers?"

Zawar put his hand over his heart in a gesture of gratitude. Sure, the gesture said. It would be proper.

I reached into my pocket and withdrew the "gift" I had brought with me: two crisp bills bearing the likeness of the best ambassador the United States has ever produced, Benjamin Franklin. I respectfully handed one of them to the mullah and the other to his assistant. Both smiled broadly. Obviously they had seen Benjamins before.

In 2003, the average Afghan farmer in wheat or poppies was lucky to pull in two or three dollars a day. So a hundred dollars was more than a month's pay. For the mullah and his aide, it was a windfall. For the American taxpayer, it was a negligible price to pay for a holy man's support.

At least I hoped that was what we were buying. I didn't delude myself into thinking that the payment had purchased an enduring friendship, and I didn't see the gift as a bribe or as a means of buying his silence. I saw it as a tangible symbol of respect for the man's position and religion. I hoped that, taking the gift in that way, the mullah might give us the benefit of the doubt and lighten up on his anti-Crusader invective.

He did better than that. The day after our visit to the mosque, Randy gave me an update on Zawar's preaching.

"Whatever you told him did the trick," he said. "The Afghans say that yesterday's sermon was very pro-American. It seems we're not infidels after all. We respect Islam, he says. We're not like the Soviets."

Amen, I thought. But I wasn't ready to celebrate yet. I knew that in a culture as devoted to deal making as Afghanistan, Tuesday's newfound friend could be Thursday's backstabber. I hoped that my gesture of good will would bear more fruit than one cheerleading sermon. We had been there only a week. Time would tell.

Over the next few days, several of our soldiers and our interpreters thanked me for visiting the mullah. Obviously, this was more than a gesture to them. As the "lifers" in this valley, they appreciated that we were doing our best to win over the people and the leadership, thus improving everyone's chances for a brighter future. I took satisfaction in knowing that improving relations with the local clergy also increased my stature and trust among our indig soldiers.

Those soldiers were constantly on my mind, because as our mission proceeded, we would have to rely more and more on them to help us keep the peace. This would mean adding many more volunteers to their ranks. So many that, we anticipated, there would be an entire ASF company—more than one hundred fighters—patrolling the Pech. Securing those soldiers would be a more complicated proposition than just borrowing Malik Zarin's nephews.

We needed recruits that we could train to help us accomplish the mission, but at the back of everyone's mind was a question: how could we be sure that the young guys lining up to help us fight the Taliban were not friends of our adversaries infiltrating our ranks? We had all heard horror stories about Green Berets in Vietnam having their throats slit in the night by indigs they had recruited and trained. Similar "green on blue" incidents had occurred in Iraq and Afghanistan, so getting the right Afghan allies wasn't an academic concern.

After some discussion of this touchy issue, Mike, one of the LDS team members, said half jokingly, "Why don't we recruit Afghans the way Helaman did with the stripling warriors?"

This was a novel and, as it turned out, fruitful suggestion. As Mike explained to the half of the ODA who weren't LDS, in the Book of Mormon, Helaman is a prophet and warrior who is trying to defend the pacifist Ammonites against an attacking Lamanite army. When the Ammonites, fearing destruction, are about to break their oaths not to shed blood, Helaman convinces them instead to give him their sons, who are too young to have taken the oath. These "striplings" become an army that vanquishes the attackers, and although every one of them is wounded, no one dies. The two thousand boys are referred to as the Sons of Helaman.[3]

"Let's hire the sons of the village elders," explained Mike. "That way, we'll have guys that have been vouched for and that have the reputation and the honor of the village elders at stake."

"Great idea," Scott added. "The chances of their sons betraying oaths or embarrassing their fathers in combat is less likely than if we filled our ranks with ragtag Afghan punks."

All of us, Mormons and non-Mormons, agreed that this was a good idea. So it was decided. I didn't know it yet, but it wouldn't be long before Mike's clever idea was put into operation.

In a rural community, word of mouth travels fast. Just a few days after our meeting with Mullah Zawar, I learned that the district *shura*, or council of elders, was about to convene and that they would like me, the region's putative new warlord, to attend. This was great news. I didn't know whether the council would act as a welcome wagon, an investigating body, or a judgment seat, but one thing was clear: this was the perfect chance to meet the neighborhood honchos face-to-face.

In Afghanistan's rigidly patriarchal culture, *shuras* served as de facto governments for huge rural areas. Generally each village would have a council of elders to manage local issues, while regional issues would be addressed by a district council composed of representatives from each village. If you wanted to get anything done in rural areas, you might have tea, as I had been doing, with police chiefs and district governors. But without the approval of the *shura*, little of what you decided would come to fruition. So I was happy to accept the invitation. Kunar *shuras* were like old-time town meetings, except that only male elders got to attend. To a Western perspective this was sexist and antidemocratic. In the Pech, it was the way things were done.

The meeting took place in a large open area next to the Manogay district house. I arrived with Scott and Mashal, expecting to be greeted by ten or twelve elders from the immediate vicinity. Instead there were seventy or eighty. They had converged on Manogay from as far away as the Waygal district to the north and Kanday to the east, some of them undertaking a two-day journey by foot to see how the new commander dealt with their neighbors in Manogay.

As Mashal briefed me on who was in attendance, his tone made it clear just how important this meeting was for our mission—and for our safety. In their *jamas* and *pakol* caps, all of them gray bearded and many of them with canes, the elders looked like a reunion of aging mujahideen—which some of them might have been. It took us ten minutes to shake everyone's hand. Then we sat on mats in a long rectangle, with me seated in a place of honor next to the district leader.

He opened the proceedings by introducing me. Evidently I wasn't just another invitee; I was the main speaker. The gist of his introduction, as relayed to me by Mashal, was that (a) the Americans are here; (b) this is their new warlord, the one with the red beard; (c) they've promised to bring us security; and (d) they want to know what your concerns are. Pretty straightforward. He then surrendered the floor to whoever wanted to speak, and I listened politely for perhaps fifteen minutes, while Mashal gave the translations and Scott took notes.

Much of what the elders said came as no surprise. Every village in this poor country needed help with infrastructure—a new well or a new bridge, a market here with no roof, a school there with no running water. Scott took it all down—a wish list of restoration projects that I hoped we would be able to undertake. Two of the elders' questions, however, were unexpected.

The first came from a thin, hunched old man who, despite his apparent frailty, obviously commanded the respect of everyone present. He said that, during last month's operation (he meant Mountain Resolve), our troops had captured a good man from his village; they would like him back. I had no way of knowing who the captured man was; whether he was truly a "good" man or a Taliban fighter; or where he might have ended up after his capture. The only honest response I could make was a weak one: I would "look into it." Given my fruitless attempt to undo my "Gestapo" move back in October, I didn't say this with a high degree of confidence.

The other question was even more pointed. It came from several of the elders, speaking at once: "When are you leaving?" The way I interpreted it, the question had a double meaning: They wanted to know how long they would be able to rely on our support. But they also wondered when the foreigners would be off their soil. They appreciated our presence, but they didn't care to see us become permanent residents.

I took this as a cue to rise and address the assembly. The elders had in effect offered a challenge, and I knew that my response would be carefully scrutinized. In my first public appearance as the valley's new warlord, I would have to present myself as calm, deliberate, and authoritative—not exactly a description of the way I was feeling. But the curtain was going up, and I had gotten my cue. I was glad that I hadn't prepared a speech, because it forced me to speak straightforwardly—to say, in unfiltered terms, what was in my heart.

"You are the elders of this valley," I began. "It is your home, your children, your future. We have been allies since we worked together to defeat the Russians and we want to rekindle that alliance between our countries. We are here to assist in the security of the valley and to help you accomplish your goals. Whatever they are. Your schools, your water, your police, your mosques, your crops. However you want us to help you, that is what we will do. We will leave when you no longer need us. When you have accomplished your goals and when the valley is safe, we will return to our own country and you will run yours."

The speech was admittedly idealistic. But I meant it, and I think they saw that. A kind of calm settled over the group, and they sat there expectantly, maybe trying to figure out whether or not to believe me.

"But we need something from you, too," I continued. "If we are to help you bring peace to this valley, we need two things from you."

I paused a second, knowing I had their attention.

"First, we need you to keep your people out of the hills next to our camp at night. We do not want to kill any innocent Afghans. If someone comes near our camp in the dark and we cannot see him, he may have a rocket or a rifle. He may want to shoot at us, so we will shoot at him first to protect ourselves. It is what you would do if someone came upon you in the dark. Please help us. If no one approaches our camp in the dark, then no one will be hurt."

Then I made my second request. This was in line with Mike Montoya's clever suggestion, made just a few days before, that we should recruit the "stripling warrior" sons of the elders themselves.

"We need your sons," I said. "Your brothers, your cousins, your fighting men. Many Afghan fighters are already working with us to build a new Afghanistan. These men are heroes and they are our friends. But we need more. At our camp we have room for one hundred additional soldiers. We will give these soldiers food and shelter and we will pay them well. Please send the word out to your villages. Any man who wishes to fight with us for Afghanistan should come to our camp. He must bring his own weapon and ammunition. And he must bring a letter from his father or an elder saying that he is loyal to the Afghan government. If he brings these things with him, we will train him for the new Afghan Security Force. And he will join us in our good fight for Afghanistan's children. Insh'Allah."

The elders took this announcement in respectful silence. Then one man asked the obvious question: "How much will you pay them?"

I told him the going rate: five dollars a day, or about $150 a month. That was what the CIA and the ODA before us had been paying the six nephews, and it seemed fair that new recruits should get the same. It wouldn't get them the Afghan equivalent of a Lamborghini, but it was twice what a farmer or laborer made. It would keep new arrivals happy without dislocating the local economy.

Evidently satisfied with the pay scale, the elders nodded appreciatively, shook our hands, and agreed that they would commit their sons to our cause. The proof of that would be the arrival of enlistees, and I expected that this would take at least a few days. To my surprise the first ones arrived the following morning. By the end of the week our security force was 108 strong—enough to completely fill the building we had designated as the ASF barracks. We had to turn others away until the quarters could be expanded. In a culture where a man's worth was measured by his fighting spirit, these late arrivals were the unlucky ones.

ODA 936 had been at Catamount for less than two weeks. Under the watchful eyes of our engineers Jimi and Jason, the camp's physical amenities were coming together. We had made our intentions clear to the local leaders and had won a diplomatic victory by extending a hand to the mullah. Best of all, we were starting to make our presence felt in the community. When we weren't hooking up generators or stacking and filling Hesco bastions, we walked the local streets, greeting folks politely, giving kids candy, and contributing whatever we could to the economy. As a way of letting people know you are on their side, it's amazing what buying a bottle of Pepsi can accomplish.

At one point in that first week, our rapport building took an odd turn. Mashal told me that, impressed by our beards, our adoption of *pakol* caps rather than helmets, and the fact that we didn't drink alcohol, some villagers felt that we must share their religion.

"They are happy that you are not infidels like the Russians," he said. "They are speaking of you as the American Muslims."

This was flattering in a weird way, but I couldn't let it stand.

"You cannot let them believe that," I said. "They will see us eating bacon. They will see that we do not pray five times a day, and that will bring trouble. I would rather be seen as a tolerant infidel than a bad Muslim. Tell them that we are not Muslims but Americans who respect their religion and their culture. That's enough. And it's the truth."

Mashal was at first nonplussed by my vehemence, but he got the point. The corrected message got around, and we were soon back to being just "respecters of Islam." If we were going to build trust with the locals, that identity was essential.

The bloodless victories of those first few days added a new layer to my thinking about our mission. We had been sent here, ostensibly, to neutralize troublemakers like Abu Ikhlas and Gulbuddin Hekmatyar. I was beginning to feel that there were two ways to defeat them. One was by the conventional method: force of arms. The other was by transforming local attitudes so that the "solutions" that the bad guys were offering no longer seemed attractive. Time would tell which combination of those two strategies would prove effective.

*   *   *

Those opening days saw one other transformation. Ever since our arrival, we had been following 10th Mountain's lead in referring to the "A" Camp site as FOB Catamount. By our third or fourth week there, that name had been discontinued, and we began calling it Camp Blessing.

The new name was Randy's idea. He felt that Catamount was a 10th Mountain "brand," suggesting a temporary bivouac, not a permanent installation. We needed a name that would signal our stewardship in the valley and have some meaning for us as Special Forces soldiers. He chose the name Blessing as a memorial to an Army Ranger, Sgt. Jay Blessing, who had been killed by an IED during Mountain Resolve. Everyone agreed it was an appropriate choice, especially since Blessing's vehicle had been hit on Route Blue, the same road we had taken to get to the camp. In calling the place Camp Blessing, we were reminding ourselves of the danger that lurked all around us even as we honored the sacrifice of a fallen comrade.

Jay Anthony Blessing, from Tacoma, Washington, joined the Army straight out of high school, earned his Ranger tab at nineteen, and served with the 2nd Battalion, 75th Ranger Regiment, based at Fort Lewis, Washington. He died on November 14, 2003, two weeks after landing in Afghanistan. He was twenty-three years old.

10

A Captain's First Duty

Don't never take a chance you don't have to.
—Robert Rogers: Standing Orders

There are commands of the sovereign which must not be obeyed.

—Sun Tzu, *The Art of War*

You know that young combat veteran you see walking around your town on plastic legs? Given his age, you might surmise that he was wounded in action in the War on Terror. Iraq, maybe, or Afghanistan. If your picture of those conflicts comes from Hollywood or CNN, you might speculate further that what cost him his legs was a rocket-propelled grenade (RPG) or a mortar round. But while you probably would be right about his deployment, you would just as likely be wrong about the cause of his wound.

RPGs and mortars play significant roles in the terrorist arsenal. Statistically speaking, though, a more lethal threat to our troops has been a variety of homemade bombs and booby traps known generically as improvised explosive devices, or IEDs. Increasingly the IED is the weapon of choice for terrorist insurgents.

An IED doesn't make you any deader than a mortar, an RPG, or the jihadist's favorite rifle, the Soviet-made AK-47. I call it more lethal because of the casualty figures. In our current asymmetrical conflicts, the ostensibly outgunned bad guys have used IEDs so effectively that they have accounted for two-thirds of our war zone deaths, mutilations, and amputations. The odds are *two to one* that what took that young vet's leg was an IED. These jerry-built weapons have been the *number one* cause of troops being killed in action. And they kill warriors and civilians indiscriminately.

It's not just folks on foot who are at risk. Al Qaeda and Taliban bomb makers have been known to pack hundreds of pounds of explosives into oil drums and to detonate them with such force that they blow a three-ton armored Humvee four feet in the air. Even with the heavier armor that the Army had adopted by 2003, that can do terrible damage to anybody inside.

Throughout our time in the Pech Valley, we were aware of the IED threat every time we pulled our Humvees onto Route Blue; this road would soon be dubbed IED Alley.[1] I was more than usually alert to it on December 11, when I was taking a split team (about half the ODA) to Abad to get supplies, use the Internet, and deliver to a B-Team meeting a couple of visiting Marines who were soon to take over 10th Mountain's security duty. The others would stay at Camp Blessing to hold down the fort.

I should have been in good spirits that day, because I was fresh off the double-play success of turning Mullah Zawar around and scoring an initial meeting with the *shura*. The day had also started with a nice surprise. We had received care packages from some friends of Roger's, and we had opened them up that morning. We were delighted to find notes of encouragement, cookies, beef jerky, and Christmas decorations to add some cheer to our radio room. I should have been feeling pretty good. And yet...

What was making me uneasy was news from outside. Even as things seemed to be looking up in the Pech Valley (Abu Ikhlas was lying low for the time being), Afghanistan as a whole was in the throes of political transition, and the passage was accompanied by an uptick in violence. Throughout the country, and especially the northeast, bombings and rocket attacks had been on the rise.

On November 27, a contingent of U.S. politicians, including Senator Hillary Clinton, had visited Afghanistan to show support for Hamid Karzai and the upcoming elections. Throughout that month, the country's grand council, the *loya jirga*, had been hammering out a new constitution; if Karzai approved it, it would become the law of the land. On December 2, one of northern Afghanistan's most powerful warlords, Atta Mohammed Nur, surrendered fifty of his tanks to the Afghan Army.

None of these developments was welcome news to the Taliban or Al Qaeda. Before Operation Enduring Freedom drove them into the hills, the Taliban had ruled the country for nearly four years. They wanted back in. The last thing they wanted was a stable government. Hence the surge in attacks. On December 8 the Taliban had threatened to kill anyone who participated in the *loya jirga*. In American terms, that would be like promising to massacre the United States Congress.

With that as backdrop, we were on high alert as we ventured out onto Route Blue toward Asadabad that December 11. By now, having done this run numerous times, we had developed a tricky evasive maneuver designed to keep us alive on this IED-littered road. *Tricky* might be too sophisticated a description. What we did was simply drive like hell.

Here's why that usually worked. As deadly as IEDs can be, their detonation is neither as reliable nor as instantaneous as the detonation of a military-class explosive. Sometimes the killer at the other end of the device pushes a button or flips a switch and nothing happens. At other times, the IED does explode, but a second or two later than the killer wanted, because he's miscalculated his own reaction time. He's sitting two hundred yards away from the road with one eye looking into a rifle scope and his finger on a cell phone Send button. A Humvee comes into sight, and he knows that as soon as it reaches the pile of trash he's put in the road as a marker, he should hit the button. The vehicle reaches the trash, but it's moving so fast that by the time he reacts, it's out of blast range. That was our evasion tactic. Most of the time it worked.

But not on December 11.

Roger was driving the first truck, with me riding shotgun. We were bouncing along the ruts at a pretty good clip. In a memoir that Roger wrote a few years later, he said that traveling Route Blue gave him "the awesome feeling of being a rally race car driver, barely missing trees, rocks, and people as we roar down the unforgiving road trying to outrun the Grim Reaper." He was doing his Dale Earnhardt best that day while driving the truck behind us was one of the visiting Marines, who had pleaded with me to let him take the wheel because he was "the best damn drag racer in Alabama."

He was a good kid, and he did his best to keep up with Roger, but apparently Alabama keeps its roads in better repair than Kunar province does. Almost from the minute we hit Route Blue, I could see in the rearview mirror that the second truck was falling behind. "Speed up!" I started yelling into the two-way. "You've got to drive faster than that."

Roger saw the problem, too. We were about to enter a stretch where the road opens up when he said, "Sir, we're going to lose them here if they don't catch up. Can you call back again?"

"Speed up! Speed up!" I yelled again. But it was already too late. A couple of seconds later, I heard a loud boom and saw the truck disappear in a dust cloud on the side of the road. The drag racer had encountered an IED.

"Back!" I yelled.

Roger reacted instantly. Not bothering to spin the truck around, he put it in reverse, glued his eyes to the rearview, and punched it (as he liked to say) back to the attack site. We were there in ten seconds, the team streaming out of the Humvee with M4s at the ready and Dave in the turret on the .50-cal. At the same moment, back at Camp Blessing, Jason was loading up our third vehicle. Over the radio he and Randy had heard first my shouted commands and then the explosion. In the few moments it took us to set a perimeter, Randy and Jason had sped out of camp, picked up a truckload of our ASF guys in Nangalam, and were racing to where we were stranded. "Backup on the way, boss," I heard him say over the radio.

It was as welcome a message as I had ever heard, because I was taking a fix on our position, and it didn't look pretty.

We were in a flat, thinly populated area in the middle of nowhere, with some ragged mud houses flanking Route Blue about fifty meters to the north and a drop down to the Pech River on the south. I scanned the rooftops for shooters. Empty. I was pretty sure you couldn't say the same for the gray hills rising away from the road. They were the same hills from which, a little farther to the east, hawk-eyed insurgents had attacked our QRF convoy in November. There were surely similar eyes on us now.

With our perimeter as tightly covered as it could be, I turned to see about casualties. The blast had thrown the second truck's gunner, our PSYOP attaché Chris Aguirre, out of the turret, leaving him with a facial gash, a broken wrist, and a "WTF?" expression. Medic Mike Montoya jumped to his aid, patched up what he could, and said, "He'll be OK, but he'll need a medevac out." The same was true for a Marine lieutenant who had sustained a concussion. The other guys were banged up—blood and bruises here and there—but nobody seriously enough to require more than first aid. Thank God and DOD for up-armoring.

Overhearing Mike's assessment, Roger was already on the satellite radio looking for medevac assets. In the Pech Valley our FM radios, transmitting by line of sight, had a significant range, but here, with the mountains and the need to coordinate with aircraft and Bagram half a country away, the necessary range could only be provided by sat radios. When we needed air support, medevac, or other serious assets, we typically turned to Channel 102 on the satcom. On this day, though, Roger wasn't able to get a clean signal on that channel, so he was relaying to Courtney at Blessing, who was coordinating with aircraft. It wasn't the most precise form of communication, and it seemed like forever before Roger got word from Bagram about available assets.

"Medevac with Apache escort en route," he said. "Coming from Bagram, so it's going to take a while." I nodded, and Roger continued to coordinate with Courtney.

The blast had attracted a crowd of truckers, farmers, villagers, and kids curious about what was happening to the bearded Americans. We set up a perimeter to prevent them or their vehicles from getting any closer to our convoy. This caused the normally light Route Blue traffic to start backing up in both directions. Jason and Randy, coming from Nangalam, managed to avoid most of this congestion, and they soon reached our position, their tires throwing up dust as they jumped out of their truck. Jason had forgotten more about vehicles than I ever knew, so I had him assess the damage. It didn't take him more than fifteen seconds.

"Toast," he reported. "This one's not going anywhere."

That made our situation clear. It wasn't good. With traffic stalled, Randy had taken over moving our Afghan contingent—Malik Zarin's six nephews—into security positions and relieving the ODA of dealing with the onlookers. The gathering crowd might be curious or it might be something else. The eyes of the bomber and his pals were on us from who knew how many directions. Worst of all, at 1600 hours on a winter day, it was getting dark.

Ben, frustrated, wanted to take a few of the Afghans and search all the cars and homes in the immediate area to find the perpetrator. I appreciated his zeal but the genius of an IED attack is that once it's initiated, the perpetrator just discards the initiation device and goes back to herding his sheep or working in his field. If we reacted emotionally and started a house-to-house hunt, we would stretch our security thin and risk harming an innocent person or damaging property. That would play into the insurgents' master plan, which was to turn as many people as possible against the invaders. So we stayed in place.

Military trainers stress the fact that in a battle zone, situation awareness is everything. What my SA was telling me was unambiguous. The safety of six Green Berets, two Marines, and our Afghan soldiers was in my hands. We were a small unit stuck in a narrow part of an insurgent-thick valley. Miraculously we had survived a hostile salvo with the only KIA being a truck. But the day wasn't over.

Mobility and speed were our best security, and right now we had neither. I knew that, immobilized on the enemy's terrain, we were very likely being set up for a direct attack: the mujahideen had used that tactic with deadly effectiveness against the Russians. So what we had to do was obvious. Salvage what we could, destroy the damaged truck so it couldn't be used by the enemy and then, before our luck turned, get the hell out of there. Or the Humvee wouldn't be the only thing that was toast.

This was obvious to our Afghan recruits as well. Randy had positioned them to the east and west of our vehicles as a security cordon, and they weren't thrilled with the job. The squad leader, a burly character named Bazir, turned to me nervously.

"We cannot stay here," he said. "When are we leaving?"

I didn't know whether he had spotted a specific threat or whether, like me, he was just acutely aware that our position was untenable. Either way, he was right. I picked up the handset for the sat radio and called Special Ops headquarters in Bagram. By the time they answered, the Apache was flying overhead and the Blackhawk medevac was landing on a small temporary LZ that Randy had prepped with the Marines. It was settling down on the side of the road, and Randy was supervising the evacuation of Chris and the Marine lieutenant. The medevac lifted off. The Apache continued to loiter in our area to give us cover as we resolved our situation. Good news there, anyway.

Not such good news from Bagram.

When they picked up, I gave the commo guy a sitrep update: "IED attack. Medevac is complete. One truck undrivable. I am requesting that the Apache destroy the vehicle so we can evac the location." My Channel 102 transmission was unclear, and Courtney needed to repeat it on his end before the Camp Vance radio guy understood the request. Jason and the team had already begun stripping the vehicle of its radios, ammo, spare tires, seats—anything that was salvageable.

The commo guy, aware that agreeing to blow up $250,000 worth of government property was above his pay grade, said "Hammerhead Six standby," and passed me up the chain of command. The next person I heard was the battle captain, relaying a denial of the request from "higher." Even through the fog of the communication relay through Blessing, it became clear that the Camp Vance head shed wanted to retrieve the vehicle by helicopter sling load. I relayed this bit of info to Jason.

"Where's the sling going to go?" he laughed. "The attachment's shot. Lift this thing and it'll fall apart."

A new, more authoritarian voice came on the radio. "What's

your position, Captain?" A higher-ranking staffer had taken over for the battle captain. I gave him the coordinates and recapped the sitrep. "We're sitting ducks, here, sir. Have to destroy the vehicle." At Blessing, Courtney relayed the message. He was getting pretty good at being my echo.

I was asking for permission because I knew that the Apache pilot was not going to use a Hellfire missile or rockets on a friendly vehicle without approval from Vance. In my trustful innocence I had figured that "Affirmative" wasn't only the obvious right answer to my request but a foregone conclusion.

I was mistaken.

"Negative," came the staff officer's voice. "We need to retrieve the asset and study it for intel. You and your team are to remain and guard it from hostiles."

To put it bluntly, that was nuts.

At that location on Route Blue, there was never a shortage of creeps who wanted to take your head off, with an AK-47 if not with a sword. In the gathering dusk we couldn't see where they were. There were a dozen of us against an unknown number of them. Sitting in that vulnerable position guarding a dead truck was exactly what the enemy would want us to do. Unless you had a death wish, it was time to leave Dodge. Anybody with half a brain would have realized that the minute he set foot on the spot.

But the staffer wasn't on the spot. He was in a head shed several hours away, weighing the pros and cons of destroying the Humvee against a different set of priorities from the ones I was facing. He hadn't just put one of his team and a Marine in a medevac chopper, and what he saw out the window of his Bagram bubble didn't bear any resemblance to a Kunar ambush.

Never in my military career had I been more painfully aware of the gulf that can exist between strategy and tactics, between the view from ten thousand feet and the view on the ground. The staffer's priority was getting an assessment or intel on the damage to equipment, a strategic consideration. Mine was simpler. A captain's first duty is to his men. To me that trumped anything Bagram had in mind.

I believed that if the staffer or Colonel Herd or a commanding general were in my position, their plan of action would have been the same as mine. But on that day, as shadows lengthened on Route Blue, I evidently was not communicating the situation clearly enough for my superiors to come to the same conclusion.

Courtney didn't wait for me to respond but repeated the sitrep on my behalf. As he told me later, "I couldn't believe what I was hearing, Ron. I thought the guy just didn't understand the situation."

Maybe so. But it didn't matter. The staffer's order, coming in over the scratchy radio connection, was clear: Stay put. Command was working on a plan to retrieve the damaged vehicle. They would be sending out either a sling-loading Chinook (which we knew was useless) or a tow truck (probably ditto).

He couldn't give us an exact ETA, but I knew it wouldn't be soon. Bagram was over one hundred miles away. If we went with his "study the asset" plan, we were going to be in enemy gun sights all night long. Somehow this made sense to a staffer in an air-conditioned war room. To me it was the equivalent of painting bull's-eyes on my guys' backs and yelling *"Allahu akbar!"*

It wasn't going to happen.

In his autobiography, *A Soldier's Story*, Omar Bradley observed soberly that while concern for one's men is a requirement of command, it cannot interfere with the accomplishment of a mission. If a commander "becomes tormented by the casualties he must endure, he is in danger of losing sight of his strategic objective. Where the objective is lost, the war is prolonged and the cost becomes infinitely worse."[2] Bradley was a five-star general who helped plan the Normandy invasion and led the Allied advance that ended World War II. I won't be so bold as to say that I disagree with him.

But the devil's in the details.

Just because soldiers' lives must be sacrificed to secure objectives, it doesn't follow that everything your superiors consider an objective is worth that sacrifice. It costs more than $1 million to develop and train a single Special Forces operator. If the "objective" Bagram was focused on was the recovery of destroyed government property, the logic of risking human assests was ridiculous even by accounting standards.

To those back in Bagram, finding out exactly how the IED had disabled our truck was evidently worth putting our lives at risk. I could picture them clutching clipboards and pencils while a mechanic poked around the undercarriage searching for answers. What was the approximate explosives load? What was the angle of impact? What was the precise nature of the damage? What percentage of optimal cushioning did the armoring provide? Maybe all of this would be good stuff to know. But in the situation we were facing, I didn't give a crap. All I wanted to know was how I was going to get my team out of there in one piece.

As Jason, echoing the Afghans, put it bluntly, "We're out here with our asses hanging in the wind. We need to get the hell out." I suspect that Bradley—the soldier's general who said that the agony of war was having to pay its costs in men's lives—would have agreed.

So I got back on the sat phone and did a little dance. "I understand that the Apache destruction is denied. Hammerhead Six out."

I turned to Jason. "No way the truck can be—"

"—fixed?" he said. "You got a magic wand?"

If I'd had a magic wand, I would have zapped us all back to camp. "OK, then," I said. "Finish stripping it and rig it."

This was Junior's meat and potatoes. As a demo expert, there was little he liked better than blowing things up. "You got it," he replied with undisguised enthusiasm.

Within ten minutes, with half of the team watching our perimeter, the other half had finished stripping the dead Humvee of everything portable, and Junior had rigged it with explosives and prepped a time fuse. We moved the crowd a safe distance away. We were ready for the blast when Randy pulled me aside for a sanity check.

"Ron, destruction was denied," he said. "Are you really willing to do this?"

"Destruction by the Apache was denied," I replied. "They didn't say anything about destruction by C-4 and an 18C."

Randy half-smiled at my convenient interpretation of the staffer's words, obviously relieved to see that my mind was made up. And I can't say that the decision was a difficult one. I was perfectly clear on what needed to be done, and just as clear that obeying the staffer's directive would have been putting my career ahead of my duty to my men. I wasn't concerned about my career. A no-brainer, really.

I turned to Jason, who had overheard our exchange. "Give us a countdown, Junior. Let's get this done."

A few minutes later the crippled Humvee was reduced to scrap metal. Bagram would have no further use for the asset. But neither would a Taliban patrol seeking evidence of a coalition defeat or armored plates to fortify a bunker position.

Along with our clearly relieved Afghan allies, we piled onto the remaining Humvees and Toyota to return to camp. Our two wounded were in the air and we were all in one piece. I'd had better days, but this one could have been a whole lot worse.

*   *   *

As Special Forces, we had been sent to Afghanistan to engage in unconventional warfare, but destroying government property wasn't what the Pentagon had in mind. I knew I wouldn't be earning any kudos from the brass. When Randy told me later, "You're betting your bars on this," I knew he was right. The fallout from smoking the truck wouldn't be pretty.

If it came to an investigation, though, I did have an ace in the hole. Back at Camp Blessing, Jason pointed this out with the conspiratorial wink of a Philadelphia lawyer.

"Remember the SOPs we had to sign off on before we deployed?"

An SOP was a document indicating the Standard Operating Procedure that the team intended to follow in any number of possible field scenarios, from communication plans to paying for intel, from reacting to ambushes to dealing with broken vehicles. The Standard Operating Procedures are decided upon and internalized by all team members and then submitted to HQ for approval, which ensures they are not at odds with the rest of the army.

"What about them?" I asked.

Jason looked like the attorney who has just saved his client ten years in the clink. "Wasn't one of those things entitled Vehicle Destruction Plan?"

"It was," I said.

"Well then," he said. "If Bagram insisted that we have an SOP for vehicle destruction, they must have anticipated that we might actually have to *destroy a vehicle*, right? You were only doing what headquarters prepared and authorized you to do."

I had to smile. I had forgotten that Vance HQ had in effect given prior approval for what I had done. I followed Jason's logic, although I wasn't sure if a military court would do the same. At the time I was just happy to be back at camp with the team intact. I didn't know yet how the higher-ups would respond.

What I did know was that our area of operations wasn't textbook territory. We were in the Pech Valley—about as gray an area of the planet, physically and morally, as anybody could imagine. There were no rulebooks here. Sometimes you had to make adjustments with your gut as you went along. Learning to do that and not second-guess the outcome was one of the biggest lessons I learned in Afghanistan.

Folks who have never been to war, or who are convinced that war is never justified, will tell you that no military objective is worth a human life. Logic and experience tell me otherwise. I think there are wars worth fighting, objectives worth dying for. But in the end it's a question of proportion: how many lives are you willing to sacrifice to attain which objective?

I don't have a formula to help me answer that question.

If I had been Omar Bradley, surveying Omaha Beach as the first wave of Allied troops fell to German bunker fire, I think I would have said that defeating Nazism was worth even this sacrifice.

On the other hand, if I had been commanding the British Fourth Army on the first day of the Somme offensive a century ago, I think I would have agreed with the writer Pat Barker. In her novel *Regeneration*, she has the military psychiatrist W. H. R. Rivers, reflecting on the loss of nineteen thousand British lives that day, comment, "Nothing justifies this. Nothing nothing nothing."[3]

That's what I think. What I know is that on that December day in 2003, stranded with my men in a darkening kill zone, I wasn't going to risk even one life for the sake of a truck.

I made my share of mistakes in Afghanistan. That wasn't one of them.

11

Commander's Intent

Act with respect for local people, putting the well-being of noncombatant civilians ahead of any other consideration, even—in fact, especially—ahead of killing the enemy.
—David Kilcullen, *Counterinsurgency*

It is critical that the commander's intent is clearly understood by all members of the detachment.
—*Special Forces Planning Techniques*, 2000

Within twelve hours after I made the executive decision to destroy the Hummer, we heard that it was met with admiration by some and disdain by others. Rumor had it that the Combined Joint Task Force commander, Brig. Gen. Lloyd Austin, was awakened the next morning by the news that a rogue captain had circumvented his authority in destroying a vehicle. I was sure I had not heard the end of the incident. But worrying about a dead truck was soon far from my mind. I had enough to think about with Becky and our kids halfway across the world and the challenges of running an "A" Camp staring me in the face.

By mid-December, the camp was well fortified, we had power, and we had reasonably comfortable quarters both for ourselves and for the indigenous soldiers who were steadily joining our command. We were building relationships with the spiritual and municipal leaders of the Manogay district, and the general population seemed at least comfortable with, and often enthusiastic about, our presence. The occasional rocket from the southern ridge wobbled wide or short, and we had weathered an IED attack with no loss of life. There was a lot to be thankful for.

But my excitement was tempered by a sense of uncertainty. It was the same feeling I had on the transport flight from Bragg, when I was thinking about Secretary Rumsfeld's unknowns and asking myself what our mission was. Our general orders were to neutralize bad guys in Kunar. Back in September, living on a functioning firebase, that sounded cool enough, if a little indistinct. Now, ten weeks into our deployment, with the responsibility of managing an entire valley, its struggling local government, its people, and an "A" Camp of American and Afghan soldiers, it didn't sound like a plan at all.

I didn't have any problem with neutralizing bad guys. I was as cranked as anybody on the team with our rescue of the QRF back in November, and if Abu Ikhlas had sent an attack force against our camp that night, we would have enjoyed the opportunity to take him down. To the counterinsurgent, a successful firefight is measurable. In Vietnam, commanders would actually use enemy body count as an indicator of success; they read a high body count as proof (against all evidence to the contrary) that they were winning.

When I thought about our experiences in Afghanistan so far, I realized that what gave me the most satisfaction, and made me feel that *we* were winning, were nonkinetic moments like addressing the *shura*, getting a smile from a child in our clinic who reminded me of one of my own, or seeing the Afghan soldiers doing their best to be like their American counterparts. It was working the human terrain and attempting to connect with the villagers and improve their lot that really got to me. As the days got shorter, my view of our mission started to evolve.

Then, on the shortest day of the year, December 21, something happened that helped me bring it into focus.

For the previous two days, we had been conducting a Relief in Place (RIP). The 10th Mountain security platoon that Lieutenant Colonel Paschal had loaned us was being replaced by a platoon of Marines. The RIP wrapped up on the twenty-first, and before that day was out, the jarheads, true to their fire-eating reputation, had secured the baseplates for their 60mm mortars, done preliminary calibrations on some ridgeline targets, and conducted a test firing of their new toys. At first I was happy to witness their zeal in getting down to business. My attitude changed when, half an hour later, four men from Darinar, a small village to our south, appeared at our gate and asked to see the red-bearded commander. I met them in front of the indig barracks.

"Why are you shooting at us?" one of them said.

"What?"

"Your shells are hitting our fields. Next to our houses."

I was dumbfounded for just the moment that it took me to realize what had happened. Then I apologized to the men, assured them that the shelling was not intentional, and promised them that it would not happen again. They went away muttering as I made a note to myself that we must visit Darinar the next day to make it right with the elders. Then I sent for the Marines' mortars sergeant.

I was angry at his carelessness, given that it might have created a diplomatic and human disaster. But I realized that, like his squad, he was a young guy itching for action, that he hadn't meant to hurt anyone, and that rapport building wasn't exactly a Marine Corps strong suit. So I was as tempered as I could be in chewing him out.

"While you are here, Sergeant," I said, "you will likely get plenty of opportunity to engage with targets. But our purpose here is not to fire our weapons. It is to make the people of these valleys feel secure. We may sometimes have to serve as a strike force, but when we are not under attack, we will function first and foremost as a defense force. These are the people we are defending. Is that clear?"

"Yes, sir."

"If the people of the village you shelled today see us as a threat and not a solution, it will not matter how many of the enemy we kill. If they fear us—worse, if we accidently kill an innocent villager—everything we are trying to accomplish here will go up in smoke and Marines will be killed. I'm sure you don't want that to happen, Sergeant."

An embarrassed shake of the head indicated that he didn't.

"All right, then. When you return to your squad, explain to your men exactly what I have explained to you. And the next time you test-fire a weapon, you will double-check your coordinates and make certain that your shells will not land anywhere near a civilian population. Understood?"

"Understood, sir."

I dismissed him, not sure whether he fully understood what I meant by "what we are trying to accomplish here" but confident that his boys wouldn't be shooting from the hip again soon. Marines were fantastic fighters. I just needed to make sure that their efforts were pointed in the same direction as ours.

The next day I asked the Marine sergeant to accompany Courtney and me on a "make nice" patrol to the village he had shelled. The Darinar elders greeted us as amiably as you could expect under the circumstances, gave us tea, and listened respectfully to our assurance that such a dangerous error would not be repeated. When they pointed out where the mortars had landed, the sergeant seemed as appalled as I was at how close they had come to a house. Fifty feet to the east and the house and its inhabitants, including several children, would have been destroyed. That hit the young Marine stronger than my lecture had.

By a fifty-foot margin we had escaped a devastating incident of collateral damage. Realizing that confirmed something I had been feeling on and off throughout our deployment: that a power greater than the Pentagon was watching over my team.

The misdirected mortar incident had a positive side effect. It got me thinking in more detail about firing weapons versus protecting people. Of course those two actions weren't mutually exclusive—sometimes the only way to protect someone was to shoot someone else—but making the distinction in that off-the-cuff lecture to the Marine sergeant inspired a course of reflection that, over the next few days, would result in a detailed reassessment of our mission. I had insisted that the young Marines recalibrate their mortars. I was about to undertake some recalibration of my own.

The process began with a reflection on what we were doing here. I realized that while the U.S. military's original mission in Afghanistan had been to remove the Taliban and kill or capture Al Qaeda fighters, it had transitioned into a counterinsurgency effort to keep the Taliban and their allies from retaking Afghanistan. The Taliban had been ousted with Green Berets using UW to fight by, with, and through the irregular forces of the Northern Alliance. As the Afghan government and armed forces were not yet up and running, we were continuing this fight with the same methods. We were battling the Taliban and its allies by using unconventional troops and unconventional methods.

A couple of days before Christmas, I was sitting alone on the roof of our team house. I was trying to clear my head, but the sight of the majestic mountains and the running river, the smells of livestock and burning trash, and the sounds of kids at play and the call to prayer just made me more alert to the gravity of our situation. It hit me strongly that while we were playing a part in the Global War on Terror, we were also fighting a very localized war whose outcome would be determined not in Washington or in Bagram, but by what we did in the Pech Valley. That was a huge responsibility and a huge risk. Nobody had said it out loud, but as far away as we were from Big Army support, failure in this mission could be disastrous for us personally.

One thing that would guarantee failure was rejection by the civilian population. If we lost the confidence of the Afghan people, the enemy would be emboldened and it would just be a matter of time before we were killed. Every theorist of unconventional warfare and counterinsurgency knew this to be true, and I had read about it often, in writings by Mao, Che, and our own counterguerrilla experts. With that sobering thought in mind, I began to map out some principles that I thought should govern our operations at Camp Blessing, as we positioned ourselves as stewards of these Pashtun villagers and wrestled for their allegiance with the ghosts in the hills.

I was just beginning this mapping-out process when Jimi joined me on the roof. At fifty-something, he was our elder statesman, sometimes joking, "I remember when we used catapults." I could always rely on him to provide a wise perspective, and as we looked out over the valley, I asked him a question.

"Jimi, why did you become a Green Beret?"

It didn't take him long to respond.

"*De Oppresso Liber.* That's just a motto to some, but if you think about it, all of our missions involve liberating oppressed people and making them allies of the United States. Every mission is a twofer. We serve our country in missions that nobody else in the Defense Department arsenal can manage, and at the same time we are positively affecting local people. It's a job and purpose I believe in."

"With all the conflict you have dealt with," I asked, "how does this one stack up?"

He seemed almost to read my thoughts. "You don't get to pick your wars, Ron. If I had my druthers I would have been a World War II commando, or maybe be on one of the teams that helped liberate Afghanistan from the Taliban—one of the classic righteous guerrilla missions. This one is grayer, riskier, less sexy, but equally important. The cards seem stacked against us given the terrain, the religion, the people's shifting loyalties, the lack of clarity on what the future holds for Afghanistan. It's not like anything we have seen before. But this is the war we have been tasked to win. I am just glad I am not the captain," he finished with a smile.

I returned the smile and looked back out over the valley as his words sank in. Apparently I wasn't the only one thinking about the difficulty of our mission. As Jimi left the roof, I knew I had to give some clarity to the team.

As a spur to my thinking, I took from my ruck a well-worn copy of *The Ugly American*.[1] This 1958 bestseller, written by novelist Eugene Burdick and naval officer William Lederer, was required reading for Special Forces soldiers. Written as a critique of U.S. diplomatic ineptitude, it described unconventional warfare in a fictional Southeast Asian country and espoused principles in dealing with indigenous people that were as valid in 2003 as they had ever been. During the Special Forces Officers course, I had used the inside cover of this book to write down the tenets of Special Operations. Three of them jumped out at me as I jotted down notes.

The first tenet was to *understand the operational environment*. This meant more than knowing where you were on the map. It involved knowing all the players—friendly, hostile, and undecided—in your area of operations (AO), and understanding the goals and motivations of the civilian population. As I read this, I realized that while we were pretty good at understanding *our* capabilities and values, we had a lot to learn about our civilian "hosts."

The second tenet was to *consider the long-term effects.* That meant the effects of every single action we might take or not take as we pursued our mission. I had already stumbled over this lesson once, when I shipped the Shamir Kowt mortar owner off to Bagram and risked creating a whole new generation of America haters. I wanted us to learn from that, and to measure every new decision against its possible outcomes.

The third tenet was to *apply capabilities indirectly.* This could be summarized by the mantra: "Let the Afghans do it." If we were to win our war here in the Pech, we would have to put an Afghan face on each accomplishment. We could instruct, direct, model, but we couldn't run things. If we were ever to create a long-term, strong ally, we had to develop the Afghans' own capabilities.

The following day, with those principles set down, and with the memory of the Darinar near miss fresh in my mind, I gathered the team together for a strategy meeting.

We met in the team house around a table full of intel reports. Team sergeant Randy Derr and I sat with our backs to a wall full of maps. Our two engineers, Jason Mackay and Jimi Rymut, sat in camp chairs, each holding a steaming cup of coffee. As medics Mike Montoya and Ben Guile settled into plastic chairs we had bought at the bazaar in town, I could hear them trading notes on an Afghan burn victim they had treated that morning. I smiled noticing that our weapons sergeants, Dave Moon and Ian Waters, were perched on ammo boxes as if to remind us of their specialty. Courtney Hinson, our air support specialist, sat with Roger Wilcox; they had become friends, and Courtney had in effect taken on the role of a second 18E (communications) sergeant. Scott Jennings, our intel sergeant, sat on a box of ready-to-eat meals next to me.

We were meeting ostensibly to do planning, but what I had in mind was very different from drafting an operations CONOP. What I wanted to lay out, that day in the team house, was a big-picture view of our deployment's purpose, so that when specific plans went awry—inevitable in a war zone—the team could improvise and execute in support of that larger design. I wanted to give the guys what military planners call the Commander's Intent, that is, the desired end state of the overall operation. If everyone understood what I meant by *success*, I believed they could more easily deliver against that goal.

I knew we had a tough task ahead of us. I admitted that I had been struggling to define exactly what our focus should be. Then I said that, with our training and with the resources we had as individuals, I believed that we were perfectly positioned to wage unconventional warfare in this valley. "We're calling our own shots here, guys," I said. "Here's what I think we should remember as we go forward."

Nobody recorded the sales pitch that followed, and I spoke from the heart, not from PowerPoint slides. But as far as I can remember, it went something like this:

"First of all, this is our war. It's not Bagram's or Abad's or Kabul's or Washington's. Whatever happens out in politician land, the Pech is our AO and it's where we must win. What's winning? What does that look like? Well, we'll no doubt be trading tracers with some nasty characters, but we have to remember that winning is not the same as killing every bad guy in the valley. Winning is the valley no longer being a sanctuary for those guys. It's the valley becoming a place where the people trust us and they're working with their new government for security and economic growth. It's the valley being such a secure environment that the enemy is no longer capable of or interested in operating here.

"Getting there is going to take a selling job. The people are the terrain we need to win and hold. To get them on our side, we need to be better salesmen than the enemy. That's not easy. Our adversaries share religious and family and tribal ties with the people we are trying to win over. On top of that, they live here and they're not going away. As long as the American commitment to the long-haul fight isn't clear, they can just wait us out. Nobody will want to commit to the Americans if they think we are going to abandon them in a year or two."

Jimi's nods of agreement were not lost on the other members of the team. Everyone knew what I was alluding to here. All Special Forces soldiers know the stories of our predecessors who had made promises and commitments in Vietnam and then watched helplessly as Montagnards, Hmongs, and other ethnic groups that had thrown their lot in with the Americans were slaughtered by the communists when the U.S. abandoned the fight. My team knew, too, that here in the Pech, there was not a lot of confidence in America's long-term investment. There was bitterness about the fact that, after we helped them defeat the Russians, we had left them to their own devices in a brutal civil war.

Randy, sitting next to me, reinforced this point with an astute observation. "We can't promise anything to anybody in this valley that our ODA can't deliver itself. Foreign policy changes every four years. We don't want to live with the guilt of promising something that the next detachment of Americans are unable to—or aren't allowed to—honor." In civilian life Randy was an ICU nurse, but he was speaking here like a veteran sales professional. And he knew, as I did, that the picture was complicated by the fact that the very people who appreciated our presence also didn't want it to last forever.

"The bottom line is simple," I went on. "We need to show the people of this district—the farmers, the shopkeepers, the mullahs, the *shuras*—that working with us is going to get them a better life than working with anybody else. A lot of them are undecided about that, because they've been let down before. Those are the people that we've got to convince. We can do that by following a few simple metrics.

"Number one is security. We have to provide real and perceived security to the valley's population. This means we'll have to collect actionable intelligence so we can drive out or kill those who threaten the peace. Our presence, but more important, our Afghan soldiers' presence, will create stability upon which everything else can grow.

"Number two, services. What can we provide that they are lacking? How can we show them that their new government and American allies are improving their lot? Business opportunities? Medicine? Schooling? Bridges? Wells? I don't know yet what they need. And we can't just throw stuff at them that we like. We have to find out their real needs and sell to that. At the same time, we have to be wise in how we spend American dollars, because we're stewards of those funds.

"Number three, buy-in. This is their home. Whatever help we give them, they've got to know that this is their fight. Remember 'by, with, and through.' That's got to drive all of our operations. We can help them get rid of the troublemakers, but then it's on them. So we hire and utilize Afghan forces—civilian and ASF—in a way that is sustainable, that will allow them to continue functioning at a high level long after we have gone home."

"Their valley, their show," said Randy.

"Exactly right," I said. "We're here to help them help themselves. No foreigners have ever been able to win over this valley's people. We need to be viewed as partners, guests, not foreign meddlers. We have to do things better than the Brits or the Soviets, with a fraction of their resources. So that when we leave, it's not just more chaos."

I let that thought sink in and saw clear, sober reflection in my ODA's faces.

"There are also a couple of things that we cannot do," I continued. "Ever. One is to show disrespect to their culture or their religion— that's a sure way to turn us into pariahs. The other is to harm non-combatants, especially children. That would be unforgiveable. This isn't just Geneva talking, this is Pech Valley reality. You've all heard about the mortars yesterday. We were lucky. If we're careless and we kill a child, nobody here is going to call it collateral damage. We'll be seen as murderers and treated as such.

"Guys, we have to put ourselves in their shoes. If a bunch of foreign military types parked themselves in your town, how would you react? If they were friendly, added to the economy, assisted in infrastructure, killed the local criminals, and provided security so capitalism could flourish, you would probably accept their presence for a time. If they damaged your property, ogled your women, were disrespectful and belligerent about your religion, culture, and everything you value, you would get your friends together, dust off your daddy's shotgun, and drive them out. Not to sound simplistic, but we need to treat these people as we would want to be treated ourselves. That's an ancient principle, and it's still a good one."

I was referring, without naming it, to the Golden Rule. The team didn't need it spelled out. Smiles told me they had gotten the message. Those smiles broke into laughter when, as if on cue, the call to prayer rang out from the Manogay mosque.

"That's about it," I wrapped up. "A wise man told me recently that we don't get to choose our wars. This is a tough one but it has been entrusted to us. I'm not talking about the war in Afghanistan, I'm talking about the war in the Pech Valley. To win the war in Afghanistan, the U.S. will have to deal with Pakistan, a real Afghan Army and National Police will have to be established, and the Kabul government will have to be strong. Those are problems for the politicians and the generals. Our war is here and now, and we are the only ones fighting it." I stole a glance at Jimi and saw him smile.

"I believe in this mission. My kids, like yours, are going without their father for a year so we could come to this place and make a difference. Let's do that. Let's win this war so they don't have to come back here twenty years from now."

That was the gist of my Commander's Intent. I was to a great degree preaching to the choir, so I wasn't surprised when the team's reaction was positive—or that they turned immediately to ideas for implementation. Mike and Ben addressed the logistics of maintaining a clinic for the civilians while keeping medics available for patrols and operations. Randy and Dave raised a personnel issue: how many ASF soldiers would we really need to be effective? Courtney, who was a little suspicious of the local leadership, wondered how much intel we could share with the district leader and police chief.

At one point Ben, who in the wake of the truck incident wasn't entirely sold on our own leadership, asked, "No matter how good our ideas, how much buy-in can we expect from the wizards at Bagram?"

That got appreciative grins all around. They broadened when Randy said slyly, "Who says we have to get their buy-in?" I didn't know it at the time, but he was hinting at a "Need to Know" policy I would soon be adopting.

By the end of that meeting, we decided that we would build a proper clinic and have it headed up by Mike and Ben. We'd had great success with our MEDCAPs during Mountain Resolve, and Manogay was well situated to provide similar assistance to villagers living along the two river valleys. As a plus, a tent was erected behind the team house as a place where friendlies could bring us information away from prying eyes. Dave laid out some security ideas for the camp, like clearing out an inner courtyard to make room for vehicles and building a Marine guard post outside the ODA compound to create a defendable inner perimeter within the camp. If our outer perimeter was ever overrun, we could fall back to the inner perimeter and continue the fight. In Vietnam, this tactic had saved countless Green Berets. Jason gave us an update on his building projects, including the indig barracks, the indig latrine, and some improvements to the Marine living quarters. We agreed that another couple of dozen local workers could be added to his crews. And we made a list of supplies we would need to turn these good ideas into reality.

It was a good, collaborative exchange. I felt for the first time since we had landed at Asadabad that, individually and collectively, Hammerhead Six truly understood and owned its mission. We had been operating largely on instinct. From here on out we had a clearly defined intent and the will to accomplish it.

I left that meeting feeling good. We had gotten agreement from the team on a common anchoring philosophy, we had aired good suggestions about how to implement that philosophy, and we had a provisional plan how to get a parallel buy-in from the "right" Afghans. In addition, the day before I had managed (I thought) to reset my gung-ho Marines' focus so that they, too, bought into the UW program. All in all, I thought, a good two days.

But there were other parties to win over, too.

12

Culture Clashes

In working with allies it sometimes happens that they develop opinions of their own.

—Winston Churchill

Having recalibrated our strategy, we had now to get our Afghan soldiers on board with it. Technically these men were guns for hire, but as our plan was to transition them to the Afghan National Army once it was up and running, we saw them not just as mercenaries but as dedicated members of an Afghan Security Force (ASF). With the stripling warriors idea, we had a good preliminary screening mechanism to ensure that the men we recruited to that force would be loyal to our cause. As a secondary screen, Jason and Ben conducted interviews of all potential recruits, to weed out those whose loyalty might be offset by a deficiency such as a bad attitude, no weapon, or no vouching letter. But this wasn't enough. Determining that a young, properly armed and vetted villager was willing and able to join us wasn't the same thing as knowing that he was willing and able to fight this war our way.

By this point, I had developed some definite ideas about how the ODA, the Marines, and our Afghan soldiers should engage with the local population. Those ideas weren't necessarily in accord with the established Pashtun tradition of reacting quickly and violently to perceived insults. In addition, the American military had some equally definite ideas about training, marksmanship, rules of engagement, and chain of command. Those ideas, too, might not square with local traditions. Turning our new volunteers into the kind of soldiers we needed might not be easy.

The first challenge was to develop in this ragtag bunch not a fighting spirit (that was the birthright of every Afghan male) but a familiarity with the fundamentals of soldiering. Some older recruits had seen action against the Soviets, and one of them told Jimi that as a child he had been given a knife and sent out to slit the throats of wounded Russians. Most of the volunteers, though, were younger. They were the sons of the mujahideen generation, and they came to us straight from their market stalls or farms—no more seasoned in warfare than a farm boy from Kansas. So job number one was giving them the Pech Valley equivalent of basic training.

On a stateside base, this task would fall to the legendary ass kickers known as drill instructors. At Camp Blessing the DIs were Special Forces sergeants—the nine noncom stalwarts of our ODA. To some degree they focused on their own specialties, with the weapons sergeants Dave and Ian covering firearms and medics Mike and Ben teaching first aid. But in practice this stovepiped arrangement often broke down, and everybody did a little bit of everything. Randy, our team sergeant, was top dog among the ODA trainers. With his ever-present Oakleys, a thick, full beard, and long hair combed back, he cut an impressive figure for our Afghan recruits.

The curriculum was a condensed version of Army boot camp's basic combat training. Stateside this takes ten weeks. To get our guys up to speed quickly, we designed a course of instruction that we believed would make them capable of running their own armed patrols in six weeks.

It started with physical training, which could be amusing.

Afghans are a hardy bunch, but they're not used to flopping around doing jumping jacks. But they were game, and they seemed to get as much of a kick out of their gyrations as we did. We also introduced them to the care and feeding of weapons, which ranged from their own rifles (some of them ancient) to our own .50-cal machine guns. Then we drilled them on combat procedures. Formations, security, checkpoints, raids, ambushes, camouflage, mapping, armed reconnaissance, rules of engagement. Everything their patrols had to know in order to engage the enemy effectively and to guarantee security for the valley once we had gone home.

Letting the Afghans do it, that was our goal. Teaching them how to do it, that was our job.

Most of our recruits embraced the training enthusiastically. As camp commander I did little actual instruction myself—that was the team's job—but I heard reports about how attentive they were, how eager to learn, how open to a pattern of collective behavior that, to these intensely individualistic men, must at first have seemed counterintuitive. I could see their involvement, even watching from a distance, as the recruits formed a tight circle around an instructor, as hands went up for questions, as smiles flashed when someone had an "Aha!" moment.

As instructors, the team was definitely hands-on, committed to demonstrating, not just talking about, each lesson. I'd drop by to check on the Afghans' progress and I'd catch Dave physically bull-dogging five of them into a wedge formation, or Jimi on his belly in the dirt, illustrating the prone firing position, or Randy hopping behind a truck in a "take cover" drill. They used rolls of wide butcher paper to diagram field movements, and plenty of charade-like gestures to overcome the language barrier. Jimi liked to say that to get your points across in the absence of an interpreter, you had to go slow, break things into segments, and "pretend you're Italian."

The training was serious business, but that did not prevent the team from developing friendly, often surprisingly warm, connections with the Afghans. Scott remembers this as the most unusual, and most gratifying, aspect of our Pech Valley experience. "We were friends," he reflected recently. "Not in every case to be sure, but to an extent sufficient to facilitate our purposes and, I hope, theirs as well. We tried to approach them as equals, sharing the same living conditions and the same exposure to risk. That helped to create a space where trust could develop. 'Friendship' sounds like a strong word, but that's what it felt like."

I saw this bond of friendship at lunch one day, when we had a visitor from Bagram, a genial physician named Doc Hale. One of the trainees, Dilawar, had taken to referring to Jimi as *kalka*, meaning "uncle." That day, he was sitting between Jimi and our visitor. When the food was set down and Doc reached for a piece of naan, Dilawar gently restrained him, explaining soberly, "*Kalka* first." Jimi still recalls that moment fondly.

On one of the rare occasions that I got personally involved in the training, I had an "Aha" moment of my own that proved both funny and helpful.

Dave was explaining the operation of the RPK machine gun, a heavier version of the AK-47. It's fired in six- to nine-round bursts. If you fire it faster than that—by holding the trigger too long—you risk burning out the barrel and destroying the gun. In teaching recruits how long a six- to nine-round burst takes, drill instructors will tell them to hold the trigger for as long as it takes to say, "Peanut butter, peanut butter, jam." This works fine for English speakers, but Dave found that the Afghans couldn't get their mouths around the meaningless sounds. I thought for a moment, did a mental scan through my tiny Pashto vocabulary, and came up with something I thought might work.

"Try *shin chai, shin chai, burra,*" I said. It meant "Green tea, green tea, sugar."

The Afghans got it. Smiles all around, including a big one from Dave. Soon his class was off and running on the RPK, and I congratulated myself on making a small advance in linguistic diplomacy.

Teaching might not sound very Green Beret–like. In fact, this nonkinetic activity is at the very heart of what Special Forces are designed to do. "One Green Beret equals a hundred rifles." That SF saying indicates that our basic job is to be a force multiplier: to mold indigenous troops to be so effective that we can leave our AOs confident they're in good hands. We're supposed to make ourselves irrelevant. In counterinsurgency, according to strategist David Kilcullen, you should "prepare for handover from Day One."[1] As I saw our mission, nothing was more important than our work as teachers. One Green Beret equals one hundred rifles. But those rifles must be taught to be effective.

Basic training was the relatively easy part, as our recruits were mostly able-bodied, alert, and willing to learn. Other aspects of building a security force were more challenging.

At the outset, all of the recruits held the same "rank." But when we started singling out the more capable individuals as squad leaders, we ran into an ancient practice of rewarding people based not on skill or initiative but on family connections, clan status, and palm greasing. In the Pech, you became a top gun not because you could shoot better than anyone else but because your father was a big shot in your village. That wasn't going to work for us. If we wanted fighting units we could trust, we needed to make Arman junior a squad leader because he was smart and knew how to follow orders, not because he was Arman senior's son.

One of our new recruits was related to an influential elder in northern Kunar. He was a good soldier but he didn't have the respect of others that you want in a squad leader. When several of our soldiers from his village were promoted to his rank, and one was promoted above him, emotions ran thick. He felt that his family had been insulted, and the soldiers we promoted felt that their families might be abused for affronting the status quo. Nobody was happy—least of all the man who had been promoted above him. Randy solved this dilemma by creating an additional squad leader position and giving the insulted soldier an opportunity to earn it. It was a sensitive navigation between two very different approaches to military command.

Privileging reputation or family connections over skill can wreak havoc on the chain of command. In modern militaries, you don't have to respect your superior officer as an individual, but if you don't respect his rank, discipline dissolves. In 2004, that concept hadn't quite taken hold in Afghanistan. We worked hard to show our indigs that unit cohesion and mission focus both depended on legitimate orders being followed, whether you liked them or not. This wasn't an easy sell in a culture where men were known to quit fighting and go home when they needed to work on the harvest, and sometimes whenever the inclination took them, whatever the state of the mission or the dictates of their superiors.[2]

Another challenge was the Islamic attitude of "Insh'Allah." Afghans invoke this phrase, which means "If God wills," a hundred times a day, as an acknowledgment of divine power. I respected the sentiment, but its effect was problematic.

In inviting God's blessing on something he was about to do, the pious Muslim was implicitly saying, "If I screw this up, it's not my fault; Allah didn't want me to succeed." That's an unworkable attitude. It allows the lazy or uncommitted soldier (or civilian) to put forward a piss-poor effort and blame it on God. Not acceptable in a military unit.

Our air support specialist, Courtney Hinson, had participated in the invasion of Iraq from Turkey, working with the Kurdish fighters known as the Peshmerga. An experience he had there showed just how dysfunctional the "Insh'Allah" attitude could be. A Peshmerga soldier accidentally shot and killed a fellow soldier while he was prepping his weapon. His unit's response was, to American eyes, unbelievable. "They just moved the body out of the way," Courtney recalled, "and shrugged their shoulders. It was like the guy who screwed up had no responsibility for what had happened. It must just have been the dead guy's time—that was the attitude."

The "Insh'Allah" attitude had a particularly negative impact on our trainees' ability to shoot straight. U.S. soldiers' marksmanship is among the best in the world because we are taught to keep our weapons on safe until we've sighted a target, to aim carefully, and to stop shooting when we can't see the target. This minimizes accidents, conserves ammo, and maximizes our hit ratio. The Afghan approach to shooting is not governed by such protocols.

The typical Afghan "marksman" prefers to keep his weapon constantly on automatic, to point it vaguely in the enemy's direction, and to release random bursts of automatic fire that he hopes, "if God wills," will find their targets. You see this kind of literally aimless firing in news clips of Middle Eastern street battles, where fighters lift their automatic weapons above a protective wall and spew lead in the general direction of an unseen foe. Safer for the shooter, but with a next-to-zero chance of actually hitting something.

And if you do hit something, it's not your fault. To some, this carefree fatalism might be philosophically comforting. Militarily it's bad news. We took small comfort from the fact that it was evidently a common practice among ACM soldiers, too: Some of the weapons we captured from them had the front gunsight filed off, so you couldn't accurately fire the weapon even if you tried. We nicknamed this kind of shooting "Spray and Pray," and getting our trainees to recognize its ineffectiveness was a major cultural hurdle that we had to overcome. Making sure that their guns all had workable sights was a step in that direction.

Despite these hurdles, the Afghan Security Force (ASF) guys gradually became more proficient. Their ability to climb the mountains at this altitude was impressive to the Americans trying to keep up. But with the extra equipment we wanted them to carry, we had to work on their upper body strength and general fitness. At first the sight of them struggling with pushups and jumping jacks was a source of some ODA and Marine merriment, but within a few weeks they had shaped up not just physically but mentally as well, and were ready for increased responsibilities. By early January Randy and I felt confident enough to entrust them with multiple recon patrols up and down the valleys.

Next to training the Afghans, doing meet and greets with villagers, and conducting patrols, the building out of the camp took up much of our time. In this endeavor, too, because we employed local labor, there were cultural challenges.

Take chain of command. Jason would eventually find permanent foremen to assist in managing the laborers, but at the beginning it was spotty. When he hired workers every day, after they were patted down, he would survey the crews and, based on previous experience, appoint two or three foremen for that day. Naturally he would pick those he felt were most responsible, had the best skill sets, and could function best as overseers of their peers. That didn't always work out smoothly. Among day laborers, as among our Afghan soldiers, tribal or village prestige counted more than expertise. Every so often, Jason would have to subdue the turmoil that ensued when he picked the "wrong" person to be a foreman.

Or the wrong errand runner. One day Jason sent Sahim, the

young English speaker he used as an interpreter, into Nangalam with a roll of bills to purchase construction supplies. He was wearing a new jacket when he went in, but when he returned, he had neither the jacket, the money, nor the supplies. Some young toughs had beaten and robbed him partly as a crime of opportunity but also because they had a longstanding beef with Sahim's tribe. Here was a challenge—cultural and ethical—that had to be dealt with head-on.

Sahim had been assaulted outside of a shop from which we had previously purchased small items like mattresses, sodas, and cooking fuel. Jason, who knew the shop, paid the owner a visit.

"Sahim is my employee and my friend," he explained. "Whoever beat and robbed him, that person attacked me, too. We don't do things this way. You will tell the boys who did this that they must return the money they stole. And they must show respect to my friend. Or no one at our camp will do business with you again."

If the appeal to justice didn't make the case, the commercial threat did. The next day, the shopkeeper's assistant showed up at Camp Blessing with Sahim's jacket and the stolen money. Sahim was never bothered again.

Afghan business owners also had a unique way of bidding on a project. In the West, when you want a wall built, you put out a Request for Proposal. Three or four firms give you sealed bids, and you pick either the lowest one or the one you feel would do the best job: if you're lucky, that's the same person. In Nangalam and Manogay, it didn't work that way. The name of the game was collusion, not competition. After we had bought a few items at what were probably inflated rates, the idea got around that the Americans had bottomless pockets and could be gouged at will. When Jason asked for bids on a large front wall we wanted built, he got three sealed envelopes—each one containing the same price of $35,000. Quite a coincidence.

Even if Bagram had been willing to pony it up, that price was too high to consider. We paid good wages by local standards, but we weren't about to be mugged by crafty businessmen working under the false impression that we were millionaires. That would have screwed us and it would have thrown a wrench into the local economy. We wanted to do business in a way that was sustainable. So we tore up all three bids, told the grifters no thanks—and put up a Hesco wall ourselves for about two grand. That taught everybody a lesson about inflated prices, and it made it easier for us as time went on to negotiate sensible fees.

We learned similar lessons on other building projects. For example, rather than throwing money at untested people in the hope of winning their allegiance, we found it wiser to grant contracts to competent people who had already shown their loyalty to the "new Afghanistan." They could do this, for example, by bringing us actionable intelligence—information that led to the recovery of an arms cache or the capture of an insurgent. Another lesson was that instead of following Afghan tradition in paying contractors per foot of wall as each foot was finished, we would get better results by paying half up front and half on completion of the project, with a deadline set in place to encourage promptness.

The deadline idea often ran counter to the "Insh'Allah" attitude. Like our indig soldiers, civilian contractors hesitated to state precise delivery dates because they saw such promises as presumptuous: only God could know the future. We learned to push back on this idea by granting a contractor full payment if the project was completed on time, 90 percent if completed a few days late, and so on. "If it's God's will that you be paid the full amount," Jason would tell them, "you will complete the job on time." I don't know how that fit in with Muslim theology, but it got results.

*   *   *

Working with Afghans remained an ongoing challenge for understandable cultural reasons. But we also had to contend with a different kind of challenge—one that was in a sense closer to home and therefore less understandable than the East-West divide. I mean the disconnects that arose between our ground-level view of the war and the view from thirty thousand feet that came out of Bagram. Our senior command was a principal stakeholder in the prosecution of the war, but it wasn't always clear that their "anchoring philosophy" and ours were in sync.

This wasn't a novel situation. Although most people in the military, whether on the front lines or rear areas, are trying to do their jobs and serve their country, troops in the field often feel that support personnel don't get what's happening outside the wire, and that bureaucrats in particular are insulated from that reality. Nor do they understand, as Courtney once put it colorfully, that for action-oriented soldiers "it's no fun hanging around the flagpole." Hence the grunt's slang term *fobbit* for someone who spends his entire tour on an FOB.

To be fair, support personnel have a difficult time juggling limited resources and trying to satisfy conflicting demands. That said, though, the perceived disconnect between boots on the ground and pencils on the desk is a perennial frustration for warriors in the field. This is especially the case when we are trying to fight an unconventional war.

We had already had broad hints about this disconnect. One was the deaf ear that Bagram had turned to my pleas, back in October, that they return the prisoner we had sent them after the "Gestapo" incident. Apparently, once a suspect was in custody, exculpatory evidence didn't matter. Neither did the fact that we had to live with the poor guy's family hating our guts and potentially collaborating with our enemies to exact revenge.

Another hint was the unreasonable reaction to my destruction of the disabled Humvee. That reaction became evident soon after the incident, when Colonel Herd, nominally our biggest supporter, expressed his disapproval that I had circumvented authorization to blow up the truck. As I've mentioned, it had irritated the Combined Joint Task Force commander, Brig. Gen. Lloyd Austin, that an alleged rogue captain in Kunar was destroying government equipment. I didn't know it at the time, but Colonel Herd was considering pursuing a court-martial against me, and was only swayed from doing so by the intervention of my battalion commander, Lt. Col. Marcus Custer. Lieutenant Colonel Custer warned me that something unpleasant was in the works and that I might want to think about hiring a lawyer. As Christmas approached, I got word there was to be a commander's inquiry into the incident, and there was talk of having me charged for destroying the vehicle. Not charged as in court-martial, but charged as in "pay for the truck."

"Damn, Ron," Roger said to me when he heard about this, "won't that max out your Visa card?"

I appreciated the joke, but in fact we were all disgusted with the way the blown-truck issue was being handled. And in terms of group dynamics, this was a tricky situation. In order to keep discipline and morale high, it was my responsibility to maintain the men's respect not just for me but for our senior command. In second-guessing an important decision I had made, higher-ups were making that difficult and threatening to undermine the command environment. When senior command empowers its field commanders, things go well. When they don't, folks in the field are tempted to make decisions based on CYA rather than mission focus. That can be disastrous.

So far the disconnect with Vance had worked, ironically, to my advantage. The men saw that my decision had been made for their benefit; the threatened inquiry became a burr under our collective saddle; and the incident brought us closer together. But the truck incident wasn't the only operation on which Vance questioned my on-the-ground perspective. Today, as I page through the journal that I kept during our deployment, I'm reminded that December and January were filled with similar disconnects between us and the brass.

Throughout December, I had been asking for a Humvee to replace the one we had lost, for some additional generators, and for Toyota trucks equipped with a signal-jamming technology that was a top-of-the-line defense against IEDs. At the end of the year we were still waiting for delivery. I had also been requesting funds to buy our Afghan soldiers uniforms, so we could literally tell our indigs apart from the bad guys. We had already had incidents in which Marines, understandably unclear about which soldiers were friendlies, had narrowly avoided attacking our own allies.

The CIA and Department of Defense were squabbling about who was going to pay for uniforms and equipment for the Afghan Security Force, and my pleas to Vance to get the matter settled had gone unanswered. Finally, on Christmas Eve, I used the satellite phone to call Brigade Quartermaster, an equipment supplier, and bought the uniforms myself, hoping that I would eventually be reimbursed. The girl in Georgia taking my order was confused about why I would be buying 130 uniforms until I gave her my APO address and she recognized that the order was going to Afghanistan. She expedited it and wished me luck. I was excited that our indig soldiers would soon be sporting classic Tiger Stripe duds—a pattern I had chosen as an homage to our Vietnam-era predecessors—but I was also irritated at the hoops I had to jump through to get it done.

Then it was Christmas—probably the strangest and certainly the loneliest one I had ever experienced. Posted to a land where this holiday is virtually nonexistent, I found my thoughts turning to home and to what I was missing. This was the second Christmas that war had put thousands of miles between me and my family.

Just before I left for Afghanistan, Becky and I had bought a small new house in Liberty Lake, Washington. I pictured our two sons, Tanner and Owen, playing there by the fire and eating sugar cookies while little Bailey enjoyed the lights and sounds of the season without her dad. Becky is a great mom, and I knew she would make Christmas special for the kids so they wouldn't feel sad about my absence. I took solace in knowing that this would be the last Christmas we would be apart. And I kept the team and myself busy to distract us from thoughts of warm homes and lonely stateside families.

As the holiday passed, the disconnect with higher-ups continued to bug us. On December 26, HQ informed us that an arms raid we had planned for the following day was a no-go: The Camp Vance micromanagers felt that the CONOP I had put together lacked sufficient detail for them to assess the risk and grant approval. As a result, a time-sensitive target never got hit and a prospective Al Qaeda heavy faded back into the woodwork—all because of intrusive bureaucratic oversight.

Two days later, HQ doubled down on this risk-averse attitude by sending me a truly ridiculous order: I was forbidden from sending anybody out of Camp Blessing without a CONOP. Which meant, technically, that if Abu Ikhlas lobbed a rocket at our front gate, or if Hekmatyar was seen having tea in Nangalam, we would

Camp Blessing, January 2004

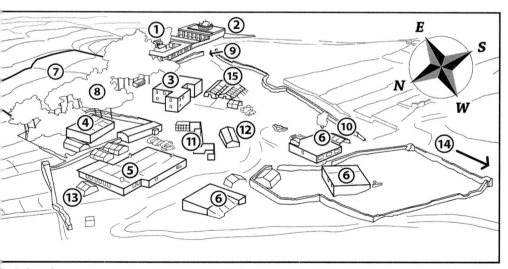

1. School
2. Mosque
3. Afghan Barracks
4. District House
5. ODA 936 House

6. Marines' Buildings
7. Helicopter Landing Zone
   (HLZ)
8. Front Gate
9. Vehicle Gate
10. Gym

11. Temporary Clinic
12. Building Supplies
13. Intel Tent
14. Firing Range
15. Shura Tent

ODA 936, April 2004.
Left to right back row:
Courtney Hinson, Ben
Guile, Scott Jennings,
James Trusty, Jimi Rymu[
Scott Pulham (camp coo[
Justin Jones (PSYOP).
Left to right front row:
Me, Randy Derr, Jason
Mackay, Ian Waters, Mi[
Montoya, Dave Moon,
Roger Wilcox.

Ben Guile on the .50-
cal. machine gun on
the road to Kamdesh

Jimi Rymut guards
the Sangar cache.

I break bread with the
Manogay *shura*, January 22,
2004. Omar is to my left,
facing the camera.

Mediating a water dispute
between Wanat and Aranus
elders in Wanat village,
April 2004

Team sergeant and medic Randy
Derr cares for a child. Our clinic
provided the only medical aid in
the Pech Valley.

The ODA and Afghan
soldiers practice
"candy diplomacy" in
Shamir Kowt village,
October 2003.

The Humvee that was destroyed by an IED on Route Blue, December 11, 2003.

After the IED attack, medics Mike Montoya and Ben Guile prep Chris Aguirre for medevac, December 11, 2003.

Randy Derr addresses the Afghan Security Force (ASF) at Camp Blessing, March 2004.

ASF soldiers practice compound and room clearing, February 2004.

Socializing with the local leadership. On special occasions they would provide us with Pepsi.

Men of the cloth. Our chaplain, Eric Eliason (far right), with his friend Taroon (second from left) and local mullahs.

The Manogay mosque, before restoration

The Manogay mosque, after restoration. Restoring the mosque adjacent to our camp was a major effort in the chaplain's renovation project.

The first class of the Manogay girls' school. Supporting this school was a hall-mark achievement of our civil affairs attaché James Trusty.

I address U.S. and Afghan dignitaries at the Camp Blessing dedication, May 2004.

Cache recovery covered by *60 Minutes II*, May 2004. Photo credit: Emilio Morenatti

Reunion with my family, July 2004

be powerless to respond until Bagram said we could go. I wrote in my journal that night, "They are putting me in a position where I have to either disobey orders to accomplish the mission or stay here in camp doing nothing. Damned if you do, damned if you don't." Sometimes I wondered if anyone in the chain of command between me and President Bush actually wanted to win the war.

To keep morale high, I would remind the team that—appearances to the contrary—the folks at Vance wanted us to be successful and that, if they fully understood what we were trying to accomplish, they would support our decisions. I sort of believed that myself, but as time went on, I started to take a different tack, acting more and more like the warrior king that Colonel Herd had called me. Rather than giving my superiors the option of second-guessing me, I sometimes just *assumed* that they would grant approval. I was beginning to adopt the "Need to Know" policy that Randy had suggested back in the Commander's Intent meeting. Like him, I saw that there were some things the higher-ups didn't need to know.

Jason gave me a big thumbs-up on this new direction. "You know, Ron," he said, "It's always better to ask for forgiveness than for permission."

As part of the new, unwritten policy, I began fudging the CON-OPs. I knew that if I itemized every risk we might encounter on a patrol, we might be confined to quarters for the duration. So when a contact gave us intel about an arms cache, I submitted a simple meet and greet CONOP, suggesting we were making a social call on elders. The intel proved good. We found ordnance in a cave and, after taking what we could use, we destroyed the rest of it in an impressive explosion. I didn't know which part of this was better for our morale: the destruction of the cache or our sidestepping of a fobbit roadblock. But we all felt good about this latest example of SF improvisation.

On New Year's Eve, a flurry of rockets fell just short of the district leader's compound, a kind of county seat that was directly adjacent to Camp Blessing. Proximity to this local seat of government was one reason I had found the Catamount site attractive in the first place. So an attack on the compound was tantamount to an attack on Blessing itself. In response, we ran a couple of patrols up into the valley, acquiring some useful intel and creating some amusement among our indig soliders as we bounced precariously up and down on a suspension bridge.

I felt good about that day until I got back to camp and found a message from a Maj. James Kim, who was heading up the Humvee investigation. He wanted to know whether I was going to waive my rights to an attorney. If I wasn't, he didn't want to waste his time or risk hitting an IED driving out to Blessing to question me. He had heard the road was dangerous.

Really, I thought, you heard the road on which I had to blow up a truck was dangerous?

Since I wasn't going to waive my rights, it was decided I would fly to Camp Vance to make a formal statement. I was to report to Major Kim. And oh, yes: I was to shave my beard before arriving.

Of all the little irritants that HQ threw at us, this was one of the most tone-deaf. If I had shaved my beard, when I returned to duty in the Pech nobody would have talked to me. The warrior king would have been reduced to juvenile status, and the respect that we were working so hard to gain would evaporate. The fact that senior command didn't get that, or didn't care, showed how isolated it was from the war on the ground.

Luckily, Major Hewitt saw the order's foolishness. He went to bat for me, and we finessed the situation by having me stay indoors most of the time, dress like a civilian, and tell anyone who asked that I was a contractor. A Special Forces tradition: improvisation.

When it came to the "inquiry," things worked out better than I expected. Major Kim turned out to be reasonable. When I took responsibility for destroying the truck and explained why I had no choice, he seemed to get it, and he said that he would not recommend that I be held financially responsible.

That was a relief, but it was short-lived. Command was disappointed that the rogue commander would not be made an example of, and they replaced Kim with another investigator. This second officer found me responsible for the truck, although not responsible for the entire amount. It wasn't until toward the end of our deployment that this ludicrous situation was resolved.

Work on Camp Blessing continued at a rapid pace even as we had to fight for HQ approvals and for supplies. The elation we had felt in December when the first Red Ring helo reached us dissipated a month later, when we were inexplicably dropped from the route and left to make our own supply runs to Abad. Apparently logistics thought it was more trouble to have pilots make a fifteen-minute detour than for us to scurry for our lives along IED-thick Route Blue. This issue resolved after a few weeks, but the delay exposed the politics and short-sighted thinking of those in a room filled with maps and coffee makers.

In addressing this infuriating situation, SF improvisation came in handy. Every couple of weeks, I would drive to Abad to get CIA intel and meet with the B-Team, and while there I would gather supplies. I say *gather*, because what I brought back wasn't always requisitioned through normal channels; it was discreetly scrounged. Fans, blankets, DVDs, Gatorade, beef jerky: if command hadn't seen fit to send these items to us out in the boondocks, I considered it my responsibility as field commander to get them for my men.

In Afghanistan, as in other frontier postings, the big bases (like Camp Vance) got the best supplies, FOBs (like Abad) got the second-tier stuff, and outposts like Blessing got what was left over. I considered that a wrong worth righting. Nobody on the team disagreed. In fact any of us who went to Abad for any reason at all would be expected to return to Blessing with loot in tow. If the brass frowned on this pilfering, I never heard about it. It was probably more common than not among Special Forces teams, who were forced to acquire for themselves what official channels had declined.

We were also having trouble being resupplied by land. The given reason for this was our site's location twenty miles from Abad up a perilous mountain road. I can't recall how many messages I got from HQ explaining that such-and-such a supply would be difficult to obtain. One that I got around the middle of January was especially outrageous. In response to my request for an additional generator and some extra fuel, it said my request could not be honored because "the jingle trucks cannot make it through Nangalam to the camp." We should therefore "look into the possibility of moving the camp to the other side of Nangalam where the jingle trucks can go."

This was beyond belief in a number of ways.

For starters, it implicitly reversed the appropriate roles of operations and logistics. Logistics is designed to support ops, not vice versa. Bagram was asking us to move our camp away from a strategically selected area so that it would be easier to get supplies there. That was ass-backward. I was reminded of the old joke about the guy who loses a quarter on Fifth Street but starts looking for it on Fourth Street because the light is better there. What would Gen. George Patton have said if HQ offered to resupply him in Paris because it was easier than shipping supplies to his troops' front lines?

Second, the message suggested that, despite all the work that two hundred professional and local soldiers had put into setting up the camp, it was still being seen as a dispensable operation—something that was not as serious as Abad or Vance.

Most infuriating of all, though, was that idea about the road's impassability. That was just wrong. As I sat reading the message in the building that we had prepared as our command center, I could look out the window and see, parked ten feet away, a jingle truck that we used virtually every day to move supplies and personnel between the camp and Nangalam. Many other trucks routinely made that run, as did our lumbering Humvees. Whoever had determined that trucks couldn't navigate the road had obviously never been anywhere near our camp.

I learned later that the support company for our battalion had actually been tasked with supporting almost everything having to do with the Combined Joint Special Operations Task Force. This was a huge stretch for its resources and manpower, and if I had known that then, I might have been more understanding. At the time, I was just furious that our efforts lacked the support I felt they deserved. That was my mind-set when I got the "impassable road" message.

That was on January 21. After fuming over it for a minute or two, I sent back a detailed report on what this "dispensable" operation had accomplished so far, what supplies we needed to continue our work—and the actual state of the road their trucks supposedly couldn't travel. I was as polite as military courtesy demanded, but I couldn't keep my sarcasm completely under wraps. At one point I complained that despite the daily sitreps I had been sending to headquarters, "there are still those at Bagram that feel this is a gypsy camp that could be easily moved with a little help from Century 21." Then I countered the road issue:

> I would like to know what intel was used to make the above assessment, or what map-reading guru in Bagram arbitrarily decided that jingles couldn't make it out here. My sitrep

reports three uparmored vehicles at my location. If the road was not suitable, how did we get those out here?...We have a jingle truck that works 24/7 for the camp and has no problem on these roads.

I went on to suggest that the Bagram misperception may have had something to do with the fact that nobody had laid eyes on us since the beginning of December. Then I gave a rundown of what we had accomplished so far.

Aside from recruiting, arming, and training a hundred-man ASF, we had built these indig trainees a barracks, secured the camp with wire, reinforced guard towers, wired the buildings for electricity, fixed an inoperable well, organized a pharmacy and clinic, put in a shower, constructed a kitchen...and, oh yeah, put up with two months of no hot water and no hot chow. I ended the e-mail with a wish list of supplies that we needed to continue our work. My response was never addressed, but the supplies did begin to flow more freely. In addition, as a kind of olive branch, Bagram even assigned a young infantryman, Scott Pulham, to be our camp cook. After two months of the local fare and meals ready to eat (MREs), Scott's cooking was a welcome change. Someone inside the bubble had gotten the message.

Our soldiers were shaping up, the supply issue was resolved, and I was becoming comfortable with my warrior king role. And the hunt for Abu Ikhlas and Company was ongoing. Intel about hostile elements came in to us on a regular basis, and if it wasn't always reliable, at least the fact that people were willing to share it suggested some trust. The occasional rocket lob reminded us that our governance of this valley was still in dispute. But so far the ghosts in the hills had not drawn blood.

13

The Prisoner

In a polity, each citizen is to possess his own arms, which are not supplied or owned by the state.

—Aristotle's view, according to legal scholar Stephen P. Halbrook

They shall beat their swords into plowshares and their spears into pruning hooks.

—Isaiah 2:4

When the Soviets were run out of Afghanistan in 1989, they left behind a shattered national reputation, nearly fifteen thousand of their own dead, and untold amounts of mortars, RPGs, rifles, and other ordnance that had been captured by the victorious mujahideen. Most of these weapons eventually found their way into the hands of warlords or local headmen, who in bad times used them to settle disputes and in quieter periods kept them out of sight. By the time the United States entered Afghanistan over a decade later, there probably wasn't a village or farm anywhere in the country without a cache of these arms locked in a room or buried somewhere on the property. Because they could easily be sold, traded, or given to insurgents—sometimes under duress, sometimes not— they constituted a threat to our troops. Part of our job was to contact the owners of arms in the territory we controlled and confiscate or buy back as many as possible.

Locating the owners meant relying on informants, and as we had already discovered, their on-the-ground intelligence didn't always have a high degree of accuracy. For every Afghan who was honestly trying to help us disarm the Taliban, another one wanted to curry our favor by ratting out a neighbor, and a third wanted to enlist us as a surrogate in a feud. We had learned that lesson the hard way in Shamir Kowt. The takeaway from that experience was, as Scott put it, "You can't assess intel unless you know who's bringing it to you—and why he wants you to know it." We got better at finding that out as we went along.

In January 2004, when we had been at the "A" Camp for six weeks, we received information that a community leader named Omar had a cache of arms at his compound in Walo Tangi, a village about three miles up the Waygal Valley. Reliable or not, it wasn't news we could afford to ignore. On the morning of January 16, we loaded up two truckloads of Afghan soldiers, along with the ODA and our interpreter Mashal, and took a dirt road north. The drive to Walo Tangi took ten minutes.

We had passed this village on routine patrols, but had never turned into it before, so we got our share of puzzled stares when we pulled into the central square, parked our trucks, located Omar's compound, and surrounded it.

On a raid such as this, to minimize the risk to yourself and to bystanders, things must happen quickly and by the book. The first order of business is to seal off the objective—in this case, the compound—so I sent Jimi and Ben to cover the back entrance, had Randy and Junior guard the front, and led the rest of us inside to begin the clearing process. Most Pashtun compounds are composed of an outer wall, a large inner courtyard, and a series of rooms built around the courtyard. Clearing a compound means scouring each room to ensure that no one is waiting in ambush. You've got to do this before you start the weapons search, because it won't do you any good recovering an arms cache if you've just taken a round in the head from some guy in a closet.

To clear the area, I first had the women and children taken to a safe corner of the compound. Then we started systematically trying all the doors. Some of them opened easily, and some we had to kick in. Omar was well-heeled by village standards, but it wasn't a massive compound, so the clearing process took less than five minutes.

We didn't meet any trouble, although we did have a brief moment of concern when one of the doors didn't budge. I gave it one, then another, good kick but nothing happened. I was starting to imagine a turbaned terrorist barricading himself in on the other side when, on the third try, I heard a deep, lowing sound. The door swung in three or four inches, and I peered in to see the large moist eye of a cow looking back at me. Laughs all around. I've had worse surprises.

We had cleared the compound without encountering resistance, and without having to resort to the "blowing off the doors" technique that Hollywood often portrays as standard practice. In fact, in the time that we spent in Afghanistan, unless we were convinced that there were combatants on the other side, even kicking in doors was an unusual procedure. Normal procedure was to try the handle or to knock and ask to be let in. By the time our stint in-country wound down, our cache recovery expeditions tended to be wary but peaceful affairs that began with "Good morning, sir" and ended with tea.

With the compound cleared, the next task was to find the weapons, which meant getting their owner to show us where they were hidden. I had Omar brought to me and we began the little dance of hide-and-seek that, we had already discovered, was a universally popular game in this part of the world. With Mashal interpreting, I offered my opening gambit. "We know that you have weapons hidden on your property. We need to know what weapons you have and where they are."

Very commanding, I thought. But I was also thinking, somewhere in the back of my mind, what I might say to a federal ATF agent who came to my house and asked me to show him my guns. I would probably lie through my teeth. That was exactly what Omar did. With a look of indignation, he spoke rapidly to Mashal. Mashal turned to me.

"He says that he is a friend to the Americans. He does not have any weapons. He is not hiding any weapons. He would like to offer you tea."

I bet he would. "Tell him," I said, "that he must not lie to me. We know that he has weapons from the Russians. He needs to show us where they are. We would like him to cooperate with us."

As Mashal translated, I could see Omar's indignation rising. He shook his head vehemently, with a look of feigned outrage. He put one hand on his chest and stared straight at me. I watched his eyes and listened to Mashal's voice.

"He swears he does not have any weapons here. If someone told you that, that person is lying. He is a weak old man and if someone told you that he has weapons, he is trying to trick you."

Omar was a daring liar, I'd give him that, and the "weak old man" bit was a nice touch. He was tall, burly, and well fed even by American standards, let alone Afghan ones. And he didn't look more than fifty.

"We are going to search your property, sir," I said. "And we will find the weapons. If you help us we will pay you for the weapons, but if you don't help us and we find them, no payment. And we will have to take you back to our camp. And then you will go to Bagram."

I thought that the threat of Bagram—the main U.S. detention

site in Afghanistan—might loosen him up. Afghans who were sent there often remained in processing for months, and those believed to be dangerous could be sent on to Guantanamo. No Afghan wanted to go to Bagram. But Omar was insistent. He had no weapons.

As part of a security force we had a young Marine with a metal detector. I called him over and showed Omar the device. It was the same type of rig that beachcombers use to locate sunbathers' lost change. But painted olive drab and sporting a beeping red light, it looked impressively official. In the Marine's hands it looked like a Star Wars secret weapon.

"This device," I said, "can find metal. Anything made of metal, no matter where it's hidden. Even if it's buried. This man will go around your property and he will find anything on it that is made of metal. If he finds any rifles or rockets or ammunition—if he finds any weapons that you haven't told us about—I must take the weapons and send you to Bagram. Do you understand?"

What Bagram had not done on its own, the combination of Bagram and American technology had accomplished. As he realized that the game was up, he started to let down his guard and he pointed, somewhat sheepishly, to the door of a room.

"There are a couple of rockets in there that my cousin asked me to hold for him. They are not mine, they are my cousin's."

We opened the door into a child's room. In one corner stood a crib. Under the crib was a rug, and under the rug the earthen floor had been disturbed. Omar motioned to the spot and we began digging. We quickly uncovered not "a couple" of rockets but about thirty of them, plus several dozen machine gun rounds.

"Let's check the rest of the area," I said to the Marine. With Omar in tow, we went outside and started plying the metal detector around his property. Much of this was covered by a poppy field, laying fallow in the January gray. When the Marine swept the field, the detector let out so many frantic beeps that for a moment you might have thought you were in a video game arcade. With some local people recruited to help with the digging, we unearthed an assortment of rockets, RPGs, RPG boosters, and machine gun rounds—a major cache, buried beneath the poppy rows.

Omar's expression went from nervous to resigned to penitent, as he realized we had caught him in false denials. But then, as the Marine approached a corner of the field and the detector began registering another find, Omar became animated. He started talking excitedly, indignant again.

"What's he saying?" I asked Mashal.

"He says that's not his. That one there, not his. Somebody else buried those rockets on his land."

Hilarious. Either Omar was a true liar's liar—someone with a deep need to deny the obvious—or he had been the victim of a cosmic irony. Either way, seeing him proclaim his innocence while he was standing in that poppy field turned ammo dump offered an even funnier moment than the terrorist cow.

The streets of Walo Tangi were too narrow to admit our trucks, so once the metal detector stopped beeping, I had the team form a fireman's brigade to transport the weapons to the square where we had parked. It was a mixed crowd, composed of our guys, the tough-looking Afghan soldiers, and about ten local kids pitching in on what must have seemed to them like a grown-up game. This went OK for a few minutes until one six-year-old took a mortar shell from Dave, who was to his left, turned right to pass it on—and saw it slip, business end down, out of his hands.

There was no fuse to the shell, but it was old Russian ordnance that had been buried for years. I wouldn't have bet my life on it being stable. The time it took to get from the kid's hand to the ground might have been the longest half second of my life, and the harmless clunk it made was an angelic sound. I don't recall giving an order, but as if on cue Dave and every other SF guy there thanked the kids, gave them some candy, and closed up the gaps in the line with Afghan adults.

The cache recovery had been successful. Now, what to do with Omar?

In 2003 and 2004, deciding which suspects to detain was left to commanders on the ground. The protocol wasn't clearly spelled out, so in determining Omar's fate I had to go with my gut. We had intelligence that he was a person of interest; we had found a significant store of ordnance on his property; and he had lied to us. I figured that we couldn't just let him go. He would have to be brought back to our camp for questioning; he would be detained there as a Person Under Control (PUC); and perhaps from there he would have to be shipped on to Bagram.

So Omar the indignant armorer became our first prisoner.

Ben thought that we should put a gunny sack over his head right there in Walo Tangi, to humiliate him in front of his friends. Bagging a prisoner like this wasn't a universal procedure, but it wasn't unknown. When I hesitated to give the order to bag Omar, Ben hotly disagreed.

"Damn, Ron, the dude lies to us straight out. He's got enough rockets for the whole village. I say let everybody see what happens, what the consequences are, when you screw with us like that."

"Secure him," I said, "and no kid gloves. But no bag."

"No bag! What the hell. We're gonna look like assholes, letting this guy walk away with his head up. You afraid of embarrassing him? He *should* be embarrassed. He should feel outright humiliated, and his people should know that."

I understood Ben's frustration. As someone who had suffered a loss of hearing thanks to an IED attack, he had a special reason to be angry about hidden armaments. And he wasn't wrong about the virtues of bagging. There was often a good reason to bag a prisoner, especially when you were close to home, to prevent him from observing your defensive layout, and in fact it was common practice to at least blindfold potential hostiles when you were bringing them into a military facility. But I saw no good reason to do that to Omar on his home turf. Doing so would play into Taliban propaganda, which painted Special Forces as an American Gestapo, intent on insulting Islam and imprisoning the faithful. Considering the long-term effects, we probably had more to lose than gain by humiliating a respected leader in his own village.

So we treated Omar with respect and made sure that his neighbors saw us do so. We put him in the back of a truck, along with his weapons, and moved off on the road back to camp. This didn't endear me to Ben, but it's not a commander's job to be liked by his men at every step of the way. Ben and I respected each other, and I knew that once this incident had passed, we would be fine.

The truck rumbled along for ten minutes, with Omar sitting quietly and looking a little dazed. When the men could see the wire perimeter of Camp Blessing rising in the distance, I ordered the gunny sack to be put over the prisoner's head.

"You want to do the honors?" I asked Ben. It was no surprise to hear him answer, "Hell, yeah."

Back in camp, we brought Omar to a tent that had served as a makeshift detention facility during Mountain Resolve and handcuffed him to a cot. Within a couple of days—when it became clear that he wasn't a physical threat—the handcuffs came off, and he was secured by Marine guards standing outside the tent. We interrogated him usually two or three times a day, with the sessions conducted by me and our intel sergeant Scott, with Mashal interpreting. We were looking for anything that would help us better understand the complicated web of allegiances in the Pech Valley.

Civilians often assume that *interrogation* is a euphemism for "torture"; that the only way soldiers in the field extract information from detainees is through the use of physical or psychological abuse. I don't deny that such techniques are used; but in Kunar in 2003 and 2004, this was not our practice. We treated our prisoners with respect, and I am convinced that this humane approach to information gathering got us more reliable information than we might have gathered from the use of more aggressive measures.

I'm not saying that harsher measures wouldn't work or would never be justified. Any commander, in considering enhanced interrogation, has to measure the ethical costs against the potential practical benefits. In our case, the practical benefits of *not* using such methods outweighed other considerations. Aggressive interrogation wasn't in our toolbox for a simple reason. Our goal wasn't just to get good intel as quickly as possible (often the goal of CIA and some Special Ops interrogators); it was to build working relationships with locals. Given our mission, we had to consider the long-term effects of everything we did, both in terms of U.S. interests and in terms of the everyday realities of the people we lived among.

In fact to the best of my recollection the only time we "tortured" Omar, it came about unintentionally, and with no lasting harm.

Omar had been with us for a couple of days, submitting to our daily visits but otherwise being left alone in the tent when we weren't questioning him. When we weren't there, his Marine guards would pass the time by playing rap music; they would turn it off during our interrogations. It wasn't superloud, but to ears not accustomed to it, it must have been grating. Scott and I had no idea just how grating until we were in the middle of an interrogation one day and, tired of Omar's evasiveness, we got up to leave.

"Please don't go," he said through the interpreter.

"Why not?"

"Because when you're here is the only time they stop playing that horrible music."

Here was an unplanned opening, and we took advantage of it. "All right," we told him. "If you give us the information we want, we'll stick around."

Omar became quickly cooperative. What we learned from the episode is that you don't need thumbscrews and waterboards to extract information. Just a minor adjustment of a detainees' comfort level can sometimes work wonders.

After a week we realized that we had probably extracted all the useful information Omar had to give us. He had been reasonably helpful, but he wasn't a major player in the Pech Valley, and there was no good purpose served by either detaining him or sending him on to Bagram. Doing that, moreover, could have a deadly effect on our efforts to build alliances among the other villagers. Keeping such a small fish in custody would have upset his friends, alienated the Walo Tangi community, and confirmed the Taliban's night letter claims that the Americans were devils who liked to break up families. So the prudent choice was to send Omar back home.

That said, I started thinking about orchestrating his return so that it might have some supplementary benefit for our mission. As luck would have it, we were scheduled to meet with the local *shura* on January 22—just a couple of days away—and I saw this as an opportunity to make Omar's release pay off.

Ever since we had been in Kunar, a major objective had been to get as many old Russian arms as we could out of circulation; that deprived our enemies of weapons, and it increased the arms that we had available for our own ASF soldiers—something that Bagram wasn't always helpful with. The Walo Tangi raid was a small victory in that regard, but busting down doors and watching six-year-olds juggle mortar shells wasn't our preferred method of acquiring the arms. We had also been experimenting with a buyback program. I had had our Afghan soldiers bring to their villages a list of weapons that we wanted to purchase, with the prices we were willing to pay, and we had had some success in getting folks to surrender at least part of their stockpiles. A "cash for cache" program, you could call it.

This was legally a gray area. At this time in Afghanistan, the CIA was permitted to purchase weapons from suspected enemies of the state, but the Department of Defense was not—don't ask me why. What we as DOD employees were permitted to do was to purchase *intelligence* that might lead to the *acquisition* of weapons. That legal technicality sanctioned our buyback program. We'd pay someone to tell us where his weapons were and then, acting on that legally purchased information, we would locate and confiscate them. I don't know how that got recorded by the Pentagon bean counters, but it worked for us.

With this system in place and with Omar's fate in our hands, I wondered if we might offer the *shura* a quid pro quo: his release in exchange for their support of the program. If the buybacks were approved by the council of elders, they could take off in a big way and lives could be saved.

The January 22 *shura* meeting was to be held at Camp Blessing under military tents, and our Afghan cook was putting on lunch for the elders. We wanted to show that we could be good hosts as well as good guests. This was the third or fourth encounter we had had with this group of village leaders. Their mood had always been one of polite curiosity; on this day, as I began by describing the buyback proposal, they seemed more anxious and impatient, as if they were waiting for me to finish so they could come back with a proposal of their own. I opened the door for that move by winding up my pitch with an offer of assistance.

"What we're here for," I said, "is to be of service to the Afghan people. Please tell me how we can help you."

The conciliatory gesture seemed to throw them, and they were silent for a moment. Then one of them stood up.

"We want you to release the prisoner Omar," he said. "He is a good man. He is one of us, a member of the *shura*. Please do not send him away from his family." Several of the other elders seconded this plea.

They sounded dutiful rather than plaintive. I had the sense that however good a man they really thought Omar was, they were mainly fulfilling a collective duty in requesting that one of their own be returned to his village. I didn't get the idea that any of them actually thought this would happen. There was a resignation in their faces that said, We've been down this road before and it's gotten us nowhere.

Their pessimism was an unexpected gift. I let the request hang in the air for a minute, as if I were pondering its wisdom. Then, with Mashal translating, I gave them my decision.

"We are here to serve you and work with you. You are the elders of the *shura*, and I trust your judgment. If you tell me that this man is a good man, an innocent man, I will respect your word. He will be released at once."

With that, motioning to Mashal to translate, I turned to Jimi, who had accompanied me to the *shura*, and said, "Go get Omar and bring him back here. No handcuffs. He's free to return to his home."

Of course this double announcement, like the quid pro quo arrangement itself, was calculated theater. Since I had already decided to release Omar, I could simply have had him brought to the meeting in the first place. But the stakes were high in Kunar that winter, there was a long history of antipathy to the West, and I knew we needed the *shura's* support to get anything done. Whatever the ethical stature of the orchestrated trade-off, I felt that it was justified by the potential results.

The stratagem worked. As soon as Jimi started to walk toward the detention tent, we could see the faces of the old men brighten with surprise. The excitement on their faces told me that the "quo" I had offered had truly impressed them. The question now was what they would offer as a "quid." I didn't have to wait long to find out. The one who had spoken first turned to me.

"Commander," he said, "you are young but you are wise. You have trusted us and we will work with you. We will tell the people of our village that the Americans are our friends, and we will tell them to surrender their weapons to you."

As quids go, that was the big brass ring. I realized that in the chess game that everyone was playing, the elders' support might, like Omar's release, turn out to be a calculated means to an end. Maybe down the line old enmities would return and the "young but wise" commander would be seen as just another meddling *kafir*. But at the moment, under that tent, this looked like a major victory in the hearts-and-minds struggle—and a small sign of a break in an ancient antagonism.

It took Jimi just a few minutes to go to the makeshift detention facility, retrieve the prisoner and his belongings, and return to the meeting. When he reappeared with a smiling Omar, you might have thought he had kicked the Soviets out of town single-handedly. Over a boisterous meal, our prisoner reunited with the other elders, and we became, at least for a time, honored guests in a ceremony of reconciliation. Sitting around a long rug under a military tent, sharing food and tea with a group of old men, I was aware that we had just lit a flame against the darkness of violence.

In the next few weeks, the *shura's* stamp of approval proved to be a turning point in our relationship with dozens of villages.

The first day after the meeting one of the elders brought us a pristine RPG launcher. I assessed it with Jason and determined it was worth the max price for a weapon: $200. I brought out two crisp Benjamins and handed them to the elder. He smiled and walked out the gate holding the bills over his head, indicating to a group of men watching him that the buyback wasn't just a ruse to lock people up. "Trust but verify" had just been tested—and we had passed.

Later that afternoon a convoy of twenty pickup trucks came to the camp to sell us a huge inventory of RPGs, rockets, a full 14.7mm antiaircraft machine gun, AK-47 ammo, and sundry other goodies. Every time a truck would unload its wares, our weapons sergeants, Dave and Ian, looked like little kids on Christmas morning. The buyback program picked up so much speed that in February we took possession of twenty-seven separate weapons caches—more than anywhere else in Afghanistan at that time.

In addition, ODA 936's public image got an immediate upgrade. Up to January 22, 2004, we had been known, with some amusement, as "the bearded Americans." On January 23, we began to be known as "the bearded Americans who could be trusted." This was an enormous boost in our ability to align with the people against the influence of the Taliban. They saw that, even as our program was taking weapons out of the reach of our enemies, the cash we were paying was putting food on villagers' tables. And we had pulled off this coup without firing a shot.

As a young commander—I wasn't sure how wise—I took away two lessons about negotiating with Afghans. First, I learned that small gestures of accommodation could have big results. A hardliner would have thought that giving the prisoner up might be interpreted as a sign of weakness. I thought this was a risk worth taking. In trying to secure alliances, I felt honey was a better adhesive than salt. Releasing Omar didn't cost us anything. And the benefits we gained by "giving in" were substantial.

The other lesson was that respect mattered. A lot. This became clear when the *shura* spokesman said, "You have trusted us and we will work with you." What mattered to the old man wasn't Omar's release per se, but my publicly stated deference to the elders' wisdom. That revealed what he called *my* wisdom: it was by offering them my respect that I had earned theirs.

In our time in that valley, I never learned a more important lesson.

When we sent Omar home, we didn't figure we'd see him again. We were wrong. During his brief incarceration, he had taken a liking to us, and he returned frequently to our camp, hanging around near the gate, chatting with us through Mashal, and on more than one occasion bringing us intel and gifts.

Afghans are fond of presenting tokens of friendship. In my time at Camp Blessing I was given rugs, clothes, candy, knives, jewelry, and opium. Omar himself was partial to rings. That was the gift he gave me on one occasion. It was also the gift he gave to Maj. Gen. Eric Olson, who visited our camp a few months after his release.

The general had come to check out our detention facility, and as he was about to leave and I was escorting him to his helicopter, we ran into Omar hanging around his old place of confinement.

When Omar offered him the ring, the general looked taken aback, but he accepted it and asked, "Who are you, sir?" He looked even more taken aback when Omar replied, "I was a prisoner in this camp." He announced this almost proudly.

"I see," said Major General Olson. "And how were you treated?"

"I was treated well," said Omar. "Like a guest. These American soldiers, they are my friends."

The general turned to me approvingly. "I wish that we could say the same about every camp."

"Yes, sir," I said, aware of the unspoken concern that lay under his comment. His visit took place in May, and we all knew that what had prompted his far-from-customary inspection tour was a *60 Minutes* report that had aired two weeks earlier, revealing the abuse of Iraqi prisoners at Abu Ghraib.

The Abu Ghraib scandal dominated the news that spring, and it would continue to dominate it for years, ensuring that most of the world—certainly nearly everyone in the Muslim world—would equate U.S. military policy with hooded, naked detainees being mocked by our troops. In Kabul and Cairo, in Baghdad and Islamabad, people would think about America and imagine only the cries of tortured prisoners.

In our remote outpost in the Pech Valley, I wished that for just one moment they could hear a smiling Omar say to the general, "These American soldiers, they are my friends."

14

The Decider

In the struggle to gain the support of the people, every action we take must enable this effort.... Gaining their support will require a better understanding of their choices and needs.

—Gen. Stanley McChrystal, Commander's Initial Assessment

Secure the Victory.

—Motto of U.S. Army Civil Affairs

Gradually I was learning what the "warrior king" business was all about. It had quickly become clear that, as Colonel Herd had predicted, my job was expanding in unexpected directions. Almost every day I was invited by the Manogay district leader to join him, the local police chief, and a handful of elders in the district house that was located, conveniently, next door to our camp. There we would have tea, I would receive gifts of friendship, and I would be asked to approve resources for community projects and to weigh in on local disputes ranging from the trivial to the grave.

As far as community projects went, I found that I had to put in place some sound fiduciary principles or else be overrun by unmanageable agendas. Locals had plenty of ideas for using U.S. government money. Our funds for nonmilitary activities came mostly from a Civil Affairs budget, supervised by a CA attaché, the appropriately named James Trusty.

CA soldiers like James are a critical element in any "hearts and minds" campaign. They coordinate the field commander's links to the local authorities, identify and assess project requirements, and in general work to "secure the victory" by supplementing military action with civic improvement. James was the perfect attaché for our ODA. I had heard stories about CA guys who saw their job as just that, a job. Not James. He was hardworking, friendly, and fully committed to improving the Afghans' lives. I couldn't have hoped for a better CA ally.

As dedicated as he was, he was also realistic. He taught me that Civil Affairs projects can be your most valuable weapon or your worst nightmare. To ensure that ours remained an effective weapon, he and I agreed to keep three principles in mind.

The first was that resources are limited. Unfortunately, this principle is often thwarted because Congress votes huge routine appropriations for the military and its contractors, with minimal oversight or accounting. This fosters two bad assumptions: one, that CA funding comes from a bottomless reservoir; and two, that you don't have to justify what you spend because it's not your money.

In fact, every penny a field commander spends on CA projects is taxpayers' money. Even if Congress was too lazy to monitor expenditures, I believed it was my responsibility to do that for them. If I spent ten dollars on something that I could have gotten for five, I'd have just doubled the cost of the war in one small area. Do that often enough, and suddenly the War on Terror costs real money, the American people start to wonder where their dollars (and their soldiers' lives) are going, and you've lost their confidence. I didn't want that to happen.

The second principle was that CA projects must show a return on investment. In determining whether or not to fund a project, you have to ask what your outlay is buying in terms of security, civic enhancements, intelligence, or good will. In the Pech, we ensured this by making all CA projects conditional. We allocated funding based on cooperation we had already received and cooperation we anticipated in the future. If we were considering which of two towns most needed our help in digging a well or repairing a road, the town that had given us good intel in the past or where the leadership had assisted us in the U.S. war effort would have the edge. By helping those who were helping us, we ensured that we were getting the most bang for the buck.

The final principle was to consider the long-term effects of your endeavors. Dropping a $60,000 smart bomb on a suspected HVT hideout may seem like a good use of limited resources—and maybe sometimes it is. But the effects of that decision may or may not serve your interests in the long run, whereas spending one-tenth of that amount on a school building will give the locals something they can appreciate for generations. The core aim of Civil Affairs is to win the long-term trust of a civilian population. I always kept that in mind.

Many villagers brought their problems to me at the camp itself. Secure on my own turf, the sense of me holding court was pronounced. I became known as the Red-Bearded Commander—a humorous honorific for the American warlord who was consolidating a fortress at the meeting of the rivers, whose warriors included Afghans as well as Americans, and who (to borrow a term made popular by President George W. Bush) was the decider when it came to dispensing money, labor, or materiel.

It was an accident of genetics that gave me a ruddy complexion and a red beard. Senior elders in Kunar would sometimes dye part of their beards with red henna as a sign of distinction, so to come by that distinction naturally was a lucky break. At the same time, the local term for "commander" was *commandon*, often shortened to *don*. By a weird accident of language, I was being addressed by the same title that "wise guys" used for the head of a crime family— somebody like the ODA's favorite mafioso, Tony Soprano.

Maybe that wasn't so weird after all. Like an Italian don, I was widely seen as the person you went to when professing loyalty, currying favor, asking for approval, or settling a dispute. In a place where executive power was notoriously tenuous, I was expected to juggle the roles of judge, jury and, if not executioner, at least executor of my lordly decisions.

This was time-consuming and, while its value in building respect and rapport was undeniable, it was never as exciting as going to patrol with our Afghan soldiers. There's a Biblical passage where Jethro counsels his son-in-law Moses to make major decisions for the people by himself but, so that he does not "wear away," to delegate smaller matters to other "able men" (Exodus 18:13–26). I could relate to that. Sometimes I longed to get outside the wire as a full-time warrior just to take a break from my "kingly" duties.

In one meeting with the district leader and police chief, I was asked to decide what should be done with feral dog packs that were harassing villagers. Wild dogs are often a problem in third world countries, and in Kunar the problem was acute. After two of our Marines were bitten on patrol, we had entertained the idea of reducing the local pack. But playing dogcatcher was low on our priority list, and we decided after some discussion to take no action at that time. That decision would come back to haunt me later on.

Sometimes the problems I was presented with seemed merely an excuse to have a high-level audience. Elders would make their way to Camp Blessing to request something as minor as a few hundred dollars for road repair, a separate meeting in their village, or even permission to give their daughters in marriage. Cases like these could be handled locally by their own *shuras* or district leader, and decisions could be relayed by courier. I wondered why so many old men were seeking the personal approval of a young American. I asked Mashal about it.

"It is a mark of status for them to meet with you," he explained. "Whatever you decide—even if you decide against their request—they will return to their villages as people who have spoken personally to the Red-Bearded Commander."

Hearing that, I realized for a moment how it might feel to be an actual king. It was a heady feeling not without psychological risks. In acting as decider, I had a responsibility to adjudicate wisely, with an eye not on my own preeminence but on the welfare of those who were seeking my guidance. I had always prided myself on being a problem solver, so I warmed to the opportunity to be one here. But it's a dodgy business, wielding power. I had to remind myself, as I played at being Solomon, that wisdom without humility isn't all that wise.

Some of the decisions I was asked to make were anything but trivial. Decisions directly impacting our camp, for example, had to be fair to the parties involved while at the same time securing our place in the community.

We were now a major player in the local economy. Transactions between us and those we employed had to be handled with finesse. So when one of our laborers failed to repay a debt, I had to act as mediator between him and his creditor. We couldn't have someone associated with Camp Blessing be known as a deadbeat. It took some doing, but I was able to persuade him that a good businessman pays his bills on time. He pleaded financial straits, but eventually agreed to an installment plan that satisfied the creditor.

On another occasion I had to meet with a local "trade union." Nangalam shopkeepers, aware that big-bucks Americans were in town, were charging our Afghan soldiers three times the usual prices for their goods. That had to stop. We paid our guys well by local standards, but this didn't justify a 300 percent markup. I explained this to the union representatives, making sure to point out that if Nangalam wanted to gouge our boys, I would request that they bring their business elsewhere. This appeal to customer power hit home, and the "special ASF prices" came down to normal.

One serious issue arose at Camp Blessing itself, when the man who owned the land on which it sat came to me to arrange a rental agreement. The previous tenants, 10th Mountain, had made only a temporary lease arrangement. Since it looked like ODA 936 was going to be here for a long haul, the landlord wanted a more substantial fee.

There was no county clerk's office in the Pech, so we had to have the district leader, a thin, soft-spoken man, verify that the so-called landlord actually owned the land. When he did so, we drew up a contract that gave us squatting rights in the old NGO establishment for $500 a month—about the rate for a closet in Manhattan. We paid him the first six months in advance. Everybody was happy.

A couple of days later, though, I was holding court when another self-styled landowner waltzed in, claiming that a small section of the Camp Blessing real estate had been in his family for years. We would have to pay him rent for that portion of the property. This sounded fishy, and my confidence in him didn't improve when the district leader failed to vouch for his veracity. But I listened to his case and was still debating when Mashal turned to me and said simply, "This man is lying."

Mashal was an educated Afghan with a good feel for people and great skill in reading situational nuances. I relied on him to tell me not just the literal meaning of words but their emotional and cultural implications. Often I would ask him to wait before translating and give me first his impressions of the speaker's intent. When he called the second "landlord" a liar, that clinched the matter.

The guy looked at me expectantly as Mashal spoke, no doubt

thinking that his plea had been translated. His face fell when I looked at him sharply and said, "You are not the first person who has lied to me about this. You are trying to cheat me in claiming this land."

There was no remonstration of innocence. He knew he had been found out and became immediately penitent.

"I am very sorry, *Commandon*," he said. "I am a poor man. I have no property. I do not want to cheat you."

Then he did something that surprised me. Moving close to me, he reached out gingerly and grasped my beard.

"Please forgive me, *Commandon*. I do not wish to cheat you."

This was my first encounter with the Afghan tradition of begging on someone's beard. At first it seemed almost aggressive, but the man's face made it clear that it wasn't. He was like a child tugging on his mother's skirt. Mashal's translation verified this impression, as did his aside to me: "To touch your beard means that he begs your forgiveness. He is at your mercy."

The man's begging may have been simply a request to grant a favor. You see the gesture used this way in the film *Osama*, which was the first Afghan feature film made after the fall of the Taliban government and a searing indictment of that government's excesses.[1] In the film a poor shopkeeper, seeking a favor from a Taliban mullah, touches the cleric's beard in supplication. Or the would-be landlord may have been invoking the Pashtunwali principle of *nanawatay*, which means the request of a repentant person that his wrongdoing be forgiven.[2] In either case, even though I wasn't inclined to be charitable, I didn't see much benefit in punishing the poor guy for a pitiful attempt at fraud. Unlike the warlords that this valley had been used to, I was willing to let the matter slide. I released his hand and waved him away.

"Don't come here again," I said. "You may go away and I will not place you under arrest. But you must not come back."

He nodded in relief and shuffled away. It wasn't the happiest encounter I had had as warrior king, but it had a good outcome. Word would get around, I hoped, that the American commander was not a vengeful person, but that if you wanted to get anything from him, you'd better talk straight.

Adjudication also took me out of camp on a regular basis, often to settle disputes between adjoining villages. Throughout the Pech, there was a backlog of these because one village *shura* would not accept the ruling of another, and the local judges were too weak to enforce either party's rights. One judge, after having his life threatened, voluntarily retired from public service—not uncommon in Afghanistan in those days.

Playing judge in such situations enhanced my credibility but also gave me the chance to defer to the authority of the district leaders who ought to have been handling these matters in the first place. I would confer publicly with these officials to build them up in the eyes of their constituencies and—so I hoped—lay the groundwork for better governance when we were gone. Since our role was to help the Afghans help themselves, I was mindful of a comment Joseph Smith, the founder of Mormonism, made when asked how he governed his community: "I teach them correct principles and they govern themselves."

As humble as I was trying to be in my judge's robes, there was one occasion when I did feel Solomonesque. This was in the Waygal region, a few miles upriver, when I was asked to settle a dispute over a cow. This had been brewing for some time, until the local district leader decided that bringing in the American commander might make things move faster.

During a storm, a black-and-white cow had fallen into the Waygal River near a village called Kawiri Khwar and washed downstream to Lalm Kats, where it was hauled ashore, slaughtered, and eaten. The cow's owner, back upriver, wanted restitution, but the cow was gone, carcass and all. Lacking this literal body of evidence, the man who had appropriated it was able to blatantly deny the theft, even though it was common knowledge in his village that he had done it; he had even bragged about his luck to neighbors who shared in the barbecue.

After listening to the two sides get increasingly agitated, I decided to have a little fun with the situation. The going rate for a beef cow was about $100 American. I turned to the man from Lalm Kats, who had profited from his upriver neighbor's misfortune.

"Do you own a cow, sir?"

Yes, he replied. He owned two cows.

"Is one of them black-and-white?"

One of them was black-and-white.

"Is the cow about this high"—I held my hand at about shoulder height—"and has it fed on hay and mountain grasses?"

Yes and yes.

"Good," I said. "I am planning a feast for my soldiers tomorrow night and I need to purchase a cow of this description." By this time I could sense Mashal holding in a laugh. "Would you be willing to sell the cow to me?"

"Of course, *Commandon*," said the thief. "It would be an honor for my cow to be used for such a purpose."

"Good," I said. "I will pay you $200 for your black-and-white cow. That is two times what it is worth. You will keep $100 and you will give the second $100 to this man, your neighbor from Kawiri Khwar. You will have a fair price for your cow and he will no longer trouble you for the cow that you never saw. You must deliver your cow to our camp by tomorrow morning. Both of you should come. We will settle the matter then. Is this satisfactory?"

Nods all around indicated that it was satisfactory. The next day the plaintiff and the disingenuous thief appeared as stipulated, the latter leading the cow that we had purchased. The transactions were made, everyone went away happy, and a day later we feasted on good Afghan beef. Best of all, the district leader was able to take credit for solving the problem—by bringing in the Americans to undo the tangle.

Someone once asked me what was the most delicate situation I encountered in my role as the red-bearded warlord. Two candidates for that honor came to mind. The first had to do with marriage customs.

Three times while I was holding court at camp, fathers asked for my permission to marry off one of their daughters to a boy in their village. The first time, I thought to myself: What business is this of mine? The sad answer was that villagers had probably been seeking warlords' permission to marry for decades, and I was just the latest in that line of authority. I didn't like thinking of myself as the successor to the likes of Gulbuddin Hekmatyar, but I gave my approval anyway to the first two requests. The third time I had had enough and I informed the father, who was accompanied by a village elder, that I had absolute confidence in such men of wisdom to approve their people's own nuptials. They accepted the ruling, and that put an end to that particular form of petition.

But that wasn't the end of my culture shock regarding marriage. In Nangalam one day, we were having lunch with a *shura* leader named Haji Rokhan, a guy we had nicknamed Brigham based on his uncanny resemblance to the Mormon leader Brigham Young. At one point he said a few words to Mashal and then turned to me, awaiting an answer. When Mashal translated, I wasn't sure for a moment whether I had heard him correctly, or whether he and Haji

Rokhan were pulling my leg. But the impassive expression on the older man's face indicated that he had spoken in earnest.

"With respect," said Mashal, "Haji Rokhan would like to offer you one of his daughters as a wife."

The "offer" idea encapsulated pretty well the status that women held in rural Afghanistan: They were not agents of their own destiny but their male relatives' property, available for trade or gifting as circumstances warranted. To most Westerners, that arrangement was rightly seen as offensive. I was no exception, but I wasn't sent to this valley to change an ancient culture, and I knew that refusing the offer on moral grounds would have been a diplomatic mistake.

If I accepted the offer, I wouldn't be the first Green Beret to go native by taking an indigenous wife. It had happened in Vietnam. And doing so might have created a valuable bond between this elder and me, cementing my regional authority. On the other hand, I was already married to a woman I loved. Becky and I had three children, I spoke to her by phone as often as I could, and despite the excitement of the warrior king life I missed her and the kids every day. The irony of the guy we referred to as Brigham offering an American Mormon a second wife was not lost on us. All jokes aside, though, there was no way I was interested in taking a second wife, Afghan or otherwise.

So the tricky part here wasn't in refusing his offer. The trick was to phrase it in such a way that the refusal would not be seen as an insult. Haji Rokhan was testing me, and the stares of those in the room, including other elders, told me that I needed to weigh my words carefully. I stroked my beard thoughtfully for several minutes, almost enjoying the awkward silence, and then spoke to Mashal. I watched the elder's face as he listened to the Pashto translation.

"I am honored, Haji Rokhan, that you would invite me to be a member of your family. Although our beliefs and traditions are similar, I will eventually return to the United States, to my own wife and children. I believe that your daughter and your grandchildren should have as husband and father a respectable Afghan who can teach them the ways of Islam better than myself. I am grateful for your confidence in me, and I hope that my actions and service in this valley will show that I extend to you the honor and respect that you deserve."

The nods in the room told me I had played the hand well. By showing cultural respect, I had proved that I wasn't a barbarian.

I looked at Haji Rokhan. His eyes, slightly smiling, flickered as if with a "touché." He had been publicly flattered by the American commander, elevated his stature in the local community—and pulled this off without having to give his daughter to an infidel. Both he and I had come out ahead. I wondered what the Pashto equivalent was for "Win-Win."

The second delicate situation occurred later in the spring, as the poppy harvest was beginning. This time I was at the District House, having my daily tea with the police chief. A young farmer came in, holding what looked like a large, molasses-smeared brick. This was raw opium—in Pashto slang, *tor*, which means literally "black."

For someone to display *tor* freely in the presence of a policeman was not in itself strange. Opium had been a staple of the Afghan economy for centuries. A lively drug trade, with full CIA and Pakistani complicity, had helped fuel the mujahideen fight against the Soviets; drug money was steady income for warlords; and even under the puritanical Taliban, profits from opium were an important source of income. In fact, despite Koranic injunctions against intoxicants, the Taliban actually *increased* production of the religiously prohibited drug, making it a driver of their "purist" economy. They justified this practice by a convenient sophistry. As a Taliban antidrug czar once explained, "Opium is permissible because it is consumed by *kafirs* [infidels] in the West and not by Muslims or Afghans."[3]

It also brought in a windfall in the form of taxes. Among a good Muslim's religious obligations is payment of a tax called zakat to support the poor. The Koran says the amount should be 2.5 percent of the person's income. When it came to opium, the Taliban raised this amount to 20 percent. The farmers in the Pech, like those throughout Afghanistan, had been accustomed to paying this tax throughout the Taliban years. This was where I came into the picture.

The farmer carrying in the brick of opium had come to me on behalf of his fellow farmers. As I had in effect replaced the Taliban tax collectors, he wanted to know how much the zakat would be on this year's crop.

This posed more of a puzzle than the marriage offer had. There the decision was obvious, and it was only the delivery that had to be carefully articulated. Here there was a real dilemma. Should I take the customary Taliban cut and use the funds for civic improvement? Should I raise the ante to discourage poppy production? Or should I take a smaller zakat, or none at all, thus keeping my team out of the drug economy?

I couldn't give the farmer an answer on the spot because I felt uncomfortable endorsing a drug that was a scourge around the world. On the other hand, I wasn't confident that raising the tax would have the intended outcome: you'd have to take a lot more than 20 percent to make poppy cultivation economically unviable. And did I want to do that anyway? Without poppies, these already impoverished farmers would have nothing.

"Come back tomorrow," I told the man. "I have to consider the question." He left, thanking me, leaving the brick of opium on the police chief's desk.

In the team house that night I shared my dilemma with the team.

The ensuing discussion was heated. Politics, religion, economics, and the role of government all weighed on our minds. At the end, the team agreed that taxing the people's livelihood would be an unnecessary burden on them and on us. Jimi made the clinching argument by asking how any of us would respond if opium was the only way we knew to provide for our families.

I wasn't thrilled about becoming a supporter of opium, but I could see wisdom in the position we were taking. If my only way to support my family was growing poppies, I thought, I'm not very confident I could say no. That was the rationale—or rationalization—I took the following day, when the farmer returned.

"For this year," I said, "there will be no zakat."

He looked dumbfounded, torn between confusion, gratitude, and perhaps the suspicion that the American warrior king had lost his mind (Allah be praised). With a slight bow, he said, "*Tashakur, Commandon*," and started to leave. I called him back, picking up the opium brick and extending it to him.

He wouldn't take it. Maybe he meant this as a bribe, or a gift, or insurance against me later changing my mind. For whatever reason, my attempts to have him retain this zakat-in-kind were unavailing. When he left, I took it with me back to the team house, where it sat on a pile of papers for the next couple of months. Once, when I wondered aloud what we should do with it, Jimi gave us a tongue-in-cheek lecture on the ways in which it could be consumed: smoked, chewed, even mixed in tea and drunk. It's amazing what information you can pick up when you spend half your life in the third world.

When our deployment ended later that year, the brick of *tor* was still sitting there. What happened to it after we left I don't know. But it may have been the first time in Special Forces history that a kilo of raw opium was used as a paperweight.

15

Ghost Tracks

As the nature of foul weather lieth not in a shower or two of rain, but in an inclination thereto of many days together: so the nature of war consisteth not in actual fighting, but in the known disposition thereto during all the time there is no assurance to the contrary. All other time is peace.

—Thomas Hobbes

This is another type of war, new in its intensity, ancient in its origins—war by guerrillas, subversives, insurgents, assassins, war by ambush instead of by combat; by infiltration instead of aggression, seeking victory by eroding and exhausting the enemy instead of engaging him.

—John F. Kennedy at West Point

Back in September, when the CIA briefer laid out our "most wanted" list, he said that going after the local Al Qaeda commander, Abu Ikhlas, would be like hunting a ghost. He wasn't wrong. It was now late January, and in the two months since we arrived at Camp Blessing we had received countless tips about the Egyptian's whereabouts but few that could be viewed as actionable intelligence. The two keys to actionability are time sensitivity and specificity, and most of the tips we received came in more than a day late and a dollar short.

When you're in needle-in-a-haystack mode, what you want an informant to say is something like this: "Abu Ikhlas is staying in the village of Samun, three miles from here. He's in his cousin's house, the second house from the road, the one with the old red motorcycle parked out front. He sleeps in the back bedroom, and he's there right now." Usually what we got was "My brother's friend's cousin saw Abu Ikhlas in the Korengal Valley two days ago." Even if the information was true—a big if—tips like that were too vague and outdated to be of use unless you were compiling a catalog of near misses.

At Camp Blessing we received information nearly every day on possible HVT locations, hidden arms caches, planned attacks, and a range of other troubles that might come our way. Much of this came from informants who wanted to support our efforts but who were afraid of retaliation if they were discovered to have helped us. We set aside a safe room in a tent behind the team house so that folks like this could communicate to us in confidence; Scott spent time there every day sifting through a morass of garbage for the rare intel gem. Often folks would provide an additional layer of cover for themselves by bringing a sick or injured child into the clinic, and leaving the kid in the waiting area while they talked to Scott. Informants would also talk directly to our Afghan soldiers, who in turn would relay intel to the ODA.

Most of the people who brought us information remained questionable contacts rather than reliable sources. Either the bits and pieces they brought us couldn't be verified, they didn't cohere into anything useful, or for one reason or another they didn't seem trustworthy. We were happy to get whatever news anyone brought us, but that didn't mean that we had to believe it.

This was particularly the case with one dodgy character who had—so he said—a particularly close relationship to our Egyptian quarry. Thick-browed and heavyset, he had started making appearances at our camp just before the New Year, announcing himself as one of Abu Ikhlas's bodyguards. For reasons he never clarified, he had had a falling-out with his boss and was now interested in betraying him—for a price. To earn our trust, the man on several occasions brought us tips about the Egyptian's location, none of which were timely enough to act on.

The CIA bounty on the Egyptian was $20,000. The bodyguard (if that was what he was) said that he would kill him for that reward, if we would only provide him the means to do so. "If you will give me poison," he said, "I will put it in his food."

It was an ancient assassination technique, suitable for a region thick with vendetta. But there was something off about the proposition. Here was a guy who was supposedly close to an Al Qaeda commander and who now hated him. Why would he need outside help in doing him in? And why poison? What did the U.S. military know about poison that hadn't been figured out in these mountains centuries ago? The more Scott and I thought about it, the more the bodyguard's plan sounded bogus. I wouldn't have been upset if the plan had worked, but it smelled like a trap.

When the bodyguard added that he would like us to provide him with a satellite phone—"so I can communicate with you"—more red flags went up. Over the next few months, he continued to bring us information, some of it useful, but we were unable to confirm his role or motives, and so we remained suspicious.

In a scenario like this, one logical step would be to work with the CIA to confirm or deny the bodyguard's story. But our relationship with the Agency wasn't always ideal.

The CIA and Special Forces grew out of the same post–World War II anticommunist initiative, and historically we have often worked together, so I have a fraternal respect for the Agency. But as a huge, secretive organization, the CIA doesn't always have perfect alignment with the various field operations (like "A" Camps) that depend on it for the big picture. That was sometimes the case in our area of operations.

We did our best to pass on relevant intel to the regional CIA contractors at Abad, but I wasn't always sure they were returning the favor. Sometimes the head shed spooks seemed as disconnected from our on-the-ground ops as did their military counterparts. An intel report would be generated from contacts in Abad, but then sent to Kabul, filtered, forwarded to the DOD at Bagram, and then either lost in the shuffle or sent to us days after the intel was generated. As a result, more than once we got CIA e-mails indicating the "imminence" of an attack that had already happened.

There was also a coordination problem with DOD. Camp Vance was full of commandos without a mission, all of them itching to get into the fight but none with an assigned area of operations. If actionable intel on an HVT became available, the mission would more than likely go to a JSOC team like TF-121, with Delta, Rangers, and SEALs ready to pounce on the quarry. But with minimal knowledge of the terrain or local population, this wouldn't always pan out well.

In short, in tracking the Egyptian Al Qaeda commander and the other HVTs, we didn't have what IT folks would call a synchronized or an integrated information system. Like companies struggling to manage customer data across multiple platforms, our intelligence network was a "smokestack" or "silo" system, where the data in one silo wasn't always visible in real time to the managers of other silos. So, with the best intentions in the world, opportunities and HVTs sometimes slipped through the cracks.

This was exactly what had happened in the months leading up to the September 11 attacks, when the FBI and the CIA and NYPD—all supposedly on the same team—didn't share information that might have prevented the tragedy. People in the business and IT communities recognized that immediately. But two years later, this insight hadn't yet reached the Abad or Bagram planning rooms.

*   *   *

As the ODA and our Afghan allies continued trying to get a fix on the ghost, it was also clear that he was trying to fix us. As soon as we set up the "A" Camp, we were harassed every few days by a rocket attack. Coming mostly from ridges to the south, these were generally little more than an annoyance. They never landed close to the camp, and usually they sailed so high above it that Jimi referred to them jokingly as the "Afghan space program."

The rockets were never closely enough sequenced for us to get a good fix on the launcher's position, and they were too far out of range to sight on anyway. We would often send off some mortars as a symbolic response, and I was torn between gratitude that they were not close enough to harm us and irritation that the ghost—or whoever was directing the fire—didn't have the guts to come out and fight like a man.

Even though this threat from the hills seemed light, security was always in the back of my mind. As an outer perimeter we eventually constructed three observation posts (OPs) ringing the camp. Two of them, OP Comanche to the northeast and OP Avalanche to the northwest, were manned in rotation by a Marine security platoon. The third one, OP Hammerhead to the southeast, was manned by our Afghan trainees. The Marines kept an all-night radio watch monitoring traffic from Bagram, Abad, and the OPs. If anything went awry, they would alert Randy or me. We weren't nervous, exactly. But we were alert.

Soon I got other reminders that the guy we were tracking was also tracking us. Actually, tracking me personally. One came in the form of a price on my head. We had been told as far back as September that, to match the $20,000 bounty on his own head, Abu Ikhlas had offered a $10,000 bounty on the new commander of the *kafir* Americans. I had gotten used to that bit of news. But then I got an even more vivid signal that I had been made a target.

I was attending a meet and greet in a village just across the river from our camp. With me were Mashal and a couple of Malik Zarin's nephews, who had started to serve as unofficial bodyguards on these junkets. A small meal was laid out on a cloth in front of us—a dish of naan and stew before each person. As I reached for the bread, the older nephew—a lanky man named Aimal—touched my arm, smiled respectfully, and took a piece of naan himself. He raised it almost ceremoniously, quickly scanned the table, dipped it into my stew, and took a bite.

At first I couldn't process what had happened. I turned to Mashal, raising my eyebrows in confusion.

"It is his honor to taste your food first, *Commandon*," Mashal said. "So that all will know. If your food is poisoned, an innocent Afghan will die. A violation of Pashtunwali and a great dishonor." (Pashtunwali was the ancient tribal code of the Pashtuns.)

Poison again. I nodded as if this made sense and turned to Aimal. "*Tashakur*," I said, and meant it. Beneath the placid veneer of the intrepid commander, my mind was reeling. If I understood Mashal correctly, someone I barely knew—a man on loan from a warlord uncle—had just risked his own life to keep me from harm. I was tremendously moved by his gesture, even as I realized its wider implications.

We had heard rumors before that the Taliban and their Al Qaeda cronies, outraged at the inroads we had made with the locals, were planning to use poison to attack the invaders. We hadn't taken the rumors seriously. Aimal's act changed that. The moment he put that possibly deadly naan into his mouth, it became clear that, true or not, the Afghans believed that it might be true—and that they were loyal enough that they were willing to put their lives at risk for me. When I learned later that *aimal* is Pashto for "friend," I figured, Yeah, your parents got that right.

Aimal wasn't alone. In the following weeks, several other ASF soldiers demonstrated the same level of fealty. On visits outside our camp, I was not allowed to leave without at least two or three body-guards, and at meals one of them would always serve as my taster. They gained status, of course, as the leader's inner circle. And I gained a sense of gratitude and camaraderie that before I had only experienced with American soldiers.

I also gained a sense of the danger that may have lurked beneath the façade of reassuring smiles. We were making inroads into the hearts and minds of many local people. But we were still in the middle of a war zone and could not forget that. Taliban and AQ and HIG, the men without faces, might be pulling the strings. But the threat could come from anywhere. Even from folks you thought you knew.

As if the bounty and the poison threat weren't enough, at the end of the month we got one more reminder of the danger we faced. A week after the January 22 *shura* meeting and the record-breaking weapons buyback agreement, the camp got hit by a rocket attack which, unlike the earlier wayward lobs, came close to disaster.

The timing didn't seem accidental. I already knew from the Egyptian's bodyguard that the buyback victory had angered him. All of the coalition's enemies—HIG, Taliban, and Ikhlas—were dipping into the same weapons pool as we were, and our buybacks had upset the competitive dynamic: every time a village sold us an RPG, that was one less RPG for Ikhlas and company—a situation that couldn't have made him happy. So probably he decided that he couldn't let such a Crusader's coup go unanswered. Maybe his guys finally figured out how to aim a rocket launcher. Or maybe he was responding to the front-page report of January 26 that Afghanistan's interim president, Hamid Karzai, had finally signed his country's new constitution. Nothing irritates an insurgent more than a functioning government.

Whatever the reason, in the middle of the night on January 31, I was awakened by a horrible screeching sound passing overhead, followed by an explosion just beyond our camp. I was up like a shot and had gotten halfway to the door when I heard a second screech and a second explosion. Opening the door, I almost collided with a young Marine running toward me yelling "Incoming!"

I had gotten so used to the misdirected missiles that it took a moment to realize that this time it was different. By the time the third rocket came in, the ODA was up and scrambling to the trucks and the .50-cal guns. I grabbed my weapon and rushed to the roof of the team house, from which I could oversee and direct the action. This meant coordinating whatever response might be needed from the compound itself and from the Marines manning our outer-perimeter OPs.

Dark as it was, the Marines' young eyes were closer to the action and might be able to identify the rockets' origin. A minute after the attack, the Marine lieutenant was on the phone to his guys, "OP Comanche!" he yelled. "You got coordinates?"

A pause, and then: "Negative. Second ridge, maybe the third. Got to wait for another round."

To our southeast a series of ridges stretched to a far horizon. The Marine could tell that the rockets had come from that general direction, but the volley had passed too quickly to determine whether it had come from the nearest ridge, one 1,500 yards beyond it, or a third one another 1,500 yards beyond that one. Shooting back into the hills would have been a guess at best, and it might have created collateral damage that we couldn't afford. We needed better eyes on before we could respond effectively.

Randy was running to the indig barracks to get their status and the Marine mortarmen were running to their positions hoping for a chance to return fire. Courtney was on the radio to see what air assets were available if it came to that. As Randy made it to the barracks, a voice from the OP crackled over the radio.

"Incoming! Five seconds."

His estimate was pretty good. You could hear the same awful announcement, a murderous buzz like a chainsaw clawing the air, and then a massive nearby explosion. The first two rockets had overshot us, and the third one had fallen short, landing in the poppy field east of the camp. Whether by luck or design, this effectively bracketed our position. The fourth round landed in the middle of the bracket, delivering a power punch to Camp Blessing's midsection.

A 107mm rocket weighs forty-two pounds, eighteen pounds of which is a TNT warhead. It has a range of more than five miles and a blast radius of forty feet. If you're anywhere in that circle you're in trouble. Luckily, nobody in the camp was that close to the point of impact; I was fifty yards away myself. But it was a teeth-rattling blast all the same. The shell hit maybe twenty yards away from the indig barracks—far enough away not to damage personnel but close enough to scorch the barracks wall.

It came with a blinding flash. Because we had limited generator power and no desire to advertise our position to potential attackers, we kept the lights outside of our buildings off at night. The only exception would be the headlamp of someone taking a midnight run to the piss tubes. This made Camp Blessing a shrouded target, but it also made the rocket explosion seem all the more dazzling.

Within seconds of the impact my team made it to their battle stations on the Humvees, the Afghans were wide awake with their arms at the ready, and the young leathernecks out on the OPs were adjusting their night-vision goggles and scanning the darkness.

From the roof of the team house I could see the fireball turn to black smoke, and I could see that everyone had apparently escaped unharmed. Nobody was on the ground, anyway. And for another minute, two minutes, three, nothing further came out of the hills.

The Marine lieutenant got a sitrep from his troops and reported no casualties. Randy reported none among the Afghans, and the ODA reported in on our team radio that all was well. As a show of force, the Marine mortars fired a couple of rounds toward a known trouble point to the south of the camp, but this act was basically symbolic, as we couldn't determine which ridge had been the launch site.

"What do you see?" I said into the handheld radio linking me to the OP.

"Can't see jack, sir," came the reply. "A thousand damn trees. Firing came from the southeast is all I can tell you."

"Roger that, Sergeant." I knew that already.

Four minutes, five, six. Still quiet on the southern front. In a situation like this, where visibility is next to zero and you've got a minimal fix on where the shells are coming from, there's not much you can do but hunker down and hope that the next volley will give you a better fix. Even better, hope that there isn't another volley.

Two things concerned me. One was that the rocket attack would be a prelude to a direct assault, and Americans would soon be going mano a mano with a Taliban strike force. Due to our firepower and the virtually impregnable wire obstacles that Jason had constructed, I wasn't afraid that attackers could overrun the camp. But out in the darkness a mile away, the young Marines in the OPs were prime targets. If a trained enemy had done good recon and identified our weak spot, they would be hit first. We had done our best to fortify the OPs, but they were still not as defendable as we wanted.

"You guys all right out there, stud?" I asked.

"Tip of the spear, Captain. We got this."

Semper Fi. I couldn't tell whether the bravado was a sign of confidence or a mask for nervousness. Didn't matter, maybe. There are times when martial zeal seems misplaced and other times when it seems just right. This was one of the other times.

Gradually the remains of the explosion spluttered out, leaving us in the faint glare of moonlight. Ten minutes, then twenty went by. An hour after the first blast, things were back to what passed for normal in this part of the Pech. With the excitement apparently over, I had Randy assign three of the ASF guys to extra sentry duty for the night and turned to see what damage the rocket had done.

Aside from that scorched wall, it had done very little. What it might have done, however, was sobering.

For the past week, in the wake of our buyback agreement, we had been collecting acquired ordnance and storing it at camp. The main storage depot was a tent about one hundred yards away from the indig barracks. On the night of January 31, it contained literally thousands of pounds of rockets, mortars, RPGs, ammo rounds, and fuel boosters. If the ghost's fourth visitor had landed within twenty or thirty feet of that depot, we would have been at ground zero of a fireworks display that made the fireball itself look like a birthday candle. Not even counting the propaganda coup that would have given Abu Ikhlas, it could easily have transformed Camp Blessing into a KIA nightmare.

Looking at the short distance between the ammo tent and the rocket crater, I couldn't believe how lucky we had been. I made a mental note that as soon as possible, we should move the excess armaments to safer quarters. Fortune favored us the next day, when two container trucks delivered supplies, and we had the drivers leave the containers themselves next to our southern wall—an example of "irregular" appropriation well-known to SF soldiers. With the help of the Afghan soldiers' motivated hands, we transferred the entire buyback inventory to the containers, a football field away from the nearest dwelling. The day laborers focused their efforts on sandbagging the containers so our new ammo dump was protected from future projectiles.

We had survived an indirect attack. Good in itself. But something that took place a day after the attack added poignancy to our good luck.

Scott and I were in the team house, discussing the latest "hot tip" about our enemies' whereabouts. There was a knock on the door, and in walked Mashal with two of the ASF trainees whose barracks had just narrowly escaped destruction. They looked indignant.

"It is a bad thing, *Commandon*," one of them said, "that rockets are being fired on the camp."

Scott and I nodded. We had to agree.

"We should find these rockets," the soldier went on. "We should go and track down who is firing on us."

Agreed again. "But we don't know where the rockets came from," I said. "The night was dark and the attack was brief. We don't know where to look for the men who did this."

What the soldier said next told me a lot—maybe more than I really wanted to know—about working with indigs.

"We will bring you there," he said. "Where the rockets came from. We know where it is and we will bring you to that place."

I fought down the impulse to ask him how the hell he knew that and instead took him up on his offer. "Tomorrow," I said. "You bring us there tomorrow."

And he did. The next day, accompanied by an armed patrol, the ASF guy led us to a spot on the middle southern ridge that, he claimed, was the point of origin for the attack. At the spot, scattered trash, batteries, wires, and stones stacked up as makeshift launchers made it clear that this had been one of our enemy's favored launch sites. There were no alarm clocks or other evidence that they had used timers, so I imagined thugs firing at the camp with impunity, knowing we could neither identify nor range their launch site with our mortars.

Thanking the ASF informant, we loaded the coordinates of the site into our ballistics computer system and GPS so that we would know where to send a response if we were attacked again. I also remarked to Ian that we needed to get a rocket launcher of our own if we were to respond the next time. His smile said how much he liked working with bigger and better weapons.

The episode also gave me an even more important piece of information. The indig soldiers had been living in our camp for weeks, during which time we had been the target of several rocket attacks. Although they had been ineffective, you would still think that an Afghan who knew where they were coming from would have shared that information with us. Yet in all that time, nobody said anything. It took a near hit on the indig barracks to have these guys come forward and cry "Enough!"

What did this mean? Did it mean that some of "our" indigs were sympathetic to our enemies? That they were ex-ACM themselves? Or simply that their commitment to *our* safety had only reached critical mass when the rockets threatened *theirs*? I didn't know the answers, and I didn't much like the implications. It seemed clear at least that the soldiers we were training to defend themselves needed a serious kick in the head to return the commitment.

Loyalty in Afghanistan was a fluid virtue. The rocket attack made me aware that if we wanted to keep the local soldiers on our side, we would have to continue to offer them inducements or a vision of the future that outweighed whatever they were being offered by our adversaries on that ridge.

16

Lost in Translation

What we've got here is failure to communicate.
—Strother Martin, as the prison "Captain," in *Cool Hand Luke*

"Traduttore, traditore."

—Italian proverb

Sometimes you catch a break.

On the last Monday in February, intel sergeant Scott Jennings and I had an unusual discussion at Abad with a former Marine turned CIA contractor. A trim, pleasant Midwesterner called Clark, he had an easy manner, surfer good looks, and a gift for taciturnity that was off the charts even by Langley standards. I get it that spies don't tend to be talkative, but this guy, most of the time, was like the Great Stone Face: He parceled out bits of information like they were Burmese rubies and he was worried that you might drop them down a storm drain. If it hadn't been for the Marine in him, he might never have spoken.

On this Monday, though, Clark displayed an uncharacteristic openness. This might have been a veiled apology for something that had happened a few days before. We had sent out a recon party of four armed Afghans in civilian clothes to watch the road going from Kandogal to the Korengal Valley. By walkie-talkie they reported two Toyotas filled with armed men driving south toward Korengal. I called Abad to see if they were friendlies, suspecting they were Afghans working for the CIA. No, said Abad. "There are no friendlies in that area."

This seemed strange enough to merit confirmation. "Ask the CIA guys," I told the radio operator. He did, and repeated the reply: no friendlies in that area.

According to the rules of engagement we had the right to at least challenge, and probably engage with, the unidentified trucks. Loaded with riflemen, they were sitting at a river crossing within sight of our recon team. There was no reason to believe that they were anything but hostiles, and I was not surprised to hear the voice of Sheer Wali, the recon team's squad leader, come over the walkie-talkie requesting permission to fire. "If they are not friendly," he said.

His caution encouraged me to try Abad one more time.

"Tell the CIA," I said, "that my indig recon team has observed two Toyotas of armed Afghans driving south toward Korengal. We are about to engage."

I had barely finished the sentence when Clark hopped on the radio.

"Hammerhead Six, those Afghans are friendlies, do not engage! Repeat: do not engage!"

This third-time's-the-charm admission didn't really surprise me, but it did piss me off that the CIA had sent a team into our AO and had not felt it necessary to inform us first. Thanks to the Agency's secretiveness, we had been seconds away from a friendly fire incident. I didn't want that to happen again. Clark could hear my anger as I hissed into the phone.

"If you ever send armed Afghans into my AO again without notifying me, I will assume they are enemy and we will kill them. There will be no second warning. Hammerhead Six out."

That was the only time in Afghanistan that I remember threatening anyone, much less an ally, over the radio. And once was enough.

After that exchange, Clark didn't exactly become Chatty Cathy. But he was friendlier. And on that February morning in Abad, he was surprisingly forthcoming.

Clark, Scott, and I were sitting in the base's dining tent, sipping water and eating cookies that Scott's family had sent him while Clark filled us in on the latest Bagram intel, or as much of it as he thought we had a Need to Know. It was the usual mix of cell phone chatter and hearsay, and I could tell from Scott's polite half smile that he was figuring it would lead us nowhere.

But then came the break.

Clark reached into his jacket pocket, took out a CD—black slipcase, no label—and placed it on the table in front of me.

"We got this off a guy we were working in Bagram. We thought you might find it interesting."

I didn't know whether *working* meant "working our sources" or "working over," and I guess I didn't much care. He was enjoying his cloak-and-dagger persona, and given how many of our recent leads had proved less than interesting, I wasn't about to look a gift horse in the mouth. I took the CD.

"You want to fill us in?"

"You'll figure it out," he said. "The video clip is labeled Shamir Kowt."

Shamir Kowt was the village about twenty miles up the Pech whose district house had been attacked by insurgents on November 1. The attack had drawn a response from a Quick Reaction Force, and we had raced out to rescue it from a Taliban ambush. It was our first rodeo, the one where, to the amusement of my comrades, I had ridden into battle in a boonie cap. We knew Shamir Kowt.

The last time we had visited the village, it was recovering from the attack, rebuilding the district house and replacing furniture that the insurgents had burned. I had approved some funding to help with those tasks, so maybe the video was a record of the rebuilding. Maybe the Agency was going to use it for PR purposes. But when Scott and I popped the disk into a computer, we found that it contained something more provocative than a village-improvement ad.

It was the insurgents' own home movie of the attack and of the subsequent baited ambush on our forces.

Back in November, I was surprised when the Shamir Kowt district official told us that the attackers had been running a videocam. I figured then that they would use it for propaganda purposes, and that it would some day be showing up on a jihadi website. Clark hadn't mentioned that, so maybe the Agency had intercepted the CD before it got to its intended audience. Or maybe there were fifty other copies of it, drawing cheers now in Riyadh and Islamabad.

Whatever its distribution history, the video was fascinating. The camera work was shaky, and the faces of the attackers were intermittently obscured by black dots. Whoever made the film wanted to applaud the acting without handing the actors over to the infidels. Despite these technical shortcomings, the story line was compelling.

The film began with scenes of the attackers cleaning and prepping their weapons—an opening that established them as professionals and the mayhem they were about to unleash as a disciplined operation. It then followed them out of their encampment and along the trails that led from their mountain sanctuary to Shamir Kowt. Then the rest of the narrative unfolded: as Scott and I stared at the computer screen, we saw clearly the attack on the district house, the insurgents' diatribe against the infidels (their leader waved a Koran, just as the district official had told us), the setting up of the ambush, the attack on the QRF, and the insurgents' joyous fist pumping as they rained bullets down on the Americans.

The video stopped at the point where the Warthog came on the scene and drove the attackers back up into the hills. The arrival of the lumbering A-10 wasn't shown, so that the clip ended by giving the false impression that the ambush was a success and no one turned tail.

"Slick job," said Scott, laconic as ever.

I had to agree. As technically amateurish as the video was, it enthusiastically conveyed the spirit of jihadi struggle. The production values didn't imply heavy Al Qaeda funding, but I wondered if its political astuteness didn't suggest the involvement of a savvy AQ "editor" like Abu Ikhlas. I could imagine some out-of-luck Kabul teenager seeing that video and thinking, "Awesome. That's what I want to do." In the world of asymmetrical warfare, the enemy can do a lot of damage with Radio Shack technology.

On a second viewing, Scott and I noticed something that we thought might be turned to our advantage. At several points in the half-hour clip, the censor had been less than precise. Every so often, one of the black dots slipped off target, and for a split second the face of an attacker was visible. When we froze the clip at those moments, we realized that this technical glitch was more than merely "interesting." The mugshots might lead us directly to our antagonists.

We didn't recognize any of the faces, but Scott figured that our Afghan soldiers might. By this time we were aware that while family loyalty was a sacrosanct value in Afghanistan, loyalty to political structures was not. The line between friend and foe was constantly shifting, and it wasn't far-fetched that some of our trainees might, in a recently abandoned lifetime, have been neighbors, friends, even allies, to the guys in the video. Now that they were on our side— and now that the bad guys were shooting at them as well as us— maybe they could give us some insight about who we were fighting. They had shown their investment in our safety earlier that month by pointing out the location of the January 31 rocket attack. Maybe they'd be willing to repeat that service.

Randy would know. He was a tough leader, but the Afghans

liked and respected him. He was as much their go-to guy as he was mine, and I knew that if he asked for their input, he'd probably get it. Scott and I ran the video a third time for Randy's benefit, then asked him whether he thought the Afghans might help.

"No point in bringing them all in here," he said. "You'd get twenty different takes."

I knew that all right. I remembered the scene at Shamir Kowt after the attack, when I had asked the local soldiers for input and got ninety would-be generals speaking at once.

"But I got two guys who might help."

"OK," I said. "Get 'em here. Where's Mashal?"

One of the requirements of becoming a Special Forces soldier is that you have to speak at least one foreign language. This is logical given that the typical SF mission involves earning the trust of a local community where nobody speaks English. Organizationally, ODAs are supposed to be composed of people whose language skills are concentrated in a geographical region: Africa, say, or Asia, or Latin America. The idea is that if you're set down in Cambodia it might be helpful for somebody on the team to know Cambodian and others to be able to communicate in Thai or Japanese. It was with that theory in mind that ODA 936 was designated as an "Asian" detachment. My SF language (aside from the French I had learned as an LDS missionary) was Mandarin. Others on the team who spoke Asian languages were Randy (Korean), Dave (Thai), Jason (Korean), and Ben (Thai and Laotian).

This would have come in handy if we had been assigned to Southeast Asia. In the rugged mountain reaches of Central Asia, our language expertise was doing us about as much good as our Combat Diver badges. But this wasn't as much a case of military snafu as it might seem.

Each Special Forces Group (SFG) is responsible for a given global region. As part of 19th SFG, ODA 936's normal area of operations would have been Asia. But after 9/11, 5th SFG, assigned to the Middle East, needed reinforcements from the other SFGs—which was how we ended up in Afghanistan. Green Beret military skill sets are transferable anywhere in the world, but in terms of linguistic fluency, an Asian-speaking dive team needed interpreters like Mashal to assist us in our efforts.

By 2003, U.S. forces had been in Afghanistan for a year and a half, so we didn't have to find and train our own interpreters: We inherited them from the troops already in place. Not all of them were as expert as they were supposed to be. We once had an Afghan-American interpreter sent to us from Bagram who spoke Dari, the second most common language in Afghanistan. In a Pashto-speaking area, he was virtually useless. It was a mark of the Army's cultural ignorance that they thought the guy could help us because he spoke "Afghan."

Among our inherited terps, the most reliable was Mashal. He had been with our detachment almost from the beginning, and he rode with us to Shamir Kowt the day of the attack. He had been terrified that day, so I was a little worried about him being retraumatized as he watched the film. But he was the logical man for the job.

The screening went better than I had anticipated. The two Afghans Randy had selected arrived looking sharp and proud in their new Tiger Stripe uniforms. We sat them in front-row seats, ran the film, and paused it each time an attacker's face was revealed. Up to the scene where the insurgent leader, darkly cocky in a black turban, was lecturing the officials, they had no reaction. But then one of them raised a hand and spoke sharply. Mashal's translation was almost instantaneous.

"That one, behind the leader. I know him."

"Which one?"

The soldier put a finger on the screen, touching the face of a haggard, middle-aged fighter who was pointing his weapon casually in the officials' direction.

"Who is he?" I asked. "You know his name?"

The soldier spoke a few words and Mashal turned to me. "No name, he says. But he knows him. He stays sometimes in the next village, beyond Shamir Kowt."

"What village?"

"Gambir."

It was a small village six miles north of Shamir Kowt. A couple of its elders had visited us shortly after the camp was set up to complain about timber poachers and ask for our help on a well project. They weren't hostile, but they weren't any friendlier than the valley norm, either. It wasn't a big surprise that there were ACM in Gambir.

We hit Play again. Throughout most of the rest of the film, the Afghans were noncommittal. A couple of times they peered closely at an undisguised face, as if trying to decide whether they'd seen it before—or maybe trying to decide whether or not to rat out a cousin. This went on almost until the end. Then, as the ambushers were retreating, the same soldier raised his hand again.

On-screen this time was the face of a young man. The beard made it hard to be sure, but I'd guess he wasn't more than twenty. He was holding an AK-47 over his head, looking straight at the camera, and mouthing the battle cry *"Allahu akbar!"* You might have thought that this expression of piety—"God is great"—would have softened his appearance. It didn't. Whatever he knew of Allah or piety or the Koran, in that frame he was a pissed-off adolescent screaming "Death to the infidels!"

The Afghan who had recognized him looked to his friend. His friend nodded and spoke a few sentences to Mashal. At one point I caught the word "Pakistan," and the first soldier snapped his head upward. Pointing to the screen, he repeated the name: "Yes. Pakistan."

"The boy comes from the same village," said Mashal. "He went to Pakistan. To a madrassa. When he was small. Then he came back and joined the Taliban."

It wasn't a novel story. Pakistan was loaded with religious schools where young boys from around the Muslim world were force-fed the fundamentalists' creed. After years of intensive study—some madrassas required their students to memorize the entire Koran—they returned to their home countries, where they typically either became mullahs or turned to jihad. Sometimes both. I had a sense of sadness as I looked at the young fighter's snarl and wondered what might have become of him if he had stayed at home.

"When did he leave?" I asked.

They didn't know. Months ago, maybe a year. They hadn't seen the young man in at least that long. But he was from the same village, Gambir.

"They're sure?" I asked Mashal.

They were sure.

"What are their names?"

When Mashal repeated my question, the two shook their heads. They didn't know. They only knew the village where the two were living.

I wasn't sure I believed them, but challenging them would have undermined the goodwill they had earned by identifying the attackers. The names weren't crucial at this time, anyway. We had the attack on disk, and we had their faces. That was more than enough to bring them in for interrogation. We could get their names then—and maybe that of their boss. I'd give a lot to know whether it was Abu Ikhlas, a local HIG or Taliban honcho, or somebody else who had planned the November 1 ambush and put out the film. The poor censorship job was a second lucky break for us, and I intended to capitalize on it as quickly as possible.

For a moment I considered hopping in the Humvees ourselves and beating it up to Gambir. But there was risk in that, and while I wasn't averse to risk, I was also a fan of Robert Rogers's fifth Standing Order: "Don't never take a chance you don't have to."

On top of that, realizing that our indigs had been showing steady improvement and these two knew the targets, I remembered the mantra: "The default answer to every question is to get the Afghans to do it." That was SF philosophy all the way, and I was happy to embrace it. So I turned first to the two trainees.

"*Tashakur,*" I said, showing my gratitude by a nod to each one in turn. Then I spoke to Mashal.

"Tell them that I am very grateful for their help, and that I have a job for them. I want them to go to that village and get the two men in the film and bring them back. They should do this tomorrow. Tell your squad leader you are going on a special mission and say nothing else. Go in civilian clothes so you don't draw attention to yourselves."

They received this news proudly. I was entrusting them with a potentially dangerous mission, indicating that they had earned my respect. They got to their feet and saluted smartly. Normally, they saluted only in morning formation. I took the salute in this instance as assurance that they understood and would not fail.

"*Tashakur, Commandon.* We go tomorrow."

If you've ever studied a foreign language, you know that sometimes the slightest difference in pronunciation or inflection can make a world of difference in what a listener hears. An ER nurse told me once that when she was just learning Spanish, she told a Hispanic patient's brother over the phone that he had cut his arm. Only the verb she used for "cut" was *cortar*, which can also mean "cut off." The brother freaked out until he learned that a better word in this case would be *cortarse*.

When I said that I wanted our Afghan soldiers to "get" the two attackers, it never occurred to me that I could be misunderstood. Since my Pashto was limited to courtesy phrases like *ahsalam alaikum* and *tashakur*, I had no way of checking what Mashal was saying. I knew only that he was an honorable man, that he was on our side, and that his English was good. There were two things, though, I hadn't figured on.

One was the inherent messiness of translation itself. In the best of times and with the best of intentions, going from one language to another can create confusion. This is so well-known a principle that the Italians even have a proverb for it: *Traduttore traditore*, or "Translators are traitors."

The second thing I hadn't figured on was selective attention: the tendency for people to hear what they want to hear, and to block out elements of a conversation that they find less appealing. I'll never know which of these elements played a greater part in the misunderstanding of my command by the Afghan soldiers. All I know is that, two days after our viewing of the ambush video, they walked through our John Wayne gate and reported to me and Scott. They looked pleased with themselves.

But they had no prisoners.

"Where are the men I sent you to get?" I asked.

They looked puzzled.

"Dead," they said. "We found them in the village and we killed them. Then we left before their friends saw us."

They said it as if it were obvious. For a moment I was too stunned to say anything. I tried to stay composed as Mashal repeated the news. I couldn't believe it, and neither could Scott. Shaking his head, he said, "How the hell did they confuse a grab mission with an assassination?"

In the fog of war a lot of things turn out differently from the way you plan them, especially when you're operating through indigs who don't see the war or the enemy the same way you do. The targets were enemy combatants, or at least they had been back in November, when they tried to take our heads off on Route Blue. I wasn't going to shed too many tears for Al Qaeda or Taliban fighters, even if at the time they had not been firing at us. We were in Afghanistan, after all, to neutralize hostile forces. It looked like that was exactly what had happened here.

In pragmatic terms, I didn't seriously regret the deaths of two jihadis. In moral terms, though, the incident was confusing. I had no way of confirming that the parties these guys said they had killed were in fact the ones I had sent them to capture. I didn't know whether they had been armed at the time they were shot or whether there had been a face-off or a firefight. In fact, I didn't really have solid proof that anybody had been killed; all I had was the alleged shooters' say-so.

I wasn't worried about legal repercussions, because our two indigs had acted—albeit unknowingly—against my orders and certainly against my intentions. But I wondered if I had made it clear enough—or if Mashal had made it clear enough—that "Get them and bring them to me" did not mean "dead or alive." I wondered what the long-range effects would be when the locals learned that two of my men had gunned down fellow villagers. Even if the slain men had been Taliban fighters, we didn't need payback from Gambir. There were practical drawbacks here as well as moral ones. In the gray arena of war, I was feeling gray myself.

A day later came the kicker.

Local contacts came to the camp and reported that there had been a shooting near Gambir. One of them claimed the dead villagers were known insurgents working with the Taliban, but nobody could confirm who had been shot or who had been responsible. I was pleased to learn that someone other than my trigger-happy indigs believed that the dead men had been enemy soldiers. But that didn't make the situation any less murky.

The two who had done the killings showed up at my door shortly thereafter. In their outstretched hands they showed me the casings of the bullets that they had used to carry out what they had thought were my orders. I thought at first that they were offering these as proof that they had done the deed. But no. Through a combination of pidgin English and gestures, they made it clear that they wanted reimbursement for the bullets.

For the second time that week, I was too rattled to respond. I took the casings and waved them off, muttering that I would talk to Randy about replacements. The interaction amazed me, and one thing about it amazes me still. As they stood before me, their hands full of shells, the faces of my two assassins were beatifically calm. Not a trace of remorse: just business as usual in the Pech Valley.

They looked as innocent as children asking for candy.

Not long after this bizarre event, I found myself back in the States for a brief respite from the Pech. As the middle of our tour approached, we had been rotating team members out for a few days with their families, and my turn came in the last week of February and the first few days of March.

I had been gone nearly six months. Although I had talked to Becky by phone during that time, seeing her in person, holding her, playing with our two boys, Tanner and Owen—all of this had a surreal quality. As I took our infant daughter, beautiful little Bailey, in my arms for the first time, tears came to my eyes: I had missed half of the first year of her life.

In the few precious days I had at home, I helped around the house with chores that had accumulated in my absence, played with the boys at every opportunity, and just relished the chance to be a "normal" husband and father. Yet the experience was also unsettling. I found myself both close to and distant from Becky, and from the loving world she inhabited. It was a world of highways, grocery stores, gardens, church, and neighbors, and after the Pech it felt foreign to me.

Becky has always been my best confidant and friend, but I felt that sharing with her the dangers of daily life at the camp would cause her to worry. So I tried to talk about the kids and about how it would be when I was home for good. I tried to talk about anything but Kunar Province. Outwardly that worked OK. Inwardly I couldn't help but think about the pressures of my command, about the guys still back in the Pech, about what might happen to my other "home" while I was here. At times I felt alone among those I loved the most. I realized that the only way I would be free to enjoy my role as a father and husband was to return to the Pech Valley and complete my mission. I had to get back to my camp, back to my men, back to the land that didn't know me as Ron Fry but as the Red-Bearded Commander.

The night before returning to Afghanistan, I made a paper chain with Tanner and Owen. Each link represented a day that I was to be apart from them. Each night they were to cut off one link to count down the days until I returned home. Becky and I believed that the simple, tangible, act of cutting off a link every day would give them a feeling of comfort and of control.

At the end of the week, as I kissed my wife and children goodbye, I prayed that I would find a similar sense of mastery as I returned to the land of *pakols* and *shuras* and jihad.

17

The Uprising

I loved working with our Afghan soldiers, but it was a huge
challenge. Their culture is 180 degrees away from ours.
—Ben Guile

Their vices are revenge, envy, avarice, rapacity, and obsti-
nacy; on the other hand, they are fond of liberty, faithful to
their friends, kind to their dependents, hospitable, brave,
hardy, frugal, laborious, and prudent.
—Mountstuart Elphinstone, *An Account of the Kingdom of Caubul* (1815)

In the highlands of Vietnam, Green Berets had recruited disaf-
fected minorities—chiefly Hmongs and Montagnards—to counter
the efforts of the Vietcong in remote areas. They lived with and
trained these civilian soldiers and, despite the obvious cultural
divide, were often successful in making them a respected military
force. At the height of SF involvement, they were directly managing an army of civilian irregular defense groups (CIDGs) numbering forty-two thousand. The fighters were assisted, trained, fed,
clothed, supported, and led by Special Forces to protect villages,
to set up fighting camps near infiltration routes, and to deny the
enemy sanctuary in contested areas.

Forty years later, the ODA at Camp Blessing undertook a similar
mission. To protect the population and deny the enemy sanctuary,
we were charged with training an Afghan Security Force of civilian

volunteers that would evolve into an Afghan National Guard and might eventually be absorbed into the Afghan National Army. Like our Vietnam-era predecessors, we recruited from the local population and saw some success in building alliances against a common enemy. Our job was not to run the war in the Pech. It was to train the locals to do that better themselves. Those who fought alongside us did so not because they wanted to accomplish our mission but because they needed our help in accomplishing *theirs*—making a better Afghan future for themselves and their children.

Our ASF trainees included some seasoned fighters but also farmers, shopkeepers, students, and other civilians. In a six-week training program, we worked them hard and saw them evolve into a solid fighting force. I've already spoken about our respect for them and about how central we believed that training them was to our mission. But it would be misleading to say that all of this went off without a hitch.

Even in its rare peaceful periods, Afghanistan was a place where warlords hired their nephews out as mercenaries, where opium drove the economy, where a daughter could be offered as a gift to an American soldier, and where an everyday reality included the chance that you would be killed by a long-buried mine. It was also a place where military loyalty was a tenuous commodity. Changing sides when it suited one's ambitions wasn't seen as shameful but as a sign of common sense. Afghan leaders had been doing that for centuries. Gulbuddin Hakmatyar, who had once fought the Taliban, was now aligned with them against us. Warlords who had fought side by side against the Soviets were now bitter rivals. So we were aware that, given the right political winds, some of the ASF men we were training might end up fighting for the other side.

The gap between our two worlds was wide. Ben, a student of

culture who was well attuned to that gap, often expressed amazement at Afghan customs which, to an American, seemed brutal and backward. Early in our deployment, he was asked to treat the badly scorched feet of an eight-year-old child. When he asked the father what had happened, he replied without a trace of remorse that when the child disobeyed him, he punished him by holding his feet over a fire pit. Ben saw this as a unique case of child abuse until a second, and third, and fourth child came in with the same burns. In fact many of the soldiers that we were training carried scars on the soles of their feet from the same childhood punishment. To them, there was nothing odd about it. It was the way things were done.

Afghan women were accorded little more respect than these abused children. Once, on a patrol, Ben's team came across an old man with a very young wife—nearly a child herself. Prohibited by custom from making eye contact with any male not her relative, she slipped for a moment and snuck an innocent glance at the strangers. Her husband began beating her mercilessly with his cane and only stopped when Ben approached him threateningly.

"If I hadn't scared him," Ben recalled, "he'd have beaten her to the ground. Maybe he did, when they got home. To us, what he was doing was obviously wrong. To him, what *she* had done was obviously wrong. Big cultural divide."

Among our Afghan soldiers, we had to struggle with both general cultural mores (like "It's OK to burn your kid's feet") and the particular customs of the Afghan soldiering tradition. I mentioned earlier that to our local troops merit promotion was a largely alien concept: it wasn't immediately obvious to them that their squad leader should be the guy who could solve tactical problems, not the son of the man who owned the village's biggest compound. I also mentioned the "Insh'Allah" attitude, which impeded our soldiers' ability, even their willingness, to shoot straight.

Other cultural challenges were ostensibly more minor. Intoxication, for example. Nobody drank alcohol, but despite Koranic injunctions against it, some of our guys were pretty devoted to their hash pipes. In fact the only voluntary dropouts from the ASF training were two soldiers who found that they could not abide by our rule that there should be no hashish in the barracks.

Sanitation was another sore point. At one time we had an outbreak of lice in the barracks, and we often had trouble burning the solid waste from the crappers because the indigs, before praying, would wash their private parts there and thus dilute the waste so much that it was difficult to ignite even with diesel fuel.

These were small irritants, but not too small to ignore. In January, Randy and I had developed a list of Barracks Rules designed to bring our trainees' behavior into compliance with military discipline. Posted in the barracks, there were six of these new regulations:

1. No guests are permitted to eat or sleep at Camp Blessing.
2. No use of drugs in the barracks, including Hashish, Opium, Alcohol.
3. All rooms will be cleaned and trash taken out of the building every day before first formation.
4. 2100 (9 P.M.), lights are out in the building, quiet time begins.
5. All soldiers will use the designated areas for showering, crapping, and pissing.
6. Soldiers will have ID cards on them at all times.

We didn't get much pushback on these rules. The Afghans understood their logic, and by February their barracks were closer to what you might find at Fort Bragg.

Then there was the Koran's five-prayer-a-day requirement. The Afghans were serious about this. Most of them carried small prayer rugs or mats in their rucks, and many wore elaborate wristwatches that showed, like specially calibrated compasses, the exact direction of Mecca from any position in the valley. Morning and midday prayers were easily enough accommodated, as the soldiers just incorporated the duty into the meal, like a Christian blessing. But a third designated prayer time was at dusk, and this created a potentially dangerous situation.

When you're on an overnight patrol, dusk is the time that you set up your perimeter and pay special attention to possible threats. Because the light's lousy, it's a perfect time for a sneak attack. So it's the worst possible time for a team of soldiers to drag out their prayer rugs and put their heads to the ground.

The first time Ben and Roger were on an overnight patrol and their Afghan contingent hit the dirt in twilight reverence, they looked at each other and agreed, "This won't do." That evening they pulled hyperalert perimeter duty themselves, but the next morning they called the team together and suggested a modification.

"We know you have to pray as the sun is going down," said Ben. "But what if half of you pray first, while the other half is doing security? Then you switch places and the security guys pray. That way everybody gets to pray and nobody gets shot."

Again the Afghans saw the logic. They were unfamiliar with our protocols, their situational awareness wasn't yet fine-tuned, and they sometimes thought less like soldiers than like the farmers that many of them had been. But they weren't stupid. They accepted the pragmatic suggestion, and from then on prayed happily in rotating shifts.

This outcome, it should be noted, was the result not just of their flexibility or of Ben's ingenuity. It also reflected the fact that, for weeks before that moment, he and Roger had made it a point to present themselves as comrades to the ASF, not its out-of-touch bosses. They ate regularly with the guys they were training, asked them about their families, asked questions about their religious practices. Having been raised Mormon but also having spent a lot of time among Buddhists in Southeast Asia, Ben was an avid student of religions, and by the time they found themselves on that patrol, his Afghans had already heard him and Roger make many courteous inquiries about Islam. So the half-and-half suggestion didn't seem presumptuous.

"Of course," they said. "Of course we can do it that way."

I shouldn't exaggerate the degree to which cultural differences were an obstacle to our training. Our weapons sergeant Dave Moon, for example, would express admiration at how readily the Afghans took on the responsibility of patrols and security. "They're way different from Americans," he'd say. "Much more indirect and soft-spoken. But any group will have a range of the warrior spirit, and some of these guys are solid, natural leaders. Even the ones who've never seen any fighting, they're ready to go, willing to try really hard."

Their helpfulness was exemplary. Courtney, the boy from a large Texas family who asked to join our ODA because he liked our team attitude, admired the Afghans because of their willingness to pitch in wherever they were needed. "When a job needed doing around the camp," he recalls, "there was never a shortage of Afghan volunteers." He also admired how hard they worked to follow instructions when, in the absence of an interpreter, the instructions had to be given in "pointy-talky" sign language. "For a bunch of farmers and shopkeepers with no military background," he says, "their willingness to work at getting better was really incredible."

On a patrol one day, when I was suffering badly from dehydration, I saw personally what Courtney meant. I had been fighting dysentery all night and probably should have stayed in my bunk.

But as commander I didn't want to let anybody down or lose face myself, and so I trudged up and down hills on wobbly legs, thinking half the time I was going to pass out. Throughout that miserable day, the Afghan squad I was leading ministered to me as if I were an ailing relative. They paused when they saw me struggling, lent a hand, and let me know with nods and smiles that they had my back. I never felt coddled, but I did feel the quiet concern of professional comradeship.

At other times, though, the barriers were definitely there, and on one occasion, the distance between the American and Afghan worldviews was so great that the survival of our mission was placed in jeopardy. Ironically it was Ben—a culturally astute member of the team—who was at the heart of a near disaster. In retrospect, we came to refer to it as the Uprising.

It was at the beginning of March. I was on my way back from several days' leave at home in Washington State, and I was still in transit at Camp Vance, getting ready to hop a helo to Camp Blessing. I didn't know it at the time, but half the ODA was also away from the camp. A team from *Time* magazine, led by writer Michael Ware, had arrived in my absence to do a story on our efforts; that day, they were up the valley at an elders' meeting, accompanied by an ODA security detail. Holding down the fort, in addition to the Marines, were Ben and Jason.

That morning, they had led a routine ASF patrol into Nangalam to check in on one of our local big shots. There was nothing unusual about the meeting, but on the way back to camp a young recruit violated one of the cardinal rules of soldiering. He was carrying his weapon, safety off, with the barrel horizontal—that is, pointing in the direction of his fellow soldiers, including Ben.

When Ben saw this, he hit the roof. He moved the soldier's barrel out of harm's way and managed to contain his anger until the troops were back at camp. Then the crap hit the fan. The way he and Jason describe it, he was instantly transformed from the Afghans' friend into a recruit's worst nightmare: the in-your-face drill instructor from hell.

Ben rarely used foul language, but on this occasion Sahim, the interpreter that Jason had hired, was having trouble keeping up with his obscenities. The Afghans didn't know many English swear words, but they understood the "F bomb" in its various permutations, and that day it wasn't in short supply.

"I totally lost it," Ben remembers. "I was so ticked at that dumb mistake, and at this guy who didn't seem to realize how serious it was, that I came down on him with all guns blazing. I was so incensed and so scared to think what might have happened that I totally went off on the kid."

Ben ended his tirade with a standard rhetorical question: "What the hell do you think that safety is for?" When the soldier failed to respond—when he had no explanation and no apology for his blunder—Ben ratcheted it up a notch.

"Hit the ground and give me twenty!"

The kid assumed the push-up position. Without saying a word, he followed the order, with Ben still fuming and telling him what an idiot he was. His fellow Afghan soldiers watched as this verbal assault continued. As he dismissed them to their barracks, he turned once more to the screw-up and snarled, "I want to see you in one hour right here. We're not done yet."

If this exchange had taken place on a U.S. military base, no one would have considered it extraordinary. When an American soldier commits a major safety breach—and pointing a loaded weapon at your sergeant certainly qualifies—he's guaranteed to get a public dressing-down. Such disciplining, customary in the Western services, serves a double function. It embarrasses the perpetrator so he never commits that blunder again, and it reinforces for everybody else the importance of safety. A soldier who gets such a chewing out won't like it. But he'll know he had it coming and, since by the time he gets out of boot camp he's seen a dozen other recruits get the same treatment, he doesn't consider it cruel or unusual punishment.

Not so for your average recruit from the Pech Valley.

Among Pashtun males, face is everything. The same culture that condones the beating of women and children sees public ridicule of an adult male as a revenge-worthy event. The proper way to criticize the soldier would have been to do so quietly and privately, citing Koran verses to drive home the lesson. By berating the kid in public, Ben had violated an invisible cultural rule: don't make a man look bad in front of his friends.

When the Afghans trooped silently into their barracks, Ben half-suspected that he had kicked a hornet's nest. When they emerged an hour later, he was sure of it. Half of them were still wearing the Tiger Stripe uniforms that I had charged to my Visa card back in February. The other half, though, had shed those symbols of unit cohesion and changed back into civilian clothes. All of them, uniformed and not, were carrying their AK-47s. Ben took one look around and knew he was in trouble.

"The guys still in uniform looked nervous but not angry," he recalls. "I figured they were showing me a vote of confidence—sort of. The guys who had changed back into *jamas*, though—I didn't know what they were thinking. This was obviously a show of solidarity with the kid I had chewed out, but I didn't know where it was going. Maybe they were just going to walk off the job, or maybe they were going to turn the AKs on me. I couldn't believe what I had gotten us into."

Angling for time, he told the men to go into formation behind the indig barracks and to wait for him. Then he went back to the team house and called the lieutenant in charge of our Marine contingent.

"I need eyes from the rooftops," he said. "We will be in formation, and things might get ugly."

"Got your back, Sergeant," said the Marine.

The rest of the story, in Ben's own words, went something like this.

"When I got to the parade ground, they were lined up OK, but they didn't look like they were awaiting orders. I was scared to death. So was Sahim, the terp that Jason had hired and who I'm sure was wondering at that moment why he had accepted the assignment. Jason was standing by, cool and confident, but I imagine he was thinking of places he'd rather be.

"I hoped my voice wasn't shaking too bad when I asked the indigs to form a semicircle facing me. They shuffled together. I sat down and asked them to do the same. They did. Then I took my pistol out—the only weapon I had with me—held it up high, removed the magazine, and laid it on the ground. I asked them to do the same with their weapons. It took one of those minutes that seem like an hour, but they did it. So I'm sitting there surrounded by about fifty guys who look like they're going to go home or maybe waste me first, and I do what I guess I have to do. I tell them I meant no offense.

"In America, I say, this is how men work together. Sometimes I yell at Jimi or he yells at me, but we are still friends. When I yell at someone in my squad, it is a way of helping him to do better. I do not mean to insult any of you or to show disrespect to the ways of this valley. I mean only to help you to become good soldiers, so that you may bring honor to your families and, Insh'Allah, to be victorious against the men who threaten the peace. If I have done wrong to this soldier, or if I have done something against the teachings of the Koran, I ask for your forgiveness and I ask you to show me what is the right way."

After that penitential speech, there was a minute or two of uneasy silence. The Afghans murmured among themselves, and then one of the squad leaders Ben had been training—one of the ones still in uniform—spoke up. In a short but powerful speech, he first explained to Ben that it was wrong to treat a man as if he were a child, and wrong to cause him shame in the presence of his comrades. Then, speaking to the troops, he assured them that the American sergeant had not meant harm, that he had often shown kindness to them, and that the group should accept his apology in good faith.

More murmuring and nodding indicated that the olive branch had been accepted. Almost as fast as the Uprising had begun, it was over. Ben breathed a sigh of relief and nodded thanks to the soldier who had stood up for him. On the rooftops the Marines stood down, the tension abated, and in minutes the mood of the camp was back to normal.

By the time the rest of the ODA returned with the *Time* magazine retinue, all of the Afghan soldiers were back in uniform. Camp Blessing appeared at peace, as if nothing had happened. When Mick Ware's piece appeared in the magazine later that month, there was no mention made of a thwarted rebellion.

Ben had a genius for getting himself into scrapes and then, almost miraculously, getting himself out. There's a cell phone video clip that somebody took of him in our team house, a smile on his face as he's juggling grenades for the indigs' entertainment. That was Ben: having the time of his life as he's coloring outside the lines. But the way that he defused the Uprising carries a lesson that goes beyond his seat-of-the-pants ingenuity.

Part of his success came from the fact that, by that March day, he had already built up a reservoir of trust, with at least one of his guys loyal enough to have his back when it looked like bullets might fly. Beyond that, though, he escaped disaster because, at a defining moment, he was able to look beyond his own cultural values to see the situation through Pech Valley eyes. He could have stood on his rights as the acting camp commandant, refused to retract his critique, and explained why the American dressing-down tradition was the "correct" response to the Afghan soldier's carelessness. Anybody who's been in the service for a while has met martinet types who would have done exactly that.

Lucky for us (and himself), Ben was smarter than that. Throughout the War on Terror, and not just in Afghanistan, coalition folks have lost their lives when cultural insensitivity has elicited "green on blue" attacks—ugly and usually preventable cases of friendly fire. Camp Blessing's Uprising might have become a "green on blue" statistic, but because Ben sought understanding and saw the wisdom of adjusting to a cultural wind, I came back from my leave to find him alive and well, not a by-the-book victim of an ASF mutiny.

The incident became part of our ODA's folklore, and it served the function of refining our cultural awareness. On the firing range one day, one trainee was verbally bullying another and the victim, having had enough, pointed his rifle at his tormentor. Dave, who was running the practice session, wanted to fire the guy on the spot; in the States, he would probably have been kicked out of the service. But Jimi remembered the Uprising and offered the more culturally sensitive suggestion that they send him home for two weeks to think things over, then allow him back for additional training. Dave agreed that taking things down a notch was a good idea.

Small postscript. The evening of the incident, the soldier Ben had chewed out quit the force, leaving his Tiger Stripes behind. The next morning, he was dragged back by his father, who wanted a full explanation of what had happened. Ben brought the two of them into our team house—a symbolic gesture of trust—reiterated his apology to the troops, and offered to reinstate the errant soldier. He refused, but the fact that Ben had made the offer mollified the father, and the visit ended without incident.

Was the Afghans' culture, as Ben sometimes said, 180 degrees away from ours? In certain respects, sure: You won't find an American anywhere outside of prison who thinks that burning an eight-year-old's feet is an acceptable practice. But in other respects, the gap was smaller than you might suppose. As Ben himself illustrated, sometimes you can bridge virtual chasms of misunderstanding with little more than humility and an outstretched hand.

That's not exactly a policy statement, especially when someone wants to chop off your hand rather than shake it. But it's not a bad extra arrow to keep in your quiver when the loudest voices in the room are crying for vengeance. It's good to remember the Native American saying: "Don't judge a man until you've walked a mile in his moccasins." We tried that out again and again in the Pech Valley. Every so often, the moccasins felt like they fit.

The near disaster was an eye-opener. Central to the effectiveness of any military unit was the principle of disciplined, collective action—a part of what strategists refer to as unit cohesion. As I thought about what might have happened, I started to think that, as a way of encouraging cohesion, some reorganization might be in order. I had already seen how the Tiger Stripe uniforms were being worn with pride and a little bit of showmanship. Perhaps it was time to build on that collective spirit and transform our militia into a real infantry company.

We intended at first to model this reorganization, including its pay structure, on that of the still-germinating Afghan National Army. But when Bagram failed to respond to our request for its specs, we decided to make them up ourselves. Up to this point we had been managing the squads as units in and of themselves, not as part of a bigger chain of command. By the end of the month we had structured the ASF contingent as an American light infantry company, absent the mortars and weapons squads. This meant three platoons of four squads each, with two ODA assigned to each platoon, Randy serving as overall first sergeant, and me as company commander. The soldiers would be paid once a month in cash, with Jason and Randy checking off each payee by name, squad, and weapon serial number to ensure that no one got left out or paid twice.

We set a chain of command based on capability, promoting to the positions of team leaders, squad leaders, and platoon sergeants the soldiers who had demonstrated leadership and performed best in PT and marksmanship. In the States this would have gone off without a hitch. Here it generated a fair amount of grumbling among self-styled generals who couldn't understand why we were treating them like privates.

We also wrote out an Enlistment Contract and insisted that it be signed by everyone who wanted to stay with the company. We had heard a rumor that some soldiers were planning to quit right after the next payday, and to head that off we decided to lock them in to a six- or twelve-month contract. This too generated grumbling, but in the end all but twelve of them agreed to sign.

Those twelve left the camp but returned the next day, begging for their jobs back. There was no beard grasping, but it was pretty clear they knew they had blown a good thing and were, if not penitent, at least sorry for themselves. I wasn't crazy about taking them back, but they weren't the worst of the lot in terms of soldiering skills, so I allowed them to rejoin the company at the lowest rank.

One additional painful but necessary action was to let go four of the trainees who *were* the worst. This didn't please me any more than it did them, but I felt it was an essential form of pruning.

This decision came about indirectly. We were having a team

meeting when a couple of the ASF soldiers approached with Mashal to make some "requests." They had a list of petty grievances, including the fact that they wanted Pepsi with their meals, just as the American soldiers had. They had been drinking well water their entire lives, were being paid three times what they had ever earned before, and yet felt that they had a right to more. The entitlement mentality was obviously something that our two cultures shared. I knew I had to nip this revolution of rising expectations in the bud, so I told my guys to pick the four worst soldiers in the indig barracks and fire them on the spot. When the four slackers were identified, their squad leaders protested that they had "earned the right" to remain part of the company.

Randy's response was as firm as it was logical. "You don't earn a permanent right. You prove that right every day, and these guys aren't cutting it."

This was a hard call, but a necessary one. Our job was to build a fighting force that could secure the valley not as our helpers but as their own self-disciplined unit once our deployment ended. With that in mind, we had an obligation to hold them to the highest professional standards of which they were capable. It would do nobody any good to fill their ranks with sunshine soldiers or entitled youth.

The pruning worked. From that point on, discipline and focus were reestablished. No ASF soldier was ever late for formation, and Pepsi was never mentioned again.

18

Fireworks

Walls are no stronger than the men who defend them.
—attributed to Genghis Khan

Philosophizing about war is useless under fire.
—Linda Berdoll

A day after returning from my leave on March 4, I found myself back at Vance talking to lawyers. On February 23, the day I had left for home, the brass investigating the Humvee destruction had told me I wouldn't be charged for the entire cost of the truck (maybe they checked my credit line and found out it was less than $250,000) but only docked half a month's pay. This was still unacceptable on principle, since nobody had disclosed what brilliant plan the Army had in mind for the truck if I hadn't had Jason turn it into scrap metal.

As things stood, we were in the middle of something called a Report of Survey (ROS), a legal procedure designed to assess culpability for property damage based on "neglect"—the last thing that had been going on that day. It was the ROS that had suggested the two weeks' pay forfeit.

Lieutenant Colonel Custer, to his credit, had told Colonel Herd that whatever price the ROS charged me should be split with him, as he supported my field decision. I appreciated the gesture, but agreeing to sacrifice even a week's pay seemed to me like admitting the decision to blow the truck was wrong. I wasn't ready to do that. So a week into March I was in Bagram again, talking with JAG officers about appealing the decision. I resented having to run this damage control, but I knew I had done the right thing, and I wasn't about to give in without a fight.

When I got to Camp Vance, I was ambushed by being called to a meeting with Colonel Herd that turned out to be a formal questioning. I found myself standing at attention in front of the colonel answering a string of "Yes sir" and "No sir" questions as a major sat nearby taking notes.

"Did you not get the order not to destroy the truck?"

"Sir, I understood that the Apache destruction was not authorized, that's all."

"Did you know that the Task Force was sending a sling-loading CH-47 and that you therefore destroyed the vehicle unnecessarily?"

"No, sir. I never received any information that there was a plan for the truck. With respect, sir, how long were we supposed to wait for that aircraft to arrive? Were we supposed to guard the truck all night?"

No answer.

"Captain Fry, do you know the cost of a Humvee?"

I may not have known it down to the penny, but I could give a good guess based on the Army's threatened bill. "Yes, sir," I said.

After what seemed like another ten minutes of the colonel's questions, I had a few of my own.

"Sir, if you think I disobeyed a direct order, why are you trying to punish me with a Report of Survey and not a court-martial?"

No answer.

"Sir, if you were in my shoes that day, with limited resources, in the gun sights of the enemy, would you have done what I did, or would you have spent the night protecting a truck that in effect had already been destroyed?"

The colonel's answer reminded me that he had a reputation as "a hard nut." "I would have obeyed the orders I had been given, Captain."

Hard nut or not, this was a shocking response. The next words that came out of my mouth risked my being relieved of command, but at that point I was going on instinct and a sense of justice. I blurted out what I thought needed to be said.

"Sir, my men are grateful I was in command that day instead of you."

Colonel Herd kept his composure, but the recorder lifted his eyes and his mouth opened slightly. I wasn't sure what my impertinence would cost me. Maybe the colonel didn't know either. In any event, that comment closed the proceedings. Herd stared at me evenly and said, "Captain, you are dismissed."

That ended it for the day. As I saluted, turned on my heel, and walked away, I thought that I had won a small moral victory, although the practical outcome of my case remained in doubt. I didn't know or care how long that would last. I felt stuck in legal limbo here at the FOB, and I was aching to rejoin my team back at the camp. I hadn't been relieved of my command, and I was anxious to get back to it.

That took another day—a day that turned out to be a particularly inopportune time for me to be away. Early in the morning of March 9—actually, in the middle of the night—I was roused out of my bunk by CSM Allen Smithee, who was at Vance coordinating logistics.

"What's up, Smitty?" I asked.

His answer made me all the more irritated that my return to the valley had been delayed by this legal fiasco.

Camp Blessing was under attack.

I threw on some clothes and hoofed it to the Operations Center, where I could listen over the satellite radio to what was happening to my guys. There were several radios there monitoring different channels. On one channel I could hear Courtney speaking to aircraft. On another, Randy—that night the camp's de facto commandant—was sending in sitreps to the battle captain at Vance. What I heard increased my resentment at having been dragged away from camp, but it also made me proud of how the team was performing. I felt envious at not being part of the fight and at the same time guilty for not being there at a time when I could have provided leadership.

In the background of Courtney's and Randy's conversations I could hear explosions and the staccato working of crew-served weapons. I was hoping most of those were ours, but the sense of urgency in Courtney's voice told me air support was going to be a necessity. Occasionally a staffer, sitting next to me in the Ops Center, would offer Randy a tactical opinion or request trivial details on the situation, and I would shush him politely so Randy could focus on the fight. From more than a hundred miles away, that was the most I could do. Randy did a great job, as expected, in leading the camp that night.

From where I sat, it sounded like the fight lasted about an hour. I listened while the firing sparkled, then ebbed, and ended with a muffled roar in the distance, which I later learned was the sound of an A-10 gun run. Around 1 A.M., when Randy's voice assured me that the excitement was over and that the camp was secure, I whispered a prayer of thanks and went to grab some shut-eye.

The next morning, when I got back to camp and was debriefed by Randy and Courtney, I got a fuller picture of what had happened.

Just after midnight that morning, Camp Blessing came under fire from a rocket barrage far more sustained than the sporadic volleys we had gotten used to. We had recently been receiving intel that a major attack on the camp was in the works, and from the intensity of the shelling, Randy thought that this might be it. He roused everybody whom the rockets hadn't already woken up and got them to battle stations. Mortars began firing as soon as the OPs identified probable launch sites on the southern ridges. Soon they were joined by our newly acquired 107mm rocket launcher and our 14.7mm anti-aircraft gun—the only other weapons that could reach those distant locations.

We had gotten used to attacks being confined to three or four rockets over a couple of minutes, then silence. This night, after fifteen or twenty minutes, they were still coming—and getting closer. Courtney and Roger, positioned in a sandbagged bunker on the team house roof, could hear a battle erupt to the northwest, just behind the camp. It sounded like OP Avalanche was engaged in a firefight. A sitrep from the squad leader confirmed they were engaged with a force trying to take the high ground above the camp.

Seeing the need for air support, Courtney got on the radio to Bagram. Then, while he was trying to get assets on station, a new threat from the southeast jumped into the fight.

In the darkness the guys at Blessing couldn't see this new threat, but they could feel their presence, in the form of firing from machine guns and RPGs. Villagers who were closer to the attackers reported the next day that there were about forty of them, that they were camouflaged in U.S. Army–type battle dress uniforms, and that they were firing from a poppy field about two hundred yards out from our John Wayne gate.

This was the frontal assault we had been warned about, and the fact that there were only forty attackers, not the 150 we had been promised, was small consolation to the besieged garrison. Rounds were zipping back and forth in front of the gate, and at one point a young Marine manning a machine gun directly below Courtney and Roger took a direct hit from an RPG. The round impacted the sandbags of the bunker and it appeared as if the Marine's position was destroyed in the explosion.

As Courtney described it, "We were taking heavy fire. We were giving as much as we got, but the buildings were starting to look like Swiss cheese. And that young Marine...I just turned to Roger and said, that kid's gone. But then the smoke cleared and I heard him say, 'Those sons of bitches!' and he's back on his M-240B sending lead back at the attackers. He's taken shrapnel to the face, but he's back in the fight."

The assault continued for another twenty minutes, until two A-10s that Courtney had raised hove into view. As they approached and Courtney yelled that the A-10s were going to do a gun run, several of the camp's Marine detachment hit the dirt; it was only after the attack that their gunnery sergeant explained to Randy that they had been accidently strafed by an A-10 in Iraq and were understandably edgy about it happening again.

As for the attackers, they did what Taliban fighters always did when a Warthog came on station: retreated to safer ground. In this case that was Nangalam. Half the force ducked into a building on its outskirts, and the other half melted away in the darkness.

At that point, with the frontal attack repulsed, Courtney had a decision to make. As the Tactical Air Control guy in charge of directing air strikes, he had full legal authority to call the shots as he saw them—there was no requirement to seek permission from higher. What he saw was fifteen or twenty armed men who had just tried to overrun Camp Blessing and who were now taking cover in a clearly identifiable building. So he called what he saw as the obvious shot: order the A-10 pilot to attack that building. So close to the camp and in a populated area, the pilot required the ground commander's initials as his approval to execute the attack. Randy didn't hesitate.

"Romeo-Delta approved."

The Warthog's most impressive, if not its most lethal, weapon is a 30mm Gatling-style "cannon" capable of spitting out seventy rounds per second of armor-piercing or incendiary rounds. When the gunner started firing, it was only a few seconds before the job was done. The second pilot followed his lead and sent another burst from his cannon into the area. Peppered by the A-10 cannons, the building exploded in a fireball.

"At first I thought we had hit the wrong building," Courtney explains. "There was a gas station next to the attackers' hideout, and I thought that the gunner had missed them and hit the gas tanks. Actually, he had hit a propane tank next to the target. So we closed down the right building, and the excitement was over."

With the attack over, the ODA, the Afghans, and the Marines took stock. They were glad to discover that only the Marine at the bunker by the team house had sustained real injuries. (When his shrapnel wounds healed, I put him in for an award.) As for the Marines at OP Avalanche, they were in desperate need of ammo resupply but they had sustained no casualties. So far so good.

But the excitement wasn't over.

Later that morning, when command got details about the fight, we entered a second phase of damage control. In destroying the attackers' lair and an unknown number of the attackers themselves, the A-10s had caused what some were now saying was a civilian casualty. A young man who had been in the building—he was actually the brother of one of our own soldiers—had been killed by the Gatling or by the explosion. He might have been an innocent civilian, or he might have been an attacker himself.

There was no way of knowing, but at this time in the war, collateral damage was a sensitive issue. Only days before, the international agency Human Rights Watch had issued a report condemning "abuses by U.S. forces in Afghanistan."[1] So while there's never a good time for noncombatants to be hurt, this was an especially bad time for such an incident to occur.

No one was more attuned to that fact than the brass at Bagram. Around 11 A.M. that morning, as I was finishing up my appeal work with JAG, I got the word that a Blackhawk was waiting to take me back to Camp Blessing. I would be accompanied by a Public Affairs officer, someone from the Criminal Investigation Division, and two FBI agents—a dream team assembled to make sure "there were no problems."

When we landed at Blessing, I found the Marines and the ASF carrying themselves with a well-earned air of pride and satisfaction. I was surprised at the damage inflicted on the camp and even more surprised that its defenders had sustained no major casualties. After congratulating Randy on his management of the fight, I pulled him and Courtney aside to tell them that the legal team wanted to talk to them. Introductions were made, and then we accompanied the FBI agents and the other investigators into Nangalam.

There we met villagers, obviously impressed with the A-10s' power, who gave us their version of what had happened while the FBI guys took measurements of the burned-out building and photographed the damage. When we left town an hour later, the investigators seemed satisfied that, while the young man's death was unfortunate, there had been no ill intent or negligence on the ODA's part, or on that of the A-10 pilots, Courtney, or "Romeo Delta." The planes had hit a legitimate target—an attackers' sanctuary— and had, unintentionally, caused collateral damage. This was the ODA's first encounter with that unhappy term.

The fact that the Army had sent a legal team out to investigate the gun run showed that they took such incidents seriously. The good reasons that they should began with the humanitarian impulse underlying all legitimate military action. If we were here in Afghanistan to protect people, it followed that the last thing we wanted was to harm noncombatants. There were also legal reasons to avoid such incidents. Geneva, the International Criminal Court, and the centuries-long consensus of Just War theorists—all of this argued for protection of innocent civilians. Not least of all, there was a pragmatic reason. Every time an Afghan civilian died in a misdirected rocket barrage, Taliban night letters condemned the perpetrators as murderers and dozens of new jihadis joined their ranks. Collateral damage was one of the enemy's best recruiting points.

Our command realized that while civilian casualties were unavoidable, they could be minimized (the official term is *mitigated*) by adhering to the Rules of Engagement. The military's goal isn't the unrealistic one of zero casualties but the achievable one of "proportionality." In the language of an official directive, the death of "protected civilians" is regrettable but acceptable "provided that the collateral damage is not excessive compared to the concrete and direct military advantage anticipated by the attack."[2] It was to ensure that this principle had been observed that the legal team had inspected the Nangalam damage.

Nobody knew whether this would end the matter or whether there would be more brass to talk to, more reports to fill out, and maybe an official investigation. But for that day at least, it seemed to be settled. The trio returned to Bagram to file reports, while I congratulated my team on a solid defense—the repulsing of the biggest attack we had seen to that point.

What we had to deal with now was the dead civilian. Nobody would ever know if he was a Taliban fighter or somebody asleep in the wrong place at the wrong time. In fact, there was even some doubt as to whether there was a civilian casualty at all: nobody ever showed us a body. Whatever the truth was, the good folks of

Nangalam weren't happy, and the alleged victim's relatives were of course devastated. The situation called for yet another form of damage control. Valid target or not, we had to make our amends.

Despite the ambiguity of the situation, most of us felt sick about the man's death and about its impact on his brother in our ASF company. It was therefore more than duty that led Randy and me, a few days after the attack, to make a penitential call into Nangalam. We actually ended up making three separate visits to the dead man's family, apologizing for the tragedy, asking for their forgiveness, and agreeing to pay them the blood money recompense demanded by the code of Pashtunwali: a goat and one hundred pounds of rice. This satisfied them legally if not emotionally, and I was struck by the fact that, even in their grief, they seemed to appreciate our willingness to honor their custom. Obviously no previous outside force had been this respectful.

My own feelings about the incident were an uneasy mix of pride in my team's performance, anger at whoever had initiated the attack—apparently Abu Ikhlas, according to our intel—and disappointment with the local villagers for not alerting us to the bad guys who were hiding in their midst. That was an old story by now. You couldn't waste too much time lamenting the fact that, as Mao had famously put it, the people were the ocean in which guerrilla fish swam. Separating them from that element was a constant struggle. In this case, it appeared that villagers to the east who might have known in advance about the attack did not have cell phones to warn us that it was coming. Still, the fact that it happened was disheartening.

The March 9 attack was the first time that our defenses had been really put to the test. They had held up well. We had intel that several enemy had been killed, and the assault had gotten no closer than two hundred meters from the camp before being driven back. The ODA had demonstrated that while it was firmly committed to the "hearts and minds" approach, it was primarily a fighting unit to be reckoned with.

The result had no doubt been a blow to enemy morale. As the SF community sometimes joked, we were like armed ambassadors or a Peace Corps with guns. In fact, with all of the machine guns captured or turned in, we had more crew-served weapons per man on our perimeter than any other military base in Afghanistan. When the ODA responded to the assault, they were able to mount an impressive display of firepower.

That fact wasn't lost on the people of the valley. When our adversary, the next day, started spreading the word that Camp Blessing had been overrun and all the Americans killed, everybody took this propaganda as laughable. Still, it was a telling example of our enemy's deviousness—like taking refuge in a village or donning American-type uniforms. Based on the intel, I was pretty sure the Egyptian was behind all this. I was getting more and more eager to meet him face-to-face.

PART III

Spring 2004

19

A Tale of Two Mullahs

Humility and curiosity coupled with overwhelming fire-power is a potent combination that will amaze and disarm suspicious locals. And when gaffes happen, as they inevitably do, they are easily forgiven when locals know by past actions that we mean to be respectful.

—Chaplain Eric A. Eliason

As the Afghan winter subsided and the first few poppy blooms appeared in the fields, our attention turned more and more to community projects. Patrols and cache retrievals continued to be part of our weekly agenda, and we never forgot that, a mortar's lob away, the hills harbored insurgents who wanted us dead. At the same time, though, Camp Blessing had taken shape not just as a heavily fortified encampment but also as the catalyst of an economic recovery that was making tiny Manogay and Nangalam more prosperous. ODA 936, building on the groundwork of 10th Mountain, had been functioning like the old town tamers of the American West. When we arrived at Catamount in December, the influence of the black hats was felt every day. Three months later, things were quiet enough for us to start thinking beyond our guns and devote ourselves to improving community life.

That spring, this meant a decisive commitment to three distinctive features of civilized living: medical care, education, and religion.

The first of these had been a priority even before we landed at Catamount. The MEDCAPs we had run during Mountain Resolve, back in November, had shown us how desperately the people of these mountains needed good medical care, and had demonstrated that providing it could easily earn us goodwill. So one of the first "buildings" we threw up at Camp Blessing was a large tent that served as our clinic. Since December, that facility had grown in size, effectiveness, and reputation. Barely a day went by without a string of patients waiting for treatment.

At any one time, the clinic was staffed by one or more of our three combat medics: senior medic (and pharmacist) Mike Montoya; team sergeant (and cardiac medic) Randy Derr; and fiery, resourceful Ben Guile, whose ingenuity in acquiring medicines and other equipment from across the Pakistan border showed his mettle as a Special Forces improviser. Together this dynamic trio created a field hospital that by spring had become the center of medical care for thousands of people in this remote area.

We realized that some of the people treated at our clinic may have been Taliban or Taliban sympathizers. More than one informant told us that when ACM foot soldiers were wounded, they were advised to secure medical care at our clinic and tell people in their villages they had been tortured. But insurgents didn't carry ID cards, and it was our policy to treat whoever showed up wanting help.

One night in the middle of March, a truck rolled up carrying the badly mangled bodies of several men who the driver said had been hurt in a construction explosion. Riddled with small rock shrapnel, they looked very much like the victims of an IED planting gone wrong, and our Marines, suspecting this, were reluctant to take them in. Ben overrode their objections. As a medic, he knew that whatever their political affiliation, we had to help them. Like good Pashtuns, we had to respect their need and give them refuge.

A quick triage outside the gate showed that half of them couldn't be saved. Those who had a chance Ben took into the clinic, where he and Mike worked on them for several hours. They survived. Maybe they returned to their villages claiming they had been tortured. Or maybe, thankful for their lives, they formed a more positive impression of the Americans' presence. Or maybe they really had been wounded in a construction blast. In terms of medical ethics—not to mention Pashtunwali—it didn't matter.

As important as the clinic in improving the quality of local life was the renovation of a primary school. The only school in town had been damaged during the civil war and was too small to accommodate more than the male youth of the valley. Besides, girls had not participated in formal schooling for years, as under the Taliban female education was prohibited. With a new sense of security and with volunteers to augment the school staff, they now had that opportunity— one that the villagers themselves wanted them to have. James Trusty, our Civil Affairs noncom, met with the local schoolmaster, and within an hour we had soldiers setting up large tents as a temporary schoolhouse. Jim then secured funds for the repair and expansion of the existing school, and by early spring it was ready to open.

I saw this as a major plus in our counterinsurgency efforts. The school would provide an opportunity to bring young women together in an educational atmosphere, to offer them an appreciation of what existed beyond the village, and potentially to improve their quality of life. Education also served to counteract insurgent propaganda about what the future should look like. And since the school happened to be located right in front of our camp, it allowed the younger generation to see Americans as friends and contributed to the building of long-term alliances. For all of these reasons, rebuilding a school was a Civil Affairs project perfectly in line with my fiduciary philosophy of using limited resources on conditional projects with a long-term positive impact.

But our most significant CA project was the restoration, throughout that spring, of damaged mosques. Many of these had been riddled by Taliban or other gunfire and then, due to a lack of resources, fallen into disrepair. They were the spiritual centers for thousands in this isolated region, and their poor condition offered us both a vivid symbol of how the Taliban had distorted Islamic values and an opportunity to generate trust by restoring their dignity.

It took a little doing to convince my team that refurbishing Muslim mosques was the best use of limited resources. But once they saw the logic of the proposal, they embraced it eagerly. Scott saw its wisdom with special clarity. Reacting to the all-too-common perception among some of our countrymen that the enemy in Afghanistan was Islam itself, he saw the need to work with our Muslim neighbors and not to see all Afghans as undifferentiated hajjis.

"Islam wasn't the problem," he later reflected. "It was part of the terrain. Hating Islam was like being mad at a mountain or a river."

Our adversaries had recently launched an aggressive PSYOP campaign, denouncing us as Christians attempting to convert the valley. At first, this put village elders wanting to support our efforts in a tough position. It took some doing to convince them that the propaganda claims—absurd on the surface to us—were false. The mosque plan helped us to set their minds at ease. It showed them that, far from trying to convert them, we were staunch respecters of their religion and customs.

The idea wasn't my brainstorm. It originated with an innovative Army chaplain named Eric Eliason, who had deployed to Afghanistan in February, had been assigned to Vance as a battalion asset, and in March had started visiting the area's ODAs, circuit rider style, to minister to their spiritual needs and see in what other ways he could be helpful. Eric was a Mormon, so there was a natural affinity between him and the LDS members of the team. We were grateful that, so far away from our home communities, we could still receive spiritual support from one of our own.

Like all military chaplains, though, Eric had been trained to minister to the spiritual needs of all troops in the battalion to which he was assigned. He did this ably, providing the same pastoral care to ODAs that had no Mormon members as he did to ODA 936. In civilian life Eric was a professor of folklore and anthropology at Brigham Young University, and the ecumenical spirit he brought to his work in the Pech reflected an openness to cultural diversity that those disciplines value. This was also evident in his interactions with local Muslims. In fact it was his curiosity about what *they* valued that led to his initiation of mosque renovation.

Soon after landing in Bagram, Eric started accompanying Special Forces A-Teams like ours on visits to *shuras* and other village meetings. Often introduced as a "Christian mullah"—a moniker that both flattered and amused him—he learned quickly that nearly every village had a mosque in need of repair. Broken windows, leaky roofs, cracked foundations, peeling paint, ragged carpeting—the list of items needing help was a long one. He knew there was American money available for construction and repair projects, and although none of it had yet been allocated to a mosque, he figured why not? Restoring a dilapidated mosque would be a worthy aim in itself, and it wouldn't hurt that such a project would put the Americans in a good light with local leaders.

So in March, Eric and his assistant, Specialist Alan Crookston, approached the battalion finance officer, made the case, and secured a disbursement of $30,000 for mosque repair. Then he came to me.

We had already met by then, and he knew that I was committed, as was my team, to treating local customs with respect and dignity. He sized me up as a potential supporter for his novel project.

I thought mosque restoration was a great idea. But before I gave my OK, I had a couple of caveats. The first one was inspired by, of all things, some reading I had been doing in Machiavelli's *The Prince*—that classic handbook for managers of touchy situations.

"Injuries," Machievelli writes, "ought to be done all at one time, so that, being tasted less, they offend less; benefits ought to be given little by little, so that their flavor may last longer." That made sense to me. I decided that rather than spending all thirty grand on reproducing the Blue Mosque in the Pech, I would divide the funds among smaller restorations in multiple villages. Why spend $30,000 in one place when $1,000 will make the recipients just as happy…and you can do it thirty times?

Second, I wanted a quid pro quo. We had observed this principle back in January, when I had released the prisoner Omar in exchange for the elders' encouragement of our weapons buyback program, and on many occasions when I approved a CA project only after proof of the recipients' friendship. On other occasions, though, we had violated the principle by doling out advance payments in a misguided attempt to buy a contractor's loyalty. I didn't want that to happen here.

"Let's make the funding conditional," I told Eric. "I'll approve a project based on the cooperation and respect that's already been shown, not as a way of winning over an enemy. So if you want your mosque painted, how many caches have you identified? What intel have you brought us? How many of the soldiers in our ASF company did your village provide Camp Blessing? Let's make it clear that we don't scratch backs for free."

"Funding as a reward, not a bribe," Eric said.

With that understanding in place, I gave the go-ahead. We decided that a good place to begin would be with the mosque next door—home of our $100 friend Mullah Zawar, who had proved, true to his word, to be on our side. Within a few days we began preliminary discussions with him and with Manogay elders about which repairs were essential and which should come first.

Over the next several weeks, that run-down building was transformed, thanks to U.S. taxpayer dollars and eager Afghan hands, into a shining model of devotional community effort. In the coming months, this success was followed by many others. Before our team left Afghanistan that summer, Eric's pet project had resulted in the restoration of twenty-six mosques up and down the Pech Valley.

As each restoration project was begun, Eric would use the opportunity to underscore its significance as a symbol of intercultural cooperation. Sitting down with the mullah and local leaders, he would deliver this message in a heartfelt speech that went something like this:

Americans and Afghans have often fought side by side to defeat evil. Together we defeated the tyranny of the Soviet empire right here in these valleys. Now the people you call "parasites" and "the uncivilized who give Islam a bad name" threaten us both. God willing, we will defeat these people, too.

You know about 9/11 and the Twin Towers, but we know that this war has hurt you even more than us because it is taking place in your country. We are thankful and indebted to you. Please see this restored mosque as a small gift of gratitude from America for your efforts. Let this mosque also be a symbol of our friendship and brotherhood and our resolution to fight evil together.

We are in your debt. God is great.

Mosque restoration was not without its challenges. As with any construction project, we had to contend with local labor traditions that we couldn't let stand if we wanted to succeed. This was an important learning curve for us, and after our return to the States, Eric and I coauthored a paper detailing the principles followed and the lessons learned.

Some of those lessons we anticipated before we began: start with small projects and make funding conditional on demonstrated friendship to the counterinsurgency mission. Others we picked up as we went along. We learned, for example, to begin by making a general offer of help to village elders and then asking them to define what they wanted done. In almost all cases, the first item on their priority list was to repair their mosque. We learned that even when locals asked us how the new mosque should look, we should throw that question back at them, and say, "It's your mosque; tell us what is the right way to do it." We learned to offer a fair, not inflated, price for work done; to secure compliance with a contract; and to mitigate corruption by having trusted local advisors—mullahs and elders—ensure that our funding was enriching the religious community and not a contractor's private bank account.

In terms of return on investment, mosque restoration was a pronounced success. On a material level, it improved a significant feature of the local infrastructure while providing villagers with employment and a sense of accomplishment. On a tactical level, the reciprocity requirement ensured that each new bucket of paint or bag of cement was paid for with increased intelligence about the enemy. Our projects weren't charity but tools, weapons really, to win popular support. That's why we preferred to spend $200 on a mosque that they wanted painted than to waste $10 million on a road in which they saw no value.

Most important of all, mosque restoration deprived the enemy of the single sharpest arrow in its propaganda quiver: the idea that Camp Blessing was a Crusader's garrison, filled with *kafirs* devoted to destroying Islam. Every time we helped a village restore the traditional center of its religious life, we took religion off the table as an argument against us. The lesson wasn't lost on the villagers we worked with. Once the restorations got under way, people frequently brought us copies of the night letters that Taliban operatives had left on their doorsteps, branding us as defilers of the Prophet's teachings.

"Look," they would say with sly smiles. "You are here to insult the Prophet and repair our mosques." After a while it became a running joke.

In the paper that Eric and I wrote, we spoke of mosques as "key symbolic terrain in the Global War on Terror."[1] As centers of both religious and secular authority, they were important "dissemination points for authoritative words about whether locals should support or resist Coalition efforts." Winning the mosques, we believed, was key to winning the conflict. That had been clear early on, when $100 had turned one mullah's pulpit from a font of condemnation to one of approval. Mosque restoration reaffirmed the lesson.

Of all the CA projects we undertook in the Pech, none of them earned us greater cooperation than helping the disciples of a "rival" religion restore their places of worship. Chaplain Eric deserves a huge amount of credit for this game-changing idea.

Eric also performed one other very significant service in support of our activities. This was his building of a spiritual and political alliance with a young Pashtun mullah called Taroon.

Taroon was born in the Pech and, like many young men throughout Afghanistan, he had been sent as a child to a Pakistan madrassa, where the curriculum consisted almost exclusively of scriptural memorization, and where the mullahs' party line was that good Muslims must wage jihad against the Great Satan. After years of such indoctrination, Taroon returned to his home valley as a hafiz— one who has memorized the entire Arabic text of the Koran and can recite (actually, chant) extended passages of it at command. This feat would be impressive even for an Arabic speaker. For a Pashtun with no command of Arabic, it was phenomenal—as was Taroon's ability, with the help of a Pashto translation (also memorized), to understand the spiritual significance of the passages even though the literal meaning of the words was unknown to him.

Back in the Pech, Taroon's learning gave him stature in the eyes of his compatriots, among whom were several of our ASF soldiers. They persuaded him to join their ranks as their mullah. Joining a coalition force was an odd decision for someone who had been educated as he had, and it was never clear to me why Taroon agreed. In fact, for a hafiz to join coalition forces was suspicious, as he might easily have been a Taliban or an Al Qaeda infiltrator, seeking to undermine our efforts from within. At any event, he did agree, and it was as our indig soldiers' spiritual counselor that Eric, our spiritual counselor, came to know him.

Their professional connection as men of God generated cordiality, then collegiality, and eventually a warm friendship. In line with our respect for local customs, and enhanced by Eric's anthropological interest in Islam, the two became each other's teachers. One task of a U.S. Army chaplain, according to a ministry handbook, is to "advise the commander on the culture, customs, and religions of the local population." As Eric fulfilled that role, he relied heavily on Taroon as a source of information.

We wanted to be sure that we didn't offend local sensibilities out of ignorance, and in securing that intention, Eric's Pashtun colleague was invaluable. "We want to be good guests here," Eric would tell him. "So please let me know if we do something that is not correct; I want to learn what is proper, to respect your traditions." Reluctant at first to speak up, Taroon soon came to see that this request was genuine, and he became our guide for Islamic protocol.

On one occasion, noticing that one of the team had put a prayer rug on the wall as a decoration, he informed Eric that this was counter to Islamic teaching. The rug was taken down. On another, he told us that the women in a Nangalam compound were unable to go about their daily affairs without their head coverings (as was permitted in a family setting) because the Marines and ASF in one of our OPs could look down and see them; the OP guards were persuaded that, as a courtesy to our hosts, they should make their monitoring of the area more discreet.

On a third occasion, Eric himself committed a blunder which, if he had been in Taliban company, might have gotten him executed. He and Taroon were seated outside discussing the Koran when Eric pulled his English copy of the book from his rucksack and, to consult a passage, placed it on the ground in front of him. To a by-the-letter fundamentalist, this would have been seen as a desecration punishable by death. Taroon just smiled indulgently, picked up the Koran, and explained that—like the Torah to an observant Jew, like the Stars and Stripes to an American patriot—the holy word of Islam should never touch the ground.

Eric likes to joke about this episode: "I desecrated a Koran and lived to tell about it." But he knows that the incident carried two big lessons.

One was the stated lesson: don't let the Koran touch the ground. Just as important was the lesson that not all Muslims were fanatic literalists, and that if you had built up a reservoir of mutual respect, even a mullah trained in a Wahabi-funded school could be forgiving. It wasn't that Taroon became less devout a Muslim, only that he realized devotion to his faith didn't require him to advocate killing Americans. In a world where Allah's mercy was often honored more in the breach than in the observance, that was a heartening development.

The friendship between the Pashtun mullah and the Christian chaplain took an important turn in March, thanks to a novel suggestion by Ben Guile. In training the indigs, Ben was seeing to it that, like U.S. troops, each of them was assigned a military occupational specialty (MOS). Aware of Taroon's special status as the indigs' mullah, he asked Eric, "Why don't you train him as a chaplain?"

Eric thought this was a great idea and so did Taroon. When Eric broached the idea, his Pashtun friend was visibly moved. By this time, with mosque restoration under way and his cultural advice obviously being taken seriously, he saw that the American mission was an honorable one, not the assault on Islam that his madrassa teachers had called it. His fellow Afghans had already recognized his special status; for the Americans to do the same was an additional honor that he was pleased to accept.

And so began for this young hafiz a course of instruction that would result in his official designation as the ASF chaplain.[2] Over a period of several weeks, he and Eric discussed how the broad work of a spiritual leader differed from the more specialized duties of a military chaplain. They discussed the chaplain's peculiar role as an unarmed soldier; the general principles of the Geneva Conventions; confidentiality when counseling soldiers; how to conduct ceremonies, including funerals; and how to comfort soldiers following traumatic events. Eric shared with his student the Chaplain's Creed—"Nurture the living, care for the wounded, honor the dead"—and found that to this young man raised in an entirely different tradition those words rang beautifully true.

He also emphasized the importance of practicing a "ministry of presence," that is, of making the dedication to soldiers' welfare not just a Sunday (or in Taroon's case a Friday) obligation, but a constant reality. When a chaplain practices a ministry of presence, he assumes the same burdens as his "congregants," shouldering the same packs, eating the same food, trudging up the same mountains, sleeping in the same cold outposts. Eric practiced what he preached—he was constantly leaving his Camp Vance office to visit us or one of the other ODAs—and he was very successful in modeling that behavior for Taroon.

The upshot of all this was that Taroon—a prime exhibit for "letting the Afghans do it"—became as adept and involved a chaplain for our indigenous troops as Eric himself was for the ODA. Proud of his new status and devoted to his job, he became a reliable judge of correctness in cultural matters, a ready ear for his men in calmer moments, and a great source of consolation when things went wrong.

Taroon's "conversion" from infidel hater to our "Muslim chaplain" had an additional outcome that was as unexpected as it was momentous.

When the mosque project had been under way for about a month, he asked for leave to visit his old haunts in Pakistan so he could—as he put it—"tell the truth about the good things the Americans are doing." This was a gutsy move, since the general Pakistani take on Americans didn't include admitting that they did "good things." Besides, Taroon was intending to drop in on his old madrassa and set the record straight with his fundamentalist teachers. When I heard about the plan, I first thought it was an elaborate hoax to get some vacation time. But Taroon seemed sincere and he had proven himself valuable, so I decided there was no reason to keep him from going. Little did I know how effective he would be as an ambassador advertising our efforts.

He was gone about a week. When he returned, he said that when he told people the Americans were bringing peace to the Pech, the first reaction was outraged disbelief.

"We all know they are devils" was a common response. "How can infidels do any good for followers of the Prophet?"

"Come and see," replied Taroon. "Come and see that there is no disrespect. See that my soldiers pray five times a day, and the Americans encourage them. See the beautiful new minarets they have helped us to paint."

Skepticism remained the general public response, but in private people listened, debated, wondered if this wild story could be true. And then gradually, first one family, and then two and then a dozen, decided to take a chance and test the tale.

During the civil war and continuing into the Taliban period, thousands of Afghans had fled the country, looking for a patch of quiet earth across the Pakistan border. Now, in March 2004, encouraged by Taroon's words, and undoubtedly those of family still living in the valley, some of them began to drift back, ending their exile and venturing cautiously homeward to see if this young mullah told the truth. This process continued throughout the spring. By the time the poppies were in full bloom, hundreds of Pech Valley residents were returning to their homeland.

As they trooped back into Nangalam and Manogay, the emotional mood of the villagers was incredibly touching. We saw reunions on the road right in front of our camp and heard, sometimes throughout the night, jubilant celebrations nearby. Reunited family members often visited the camp to thank us for what we had made possible. This was gratifying to us, and especially to our

ASF soldiers, who were proud to have played a role in this mass reconciliation.

I doubt that anything Hammerhead Six did in our time there gave me greater satisfaction, or had a greater strategic impact, than this return of the oppressed. By that spring we had not yet succeeded in tracking down Abu Ikhlas or any of the other big-time cutthroats. But to judge from the reverse migration of these displaced families, we had evidently made some headway in transforming their bloody playground into a place that decent folk were not afraid to live in. We had not eliminated Ikhlas and associates from the valley but we were taking the valley *from* them one village at a time.

If we could sustain that modest victory, I told myself, I would be willing to call our mission a success.

20

Eye for an Eye

Eye for eye, tooth for tooth, hand for hand, foot for foot.
—Exodus 21:24

The old law of an eye for an eye leaves everybody blind.
—Martin Luther King Jr.

As the February killing of the two videotaped ambushers indicated, our Afghan soldiers sometimes interpreted the Rules of Engagement too flexibly. We were reminded of that again late in March, when two of our ASF trainees, believing that they had cornered some fleeing HVTs (Hekmatyar was rumored to be in the area), opened fire on a trio of unarmed civilians. They had been near a checkpoint, pushing a disabled truck at night with the headlights off, and when our guys approached, they apparently got nervous and started to run. Why they panicked was unclear. What was disturbingly clear was that our soldiers shot first and asked questions later, leaving all three of the civilians severely wounded.

When they approached the victims and discovered their mistake, the soldiers rushed the wounded men to our clinic. Mike had heard the commotion and was on the spot when the truck arrived bearing the three bodies. I was awakened by the Marines on radio watch and had a couple of minutes before the victims arrived. When they rolled up, I was shocked at the carnage I saw. The three unlucky souls had huge entry and exit wounds all over their bodies. The

AK-47 rounds had left bones protruding, tendons and muscles torn, and blood everywhere. The sight turned my stomach and jolted my body with adrenaline.

At the same time I was sickened by a knowledge of suffering that went beyond the physical. These three horribly mangled Afghans, who had lived a hard, thankless life in these isolated mountains, were human beings with families—perhaps children like mine. Seeing them struggle for breath as their bodies swam in blood was a sight that I carried with me for a long time afterward.

A quick, desperate triage told Mike that for two of the wounded men it was too late. The third one, riddled with six bullets, was close to joining his two friends. But Mike was confident he could save him and had the soldiers rush him into the clinic. Then it was all hands on deck, with Ian Waters opening Kerlix bandages, James Trusty starting an IV, and me putting pressure on a bleeding arm. The victim was conscious enough to keep apologizing to me that he understood why the soldiers shot him, that his activities must have seemed suspicious, and that he was sorry—a weird comment from somebody full of bullet holes.

After a few minutes I was relieved by a Navy corpsman from our Marine contingent, leaving the medics to work on him through the night. Walking out of the clinic, I was swept by a wave of sick responsibility, apprehension for the backlash that was probably coming, and of sadness for the victims' families. I was up all night piecing together how this could have happened, answering questions from higher-ups, and trying to figure out how to defuse a situation that our enemies would certainly try to turn to their advantage.

As the team fought for the third victim's life, Randy went to the indig barracks to deal with the ASF troops' frustration. Tensions ran hot with the indigs and Americans alike. I was glad that Chaplain Eric and his buddy Taroon were nearby. They had hiked up to one of the OPs earlier that day, doing their "ministry of presence" thing, but had returned to the camp when they heard the gunshots. Now, their presence helped to calm a situation that could easily have spun into chaos.

While all of this was going on, Scott and I met with the two soldiers who had done the shooting.

They were devastated. They knew that they had violated one of Islam's central principles: the sanctity of human life. Even though in Afghanistan that principle was widely ignored, and even though the shooters had thought their targets were anything but innocent, the ugly fact remained: they had taken the lives of two guiltless civilians. This was a transgression against the basic Koranic injunction that, unless it be for "just cause," killing one person was like killing the entire world (Sura 5:32). There's a world of fudging available in that "just cause" proviso, but that wiggle room didn't apply in this case. Our soldiers knew deep in their guts that they had done wrong.

They also knew, on a practical level, that they might be punished for their crime not just by Allah but by the male relatives of the men they had slain. That was standard practice in northeastern Afghanistan, where the Pashtunwali principle of *badal* demanded that the shedding of blood be repaid in kind. In this case, the likelihood of swift retaliation was high, because relatives of one of the victims were ASF soldiers in the shooters' own platoon.

Given this complication, I wasn't surprised when upon my entry into the tent where the shooters were held, they pleaded with me to be protected from their bunkmates' vengeance. Both began crying, and one curled himself into nearly a fetal position, shaking with the realization of the fix he was in. I looked at Scott and he just shook his head. They wanted me to transfer them to the States or at least out of Kunar, and I assured them we would figure this out. I needed to know what had gone wrong before we could take any action.

"Why did you shoot?" I asked.

Looking simultaneously stricken and dumbfounded, they answered in unison.

"Because you told us to. You said in rehearsals if the enemy tried to escape we could shoot them."

My turn to be dumbfounded. I didn't remember exactly the wording I used in sending them off to that checkpoint, but I was willing to swear that I hadn't said, "If you see three unarmed guys pushing a truck, open fire."

Probably what had happened was some combination of the old "lost in translation" issue and the soldiers' overeagerness to kill an HVT. In any event, they were no longer in any doubt that they had misconstrued my orders. If they had felt justified at the moment they pulled the trigger, they knew they were wrong soon after the shell casings had hit the ground.

The whole mess was unnecessary, because our vehicle checkpoint (VCP) protocol was simple. You set up an obstacle on the road, stop the vehicle, check the occupants and the cargo, and wave people on their way. We usually ran VCPs with a joint detail of ASF and Marines so the Marines could supervise the operation and the indigs could identify bad guys. Sometimes a vehicle of perfectly innocent Afghans would approach a checkpoint, be intimidated by seeing armed soldiers, and quickly go back the way they came. Normally, we'd let that pass. But based on the intel we had of Hekmatyar possibly being in the area, we had kicked things up a notch, instructing our VCP details to pursue and search any such "fleeing" vehicles. On the night of the shooting, we had set up one of these standard checkpoints, charging an ASF squad hidden two hundred yards ahead to pursue any vehicle that the Marine squad leader had radioed ahead was suspicious. We had rehearsed the responsibilities of all parties and placed them in position as darkness fell.

The plan was fine, but then came the fog of war. Based on our conversations with the shooters, the Marines, and the rest of the ASF squad that was on site, Scott and I got a clearer picture of what had happened. Apparently a Toyota pickup with no headlights was stopped at the VCP and sent through. But when the vehicle neared the pursuit squad's hiding spot, it had engine trouble, and two of the passengers jumped out to push it up a hill. Startled by the sudden arrival of a dark truck with two males outside of it, one of the ASF soldiers yelled "Stop!" The civilians, startled in turn, ran toward the river. The ASF had not been alerted that they were suspicious, but thinking that only guilty people run away, they forgot the rehearsal parameters and opened fire. They had made a split-second bad decision, with terrible consequences.

As upset as the shooters were at these consequences, they were also worried that things were about to get worse. Our interrogation was making them even more distraught than they already were— and even more fearful of punishment. At one point, one of the soldiers stood up, walked toward me with one of the most miserable countenances I have ever seen, and grasped my beard.

This was the second time I had experienced this oddly personal gesture of *nanawatay*. I knew from the incident with the lying "landlord" that it indicated a plea to be forgiven. And in this case, unlike the last one, I was inclined to be forgiving. I was puzzled and angry about what had happened. But I also felt sorry for the two soldiers, who were following what they thought was my intent and whose abject demeanor suggested that this would probably be the last time they would shoot from the hip.

It was war, after all. I wasn't happy about the mistake, and I certainly couldn't overlook it. But in a decision about their fate, I wanted to tread softly. At the end of the day, these two well-meaning screw-ups were *our* screw-ups. Our friends. In the Pech Valley, that was a category you didn't want to sacrifice lightly. It may seem harsh, but I confess that at this point I was less sorry for the dead civilians than worried about the effect that the shooting would have on our troops.

When Randy returned from the indig barracks, the ODA members not involved in caring for the wounded civilian discussed what to do next. One way to solve the problem would be to dispense Afghan-style justice for the egregious error. According to Pashtunwali, that could mean executing the two shooters ourselves or handing them over to the Afghans to exact *badal*. This option would satisfy the victims' families and probably defuse the antagonism that was likely to arise once villages up and down the Pech got wind of the incident.

This would satisfy tradition. But it didn't feel right.

The second option was to honor their plea for *nanawatay*, that is, to forgive them and work with the families and relatives in our ASF to have them atone for their error in other ways. That didn't mean that they wouldn't be punished, only that the penalty would be tempered by mercy. This option was appealing to us as Christians, but it posed a risk to our mission, to the cohesion of our ASF troops, and to our reputation with the families and villagers. If we were soft and did not respect the local version of justice, justice later might be exacted on us. It was a classic case of Justice versus Mercy—a dilemma that a handful of Special Forces soldiers were trying to figure out at 3 A.M. in the middle of the Pech Valley.

The blunder had happened on my watch and, even though it had violated my own intent, it was up to me to resolve. That thought was running through my mind as the chaplain came in and informed us that the ASF soldiers were waiting for a decision in the large tent that we used for *shura* meetings.

We walked out to the tent. Inside were more than a hundred of our Afghan soldiers. The ODA, the chaplain, Taroon, and Mashal stood near me as I faced them. As I scanned the group, I saw the two Afghan shooters. They had slinked to the back but their faces, drawn with anxiety, were lit by lamplight. Seeing them there, fearful but submissive to whatever would come, I suddenly knew what I would say and what we would do.

I started by telling the soldiers how proud I was of their dedication and their bravery. I said that every member of the Hammerhead Six team was honored to fight side by side with them. We left our country to help them improve theirs and we felt a real brotherhood with them. "The risks you have taken are honorable," I said. "In twenty years, your children who grow up in a free Afghanistan will talk about their fathers as heroes, the ones who showed courage enough to stand up and improve the country.

"Look to your left and your right," I said. "See that you are all brothers, we are all brothers, in this struggle. We must continue to work together, to protect each other, to share our burdens, even in dark times like this. Because of today's tragedy, people will be angry for a while, but they will continue to realize that we are here for their protection. They should know that the two soldiers who did the killing were acting not out of anger but in line with what they thought was right. I gave the orders to man the checkpoint and the soldiers made a mistake, but they were trying to fulfill their mission just like each and every one of you would do. I will take responsibility for the actions of these two soldiers and I will make peace with the families of the dead men in accordance with Pashtun law and custom.

"A terrible and sad event has occurred," I said, "but everything is according to God's will. We can only do our best."

I ended the impromptu speech by telling them how much my men and I relied on our own spiritual advisors, including the "American mullah" Captain Eliason, to bring us closer to God in times of trouble. As he and Taroon took turns offering spiritual comfort to the men, I could see the tension and apprehension leave their faces. They seemed to accept the decision as an appropriate one, although they were no doubt wondering exactly how we were going to make peace with the families.

Throughout that tense meeting, I was speaking from the heart, and in the emotion of the moment, I got choked up. The Afghan soldiers' faces showed that they were moved as well. This was especially so for the men responsible for the tragedy. Their faces in the lamplight showed incredible relief and gratitude. I felt at that moment that either one of them would have taken a bullet for me.

In the morning we met with local elders, who were understandably upset. They supported us, they said, but their people wanted justice. The word had spread, and there was more work to do before this issue would be settled.

To show respect for the two victims, we had their bodies wrapped in blankets, helped their relatives load them onto trucks in preparation for burial, and medevaced the wounded man—patched up but still in serious condition—to a Bagram hospital. This was an unusual use of a military asset, and it reinforced the sentiment of mutual respect. But we still had to deal with the possibility of revenge.

After talking individually with the relatives of the dead men who were under my command, I was convinced that they would honor their word not to exact vengeance, but they weren't the only kin that might want to do so. So, a day after the incident, I accepted an invitation to visit the victims' families to lay the matter to rest.

The home was north of our camp in the Waygal Valley. Randy, Scott, and the chaplain accompanied me with a squad of ASF. Jason and a second squad patrolled up the Waygal on the other side of the river to be close by in case we needed some assistance. As we pulled up to the compound, Randy called in to Camp Blessing, giving instructions that if there was a fight and we called for mortar fire, these were our coordinates: we would adjust the mortar fire as necessary if things got hairy. Then Scott, Eric, Mashal, and I walked through a courtyard and into one of the compound's houses.

My hope, as we walked in, was that we would engage in a successful negotiation, determining the blood money that we should pay to compensate the family. With his anthropological savvy, Eric had prepped me on what to expect in this kind of dialogue. But we all knew that there were other ways the situation might evolve. Negotiations might turn touchy, or there might be none at all. There was significant risk in meeting with angry family members.

Inside was a large room with carpets on the floor. We were joined there by local elders. As we sat in a circle, the scene looked like a *shura*. But it felt less like a governing council than like a lynch mob.

Several times in Afghanistan I felt adrenaline kick in before I realized why. This was one of those times when my subconscious knew we were in a sketchy situation and I started to bring my physical resources online even before my consciousness had sorted things out. By the time I became fully aware of the gravity of the gathering, my pupils were dilated, my heart pumping fast, and my vision acute. I was thinking, This is live. This is happening in real time. Do something and make it count.

There were a dozen men at the meeting, every one fixing us with glowering eyes. Some of them were introduced as family and several men at the back of the room, who were not introduced, were half-trying to conceal their AK-47s. I wondered how many others were in the hills overlooking our security detail outside. A family meeting like this—on their turf at a designated time—would be an ideal setting for another "baited ambush." Randy had sensed the danger when he gave the Camp Blessing mortars our coordinates, but I had been confident that the meeting with the family would be cordial. It seemed now that I might have been mistaken.

The stakes were high, and success or failure in discussions might be confirmed with instant feedback from 7.62mm bullets. If this had been a casual tea visit, I would have rested my M-4 against the wall behind me. This day I laid it next to me with the business end pointing toward the men at the back. I knew that Scott would take responsibility for dealing with those on his side of the room if things went bad.

With that mental rehearsal complete, I focused on the father of one of the victims: the man who had been chosen to represent the family. I knew that my greatest weapon at that point, and our best chance of getting out of this room alive, was my ability to reason with him. I started with an apology, explaining that the killing of their relatives was a terrible mistake, that the soldiers responsible were broken-hearted and remorseful, and that we hoped that, with their help, we could come up with a response that would satisfy the traditional code of Pashtunwali.

"We have come here with sorrow in our hearts," I said. "What do you require of us to atone for this great wrong?"

I had heard stories about the Law of Talion—the "eye for an eye" legal principle that still governed so much of the non-Western world, and that Pashtuns knew as the law of *badal*, or "revenge." But I still was not prepared for the initial answer. The family representative, his black eyes fixing me like a falcon's, spoke with a calm that belied the violence of his words.

"They must die. You will hand them over to us and we will kill them. We will kill their families also. It is the law."

Families, too. It took me a second to take in the enormity of what he was demanding. There was no question that the guys we trained had screwed up badly, or that, according to local law, recompense had to be made. But there was another law in play here, one that decent people had honored for a couple of thousand years, and as cognizant as I was that we might not leave here alive, there was no way I was going to let two families be slaughtered to satisfy tradition.

Besides, I was pretty sure that the demand was an opening gambit, not a final judgment. I was no scholar, but I doubted that Islam—the religion that worshipped Allah the Merciful—would demand the obliteration of entire families for the death of two men. There was a Koran passage somewhere that counseled the relatives of a slain man not to exceed "just limits" in the exacting of vengeance. If anything was excessive, it was this opening demand.

Pashtunwali was another matter. I had enjoined my men to respect the local customs in all ways that we could. But respecting their culture didn't mean we could abandon our morals or serve as rubber stamps for traditional brutality. If it *was* traditional, which I doubted. I had heard that *badal* meant "exchange" as well as "revenge," and two families slain for two men didn't sound like a reasonable trade-off.

I looked at the man's falcon eyes, unblinking, and then turned to Mashal.

"Is this man serious?" I asked. "Is this the law?"

Mashal shook his head almost imperceptibly, telling me what I needed to know. This was a game—a test of my ability to negotiate an honorable outcome. Falcon Eyes might truly care about justice; I didn't know. But what was at stake here wasn't just the fate of some trigger-happy trainees. It was the very authority of our presence. What he really wanted to know was: how far can I push this young American? So even if I thought that the Law of Talion deserved respect—I had my reservations about that—I had to call his bluff or slink away. Trying not to make my survey of trigger fingers too obvious, I returned his stare.

"That will not happen," I said as evenly as I could muster. "The soldiers were wrong, but they are my men, and we will punish them according to our law. We will also pay the dead men's families recompense, according to your law. But if you want to kill these men and their families, you will have to kill us first."

I looked at Falcon Eyes's face as Mashal translated, searching for anger or disbelief or surprise. I couldn't detect any. After the longest ten seconds of my life, he gave me a slight nod and spoke again. Mashal listened and then turned to me.

"We will now have tea," he translated, "and we will come to an agreement on the amount that must be paid."

I have never heard a bell ring out as beautifully as that little word *amount*. It meant that, whatever the circle decided in the next hour or two of back-and-forth, there would be negotiation, deference would be paid to Pashtunwali, and the payment that would cancel the blood debt our wayward soldiers had incurred would be measured in rice, goats, and cash, not innocent lives.

The Afghan system of justice, influenced by Islamic law but not identical to it, is a form of retributive justice that strikes some Westerners as calculatingly cold: to measure the worth of a man's life in livestock and grain seems to devalue his humanity. Maybe so. But in the Pech Valley, after seeing many times how this system attempted to repair injustices by paying recompense to injured parties, I saw that there was something logical about it.

Something humane, too. The intent was to provide assistance to a family that had lost someone, rather than to invoke an abstract principle that demanded proportional vengeance. In this case, this meant that the victims' families would eat better that spring and beyond. That's not the same thing as having your husband or father back, but it's not a cold calculation. Rather, the Pashtun way of settling the score was to involve victims' families in determining an amount that would satisfy them that a debt had been paid. This gave them more power than victims get in many systems, and it allowed them to heal and move on.

Most Western justice systems, more oriented toward penalties than recompense, would probably have tried the shooters on a manslaughter rap, for "recklessly causing the death of another." If convicted in many U.S. states, they could have spent several years in prison. That would have satisfied the law. I'm not sure it would have satisfied justice or facilitated healing for the victim's families.

The incident ended as well as could be expected, but it took an emotional toll. The day after the shootings I was up before dawn, turning over thoughts not just about how to manage the fallout but also about my own challenges as a leader. Aware that thousands of people in the Pech Valley were looking to me to secure them a better life, I felt sometimes in need of spiritual solace. I wrote in my journal that evening: "I should be turning to the Lord much more than I am to be inspired and guided to fulfill this responsibility. The people of this valley are truly suffering and I want to be a tool in the Lord's hand to execute judgment on the wicked or to be an instrument of hope and progress to those who would be open to peace and happiness."

Those were my thoughts on March 24, 2004. This was two days before Chaplain Eric conducted an early Easter service for the ODA. In that season of hope so central to all Christian faiths, I shared some reflections on Moroni 10:32–33 about becoming "perfect in Christ," while admitting in my journal that I was "tired and drained."

This wasn't a simple matter of physical exhaustion. It was more a psychological weariness, brought on perhaps by months of the cat-and-mouse game in which the Egyptian and our other quarries remained unseen. By April, I was tired of that game and itching for a fight.

21

High Noon

I've got to. That's the whole thing.
—Marshal Will Kane to his Quaker wife in *High Noon*

Who dares wins.
—Motto of the British Special Air Service

Twenty-five million dollars. Almost before the toxic dust of the September 11 attacks had settled at Ground Zero, the United States had offered that reward for Osama bin Laden. It was a bounty to be collected whether the Al Qaeda leader was taken dead or alive. Like in "the old poster out West," as our Texan president, George W. Bush, had quipped to the press.

The government had also put a bounty on our Pech Valley nemesis, Abu Ikhlas. Consulting some esoteric algorithm, DC bean counters had determined that the payout for the Egyptian's death or capture would be $20,000. To make things even more interesting, soon after our arrival in the Pech, Ikhlas had responded by announcing a $10,000 bounty for the Red-Bearded Commander of the American infidels. I wasn't sure whether I should be grateful or insulted that Ikhlas was less well funded than the FBI.

It was now April. The nights were nearly bearable, our Afghan soldiers were taking on more and more responsibility, the rocket attacks had been reduced to light incoming, and the valley floor was awash in brilliant red, white, and pink poppies. In terms of unconventional warfare, we had accomplished a lot. But so far, two years into the hunt for bin Laden, no one had come forward to claim the FBI rewards.

Given the sums involved, and given that the average Pech Valley farmer made about a thousand dollars a year, you had to wonder why.

Maybe they were afraid. It wouldn't be hard to be intimidated by the world's most famous terrorist or his lieutenants. In a world where the Law of Talion had real teeth, turning in even a regional player like Abu Ikhlas might bring down retribution on the informer and his family. Maybe what kept Al Qaeda leaders protected was an Afghan version of the mafia's code of silence: keep your mouth shut or we'll shut it forever.

Or maybe the locals were showing their allegiance to another mafia-style trait: the almost religious devotion to one's own kin. Both bin Laden and Ikhlas were said to have relatives who had married into local families. That would put upon those families—and by extension their neighbors—the obligation to protect and shelter them. Failing to do so would be a violation of a familial duty.

In tribal cultures throughout the Middle East, this obligation to protect extends beyond the family to guests—even accidental guests like Navy SEAL Marcus Luttrell. In 2005, when the Taliban was hunting down this lone survivor of the Operation Red Wings disaster, Pashtun villagers less than five miles from Camp Blessing had taken him in and put their own lives at risk rather than surrender him to his would-be executioners. To do less would have been an affront to hospitality.[1]

Maybe something like that was happening in 2004, too. Maybe there were villagers up and down the valley who weren't particularly crazy about Abu Ikhlas but who saw surrendering him to us, with or without the twenty grand, as a violation of a good host's obligation.

Or maybe there was a simpler explanation for why no one was biting. Maybe there was something wrong with the bait.

In America, our measure of value is the dollar. It's not surprising that a cadre of American spooks, in working out an inducement to turn in bin Laden, came up with a high-dollar figure designed to impress. Twenty-five million dollars *is* impressive—to us. But an Afghan villager has a different frame of reference, and not just because his currency is the afghani rather than the dollar. He doesn't think in terms of currency but in terms of what it can get for him and his family. How much rice, how much gasoline, how many stock animals? Maybe the problem with the $25 million bounty, and even the $20,000 bounty, was that they didn't translate easily into livestock.

I'm not being facetious. In more than one discussion with tribal elders I got blank stares when I mentioned the bounty figures. One of them once asked me bluntly, "How many goats is that?" I didn't have an answer for him. Twenty-five million dollars would buy what? A million goats? There may not be that many goats in all of Afghanistan. Who wants to cash in on a bounty whose actual purchasing power is not believable?

For whatever reason the bounties lay uncollected, I was growing increasingly frustrated with our invisible ghost. Even though the rocket attacks of the "Afghan space program" had become sporadic and ineffectual, their director was still out there, and even though we seemed to have pushed him to the margins of military relevance, knowing that he wasn't corralled remained a thorn in my side. It festered every time I asked a village elder about the Egyptian and was met with a disingenuous stare that said, "I have no idea what you're talking about."

I was starting to think that, as a strategy for flushing him out, the astronomical bounty was a waste of time. Maybe it was time for a new approach.

*   *   *

That new approach came to me one day while I was meeting with a group of elders from the Korengal Valley. They had come to our camp to secure some Civil Affairs resources—money, lumber, and concrete—for an irrigation project, and James Trusty had called me in to give the project approval.

Up to this point, I had generally withheld resources from the Korengal, as that was where Abu Ikhlas was usually reported as residing, and the ridges above Korengal were where most of our rocket attacks had been coming from. The Korengalis were isolated from the local government and just wanted to be left alone. Their economy had been destroyed when the new Afghan government outlawed the timber industry, believing that it was helping to fund the insurgency. This made it hard for these people to trust or seek interaction with their government. In an effort to improve relations with the elders and to gather intel, I had recently agreed to release small amounts of resources at a time so they would be forced to visit our camp more frequently. This was a goodwill gesture that showed the elders they could gain more by cooperating with us as the other villages were.

I listened politely as they described their needs and then nodded an OK to James and wished them good luck. It was an easy decision and my mind wasn't on irrigation anyway: I was distracted thinking about Abu Ikhlas—about the lack of luck I was having in locating his lair and the lack of help these elders had been providing in that effort.

And then, in one of those out-of-the-box flashes that come to you sometimes, the thought hit me that if I couldn't get to him, maybe I could get him to come to me. Maybe I could send him a message that would make him want to meet me face-to-face, to settle this cat-and-mouse nonsense once and for all.

How do you get a mouse to come to a cat?

That was the question on my mind as the Korengal contingent was thanking me and getting ready to leave. I'm not sure I had thought out the answer before they got up, but I did have a vague image of a new approach.

I had been treating Abu Ikhlas as a powerful warlord: someone I wanted to destroy because he was a threat. What if I reversed direction on that thinking? What if I let him know that I was the warlord and that he was too weak and cowardly to stand up to me? What if I took a tip from the tribal code of honor and used shame, rather than money, to bring him to heel? Could calling the mouse a mouse flush him out of his hole?

It was worth a try. As the elders were about to rise, I stopped them by saying, "Please. I would like to ask one question before you leave."

They sat back down, looking a little worried, probably wondering if I had reconsidered my approval of their project.

"Why is it," I asked, "that the Egyptian is now employing women to attack the camp?"

Their expressions said that they had no idea what I was talking about. I let them mull it over for a second and then elaborated.

"Last night," I said, "we were attacked by two rockets and a few rounds from a machine gun. They came from that ridge to the sunrise."

I pointed to the hills that lay about half a mile away to the southeast of our camp.

"My eyes are good, but the ridge is so far away I cannot see who is firing at the camp. I do not think an Afghan fighter would hide so far away. An Afghan fighter, a true warrior, he would come out into the open; he would fight like a man. So it must be women who are hiding so far away in the hills. The Egyptian must be using women to do his fighting."

The elders' expression went from bafflement to concern, as if they were uncertain who I was accusing of cowardice. I had phrased the insult carefully because I knew that in their culture, courage was considered a paramount masculine virtue, while a man's greatest shame was to be accused of a cowardly failure to take revenge. In dozens of Pashtun proverbs, a fighting spirit is valued above all other virtues. "Sweet is the fellowship of the sword," for example, or "Where a brave man fights, a dog runs away." Or this mother's Spartan-like warning to her warrior son: "May you rather die in battle than be disgraced by the enemy." The country of the Pashtuns was a home of the brave, a heartland of "eye for an eye" retribution and of knives being drawn in anger at the faintest slight to honor.

It was the heartland, too, of an ancient, feverish machismo that saw women as problems. They were fragile vessels of purity to be "protected" by seclusion, but they were also dangerous objects whose sexual attractiveness could invite the dread beast Dishonor into the family. They were *different* from men, and they were destined to play different roles in the world according to both tribal and Islamic tradition. No Afghan man—not even the gentlest one—wanted to be thought of as behaving like a woman.

That being said, for a man to be accused not just of cowardice but of having women do his fighting was even worse than being called a woman himself. No true man would stand for such an insult. I was betting that if this message got through to Abu Ikhlas, he would be forced to leave the hills and confront me directly.

As I was mulling over the insult myself, I found myself warming to the situation, and before I knew it, I had taken a second step in calling my nemesis out.

"The Egyptian is a coward who hides behind the burkas of women fighters. He is not a man of honor or a fighter worthy of Islam. I believe that he is a disgrace to Islam. I believe that it is

God's will that he be killed. I believe that if I kill this unworthy man, I will be doing God's will."

I knew that in proclaiming myself Allah's would-be servant I was skirting the shores of blasphemy, but I was getting into the role and I didn't care. I could feel my adrenaline spiking as I continued.

"I ask in God's name that you get a message to this unworthy man. I will fight him tomorrow. One man to one man, in any way he wishes. Knife or gun or the hands that God has given us. If he is a man, we will fight and one of us will kill the other, and it will be God's will that decides."

Caught up in my own theatrics, I swept my arm out toward the ridge again. Then I lowered it, pointing to a lone tree in a field of poppies next to the Pech River.

"There," I said. "He can choose the weapons. Tell the Egyptian that if he is not a woman, he will meet me there tomorrow at noon. I will wait for him there, and God will decide."

We all got up, and they went back to the Korengal, probably wondering how the Red-Bearded Commander had managed to transform himself, in a matter of minutes, from a dispenser of resources to a would-be gladiator. I was wondering that myself. But the die was cast, and I didn't regret it. Knowing how fast word of mouth operated here, I knew that our Al Qaeda ghost would receive my challenge before nightfall. How he would choose to respond, I hadn't a clue.

James, who had witnessed the whole little drama, raised his eyebrows in a kind of stunned appreciation. "That went well," he said, smiling wryly.

Back in the planning room, Junior and Mike were cleaning weapons and arguing about baseball. They looked up when James and I walked in.

"Gentlemen," I said, "I have some news to report on the Abu Ikhlas front."

When I told them what had happened, they both cracked up—as did the rest of the team when I called them together. I don't remember all the details of the ribbing I took, but I think it included phrases like "pistols at twenty paces" and "Go for it, D'Artagnan." The duelists I got compared to tended to be pop culture stars rather than historical figures—Marshal Dillon rather than Andrew Jackson—and there was a good deal of joking about meeting in the middle of the street at high noon.

This was appropriate, I suppose, because I currently held the camp title for fast-draw tomfoolery—a distinction that gave our head weapons sergeant, Dave Moon, no end of dismay. As our weapons expert, he had built a firing range at the back of the camp and had occasionally entertained our Afghan trainees by demonstrating his quick draw skills in knocking tin cans off a post. When I outdrew Dave himself one day in a contest, I became the camp's champion gunslinger, much to the Afghans' delight. Not understanding U.S. military organization, they apparently believed, before we corrected them, that it was because of this prowess with the sidearm that I had become the ODA commander. The misperception added to the humor of my fast-draw title.

Dave made the most of the weird situation. "Pity you don't have your trusty six-shooter, Marshal," he grinned. "Looks like you'll have to make do with the Beretta."

Soon, though, the laughter subsided, and we started to consider just how big a hole I had dug myself.

There were serious questions here, with serious stakes. What if Abu Ikhlas showed up with an army of retainers? What if he shelled the poppy field from a distance? What was the protocol for a duel in Afghanistan? Did they even have duels in Afghanistan? We spent most of the evening and the next morning discussing our options, and finally decided that, as crazy as it might sound, the smartest choice—or the least dumb one—was for me to do as I had said. I would walk into the poppy field alone, wait for my adversary to appear, and pray that I made it beyond high noon.

In discussing the upcoming duel as we would any other operation, we agreed that the most probable course of action for Abu Ikhlas was to be a no-show. Second to that was him arriving and being killed—the best outcome for us but probably the least likely one. The most dangerous possibilities were that a surrogate for Ikhlas would arrive in an explosive vest or a sniper would tag me from a distance as I waited for the show. To provide some protection against this last scenario, we decided that Dave would position himself on the team house roof with a sniper rifle, hoping (to quote Robert Rogers's Standing Orders) to "ambush the folks that aim to ambush you."

There wasn't any certainty here, but unconventional warfare is a game of calculated risk, and I figured that risk was worth it if we could nab the Egyptian.

At five minutes to twelve the next day, with my team's weapons locked and loaded in case things went south, I walked the two hundred yards from the "A" Camp's perimeter into the poppy field. There I ceremoniously removed my Tiger Stripe fatigue shirt, put it on the ground, and laid my M-4 rifle on top of it. Standing there with a 9mm sidearm on my hip and a Yarborough knife hanging from my belt, I did my best to appear calm. But I could feel my heart rate increase and my vision sharpen as the adrenaline began flowing at the anticipated fight.

Waiting by the side of the field were about a hundred villagers who had heard on the grapevine that the commander of the American soldiers was about to go mano a mano with the neighborhood bully.

Scattered in the front row were three or four elders. Placing my right fist on my heart, I nodded to them in the traditional greeting of respect.

Afghans love a good contest, and during our time at the "A" Camp the locals loved to see us display our prowess with weapons, so I wasn't surprised to see these assembled onlookers. In fact, for my purposes I figured the bigger audience the better. If I succeeded in killing the Egyptian, not only would I rid the valley of its chief tormentor, but I would prove to the Muslim faithful that—recalling my challenge—God was on the side of the bearded Americans.

If I didn't succeed...well, to tell the truth, I didn't give that outcome much thought. Maybe that was because of my Special Forces training, where they inoculate you with the mantra "Failure is not an option." Maybe it was because, getting into my gunfighter persona, I was sure that no Cairo-born thug could outdraw Marshal Dillon. Or maybe it was just an ordinary soldier's protective mantle: the belief that whatever happened was in God's hands, and that if you did your best, live or die, it would come out all right. I could joke about Insh'Allah, but on some deep level I believed it, too.

As the seconds ticked up to high noon, I found myself feeling at once calm, expectant, and eager for victory. I'm not a bloodthirsty person, and even in wartime I don't take pleasure in killing. But at that particular bated-breath moment in that flourishing poppy field, I fervently wanted my enemy to show himself. I wanted that man-to-man moment, and I wanted his blood.

I had said publicly that he was a disgrace to Islam. Maybe that was overreaching, because I wasn't a Muslim, and his goodness or badness *as* a Muslim was something for the mullahs to decide. But he was also a man, and as far as I was concerned, he was a disgrace to humanity. If it had fallen to me that day to end his life, I would have done so without hesitation. I would have taken it as a moral privilege—the day's gold ring.

As a light breeze ruffled the poppies, I looked at my watch. It was two minutes to noon. Then one minute. Then twenty seconds.

When T hour finally arrived, with Abu Ikhlas nowhere in sight, I checked my watch again. I shrugged my shoulders. I turned slowly in a circle, scanning the horizon. I tapped the watch, looked mystified at the crowd, raised my arms, palms upward, in a gesture of disappointment. I was the kid who got to the circus as the gates were closing, the luckless groom left at the altar by a runaway bride.

In another few minutes I ran through this charade again. And once again at ten minutes past the hour.

At a quarter past twelve it seemed time to draw the curtain on the farce. Obviously our ghost was not going to show. Spectators started leaving the field to return to work. I had milked the scene for all it was worth, so I bent down, picked up my M-4, and put on my shirt. Then, accompanied by a few well-wishers, I walked back to camp.

I can't say that I was amazed at the outcome, or that I wouldn't have preferred to have engaged in the fight. As bloodless victories go, though, this was a good one. And maybe, even without the physical contest, it made a theologically provocative point that served our interest. After all, you could say that if Abu Ikhlas was truly a servant of God, he would have put his fate in God's hands, not cowered in the hills. That was the way I read it, anyway—and the way I hoped that the local faithful would read it, too.

How Abu Ikhlas read the theology no one could say. But how he read the politics became clear soon enough.

Even though he didn't make the fight, his spies had obviously been there, and news of the show, including my elaborate display of disappointment, reached him quickly. Apparently he wasn't pleased at being shown up as a coward—and maybe a doubting Thomas— in what used to be his own backyard. Before evening chow, we received word from one of our informants that the bounty on my head had been increased. The new reward was fifteen thousand dollars.

I hadn't been interested in earning the Egyptian's respect, but I had clearly gotten it. In terms of the price on our heads, we were now almost equals.

And, as the "A" Camp commander, I experienced a windfall in credibility. Everywhere we went—among the locals, the police, the elders, and our own Afghan soldiers—we could sense that a new level of respect had been established. In this nation of fighters, my challenge to the Al Qaeda leader had earned us moral capital that would serve us well. At the same time, the Egyptian's standing took a nosedive. Before long we got reports that he was having trouble hiring fighters or acquiring arms. He had lived to fight another day, but at a significant cost. I had taken a gamble and for whatever combination of reasons—daring, timing, luck, divine Providence—I had come out unscathed. I was grateful, humbled, a little surprised.

And bummed that I hadn't gotten to show off my gunslinger skills.

22

The Waiting Game

They're still waiting for the prey to come into focus.
—Michael Ware in *Time* magazine, March 29, 2004

I want to keep up the pressure on the bad guys but I have to admit, I am thinking a lot about transitioning and getting out of here.

—from my journal, April 12, 2004

Time magazine's Michael Ware had visited our camp in the first week of March, while I was stuck at Bagram, fighting to extricate myself from legal quicksand. His story on Camp Blessing, which hit the stands at the end of the month, was a fair-minded picture of the danger my team was facing, but it was more interesting for what it didn't say than for what it did.[1]

According to *Time*, the entire point of our "secret" camp was to force Osama bin Laden out of hiding. "The men of Camp Blessing," the story began, "know they are bait....They are dangling far from safety to attract a big catch." Yes, we "launched numerous reconstruction projects," and yes, we had secured more weapons caches "than anywhere else in Afghanistan." But these accomplishments were apparently ancillary projects. The real point of ODA 936 going native in Kunar was to provide an answer to the question "Where's bin Laden?"

It was true that we were part of the hunt for bin Laden. Even though we knew that catching him would not stop, and might even encourage, those warring against the West, such a coup would still have made our year. Ben, who loved being out on patrol, was so assiduous in his quest for this number one quarry that, as he jokes today, "I stuck my head into every cave in the Pech Valley." If, as Ware put it, the prey came into focus, we would have made a catamount's pounce look lethargic.

But to think of eliminating OBL as our sole—or even our major—focus was to misunderstand our mission and to reduce unconventional warfare to simplistic "catch 'em." Left out of the *Time* story was any mention of our surviving rocket attacks, the challenges of building an Afghan Security Force, MEDCAPs, mosque restoration, or *shuras*. In other words, most of what we were doing, day after day.

As for being bait: I don't think so.

But *Time* wasn't entirely wrong. We *were* in anticipatory mode, just not zeroed in obsessively on Osama bin Laden. Intel came in frequently from informants and from the CIA about HVT sightings. One report had Gulbuddin Hekmatyar in a nearby village, and our Afghan soldiers' eagerness to capture that big fish had precipitated the checkpoint shooting of March 23. Less notorious targets also figured in the intel, while Taliban night letters constantly reminded us that these recently ousted pretenders to the Kabul throne were still angling to get back in power. As Afghanistan prepared for a national election that summer, the night letters became more frequent, although mostly in villages several miles from our camp, where our circle of influence wasn't as strongly felt.

And always, of course, there was Abu Ikhlas. My daring him to meet me man to man had led to him being an embarrassing no-show, but that didn't mean that he was out of the picture. On the contrary, we knew that, his honor having been impugned, he now had something to prove. It was all the more likely that he would intensify his efforts to vilify the "haters of Islam" and drive us from "his" valley.

Intel said as much. By the beginning of April, the buzz was clear that, sooner or later, the camp would be attacked again. The March 10 assault, we were convinced, had been only a prelude. The next time around we expected a larger direct attack. The big question, as always, was when it would come. So we were keeping our powder dry and waiting for the enemy to show.

There was another kind of waiting that crosscut this one. By April we had been in Kunar for eight months, with the only respite for me being a week's leave at the beginning of March. It was great to be back home even for that short stint, but it made my return to Afghanistan emotionally complicated, almost as if I'd been sent to a second deployment.

As Captain Ron Fry, Special Forces 18A, I was proud of what Hammerhead Six had accomplished and was primed for whatever challenges, including a firefight, might yet befall us. But as Ron Fry, the husband of Rebecca Fry and the father of our three young children, I was getting close to having my fill of Afghanistan. Every other day or so I would go on the team house roof to call Becky on the satellite phone. Just five minutes hearing her voice and talking to the kids would put things in perspective and keep me going. But it was hard to ignore feelings that were calling me home. Many of my ODA teammates were also husbands and fathers, and I knew that they were experiencing this tension, too.

In an "A" Camp, you never get a reprieve: You're always outside the wire. In most FOBs and at Bagram, when you came back from a mission and parked your vehicle within the gates of the base, it was like being back at Fort Bragg. Occasional rocket attacks notwithstanding, you could enjoy a relatively humdrum existence, playing cards, watching TV, hanging out in the mess hall. At Camp Blessing, we had the responsibilities of propping up the local government, running a clinic, and managing more than a hundred Afghan soldiers living with us every day. This made a one-year deployment seem much longer. None of us ever fully relaxed.

The tension was further complicated by the fact that, on the heels of Mick Ware's story, we had been discovered by the American press and were becoming minor celebrities within the coalition. Alert to the propaganda value of a successful mission within a wider war that wasn't going that well, military honchos started to visit Camp Blessing to see what we were about and, I thought cynically, to take credit for what we were doing. On one level I considered this attention an eleventh-hour apology for months of neglect. On the other hand, I was pleased to see us getting some recognition and hopeful that it would inspire similar efforts elsewhere and get us needed resources.

April started with a visit from a major general, Eric Olson, the commander of the 25th Infantry Division that would soon be taking over operations in northeastern Afghanistan. He was accompanied by Maj. Jeb Stewart (who had replaced Major Hewitt as the B-Team commander) and the usual entourage of majors and lieutenant colonel staffers and senior NCOs. Stewart, a namesake of the famous Confederate general and a strong UW advocate, did a good job of prepping the visiting brass, and I enjoyed giving them tours and discussing our mission as I stood before them in a full beard and Oakleys. We were also able to give them a live-fire demonstration, which they enjoyed. It was Major General Olson who, on his way out of camp, was given a ring by our prisoner Omar; and who, after talking to him, expressed the hope that prisoners in other camps could speak as well of the Americans as Omar did.

A couple of days later, a second group of higher-ups came to check us out, this one led by our battalion commander Lt. Col. Marcus Custer and the battalion's senior noncom, Command Sgt. Maj. Ron Webb. They too seemed impressed with our progress, and they reacted like little kids when we let them play with the weapons. It's always interesting to see how kinetics—even simulated kinetics—fascinate those who spend much of their time in planning rooms. Lieutenant Colonel Custer had been a huge supporter of the "A" Camp, and I always enjoyed discussing UW strategies and history with him. He had had some unique UW experiences early in his career in Honduras, Nicaragua, Panama, and most notably El Salvador, where in the 1980s he was part of a small team of Green Berets that assisted the government in defeating an insurgency.

In both of these visits, it was good to be able to show off our weapons capabilities and to get some top-down approval for our "A" Camp experiment. But what I wrote in my journal after Lieutenant Colonel Custer left expressed well my mixed feelings at this time. Our Afghan soldiers were just about to complete their basic training. I wrote, "I am looking forward to graduating these guys and having the *shura* meeting on Sunday. Then we will just have to knock out the attack and then we will be ready to head home. I talked to Becky today for a long time and it was nice to hear her voice. We are excited that this is almost done and things will be 'normal' soon." There was that same tension again between soldiering and home.

The enemy was still out there trying to stay relevant. His favorite tool was still the IED. At least once a week someone came to Blessing to tell us about the location of one of these deadly devices. This became so common that we hired a local man who had been trained by the UN in mine clearance. We would send him out with an ASF squad to disarm mines and IEDs and bring them in for destruction on our firing range.

On one occasion we also had an Air Force asset fly over Route Blue to destroy any IEDs that could be triggered by radio frequency transmissions. I was on the team house roof with Courtney as the plane flew the route. We counted twenty-three explosions in less than a minute. It was sobering that the enemy had been able to place that many undetected devices but a relief to know that we had undone weeks of their efforts in such a short time.

The basic training graduation fell on April 9. We had the Marines cover all of the OPs so the entire ASF could be free to participate. They formed up proudly in their Tiger Stripe uniforms. Taroon offered a prayer, I gave a brief speech of congratulations, and the soldiers all received certificates for a job well done.

This was one of the best days we had at Camp Blessing. Morale among the Americans and the Afghans alike was very high. The Afghans felt recognized, accomplished, and validated as heroes of the Pech Valley. A popular squad leader named Ghorzang, a steely-eyed veteran of the Russian conflict, gave a colorful and memorable speech about their mission and their loyalty to their American brothers in arms. Randy and I were each given a huge Afghan "lei" made of folded Pakistani rupees—a traditional celebration gift that I still cherish. Then we took a group picture of the assembled company, with praises being sent up to Allah and with many of the men, Afghan style, holding hands. It was a great day for them, and a perfect present on my thirty-second birthday.

Five days after this ceremony, we had a visit from *Time*'s journalistic rival, *U.S. News and World Report*. As happy as I was that we were again being recognized, it was a bittersweet day, as Courtney's tour had ended and he was being sent home. He had become a good friend and had done a solid job for us; he would be missed by every member of the team. The *U.S. News* reporters seemed pretty cool, and their lead writer, Mark Mazzetti, seemed to take due notice that we were as much about digging wells as packing guns. But it would be some weeks before his story appeared in print.

On the morning of April 18 we had an appointment with the Chapa Dara district *shura* in the village of Kanday, about eight miles east of Camp Blessing, to discuss security matters, information exchange, and the surrender of caches. We had been receiving caches from this part of the valley almost daily; while I was on leave, Scott had recovered over twenty HiLux trucks full of ordnance from a former mujahid commander who was now a police officer in Digal, the village next to Kanday. So this was an important area in our sphere of influence.

Unfortunately, our plan to head there on the eighteenth had run into a snag, because a four-star general had decided to visit us on the same day. He couldn't say exactly when he would arrive, though, and Vance had denied our CONOP to go to the *shura* to make sure we were present when the general arrived.

I was flattered by all these dignitary visits, but standing up a *shura* wasn't going to happen: We were going to carry out the operation as planned.

To get around Vance's "permission denied" order, we altered our call signs and contingency codes so we could use the satcom without HQ knowing what unit was conducting the operation. Our call sign "Hammerhead," for example, became "Guppy," and our code for requesting a QRF if we ran into trouble was "Send in the Clowns." We decided that if the general showed up while we were still in Kanday, Randy would give the tour and stall; with any luck, we could meet the *shura* and the brass with no one the wiser.

As we rolled out of the gate, I got a radio call that the general was delayed and that we could therefore execute the Kanday visit if we were back at Blessing in four hours. So our stratagem wouldn't be necessary.

We hit the road early to be in Kanday by 0900, but broke down halfway there with two flat tires. Hijacking a villager's truck for the day (and overpaying him to chauffer us), we arrived an hour late at the *shura*, where we were greeted amiably by probably a hundred elders. Not the kind of gig you want to blow off. The meeting went well, although with that many attendees it wasn't short. Around midday, after agreeing on some security issues and feeling comfortable that Kanday was not hostile territory, Scott and I politely eased our way out. Jumping in the truck, we raced back south, hurtling along the lousy roads like the Dukes of Hazzard. We were about to congratulate ourselves on making it back on time when Randy's voice came over the radio.

"The VIP is still at Abad. Don't break your necks."

So we had a breather, as we contemplated the "hurry up and wait" aspect of the top brass timetable. Back at Blessing, we had time to change our T-shirts and speak briefly with Chaplain Eric about the mosque project before two huge choppers appeared on the horizon. These were MH-47s, the Cadillacs of the helo world, and when they landed we saw why. Out jumped not one but three generals—a four-star, a three-star, and a one-star—plus Colonel Herd, Lieutenant Colonel Custer, Major Stewart, and an assortment of other birds and high-level noncoms.

The generals were down-to-earth and had some great questions. In 2004, there were not that many soldiers still in the Army who had done what Hammerhead Six was doing in the Pech, so I was in my element, addressing them very comfortably as a subject matter expert on Special Forces "A" Camps. At one point I must have gotten a little too comfortable and forgotten the proper deference to rank. I could see Major Stewart smiling and stroking the lapel of his battle dress uniform, sending me a hint that I was talking to the Army's top command.

The highlight of the visit was the live-fire demo of several of

our captured weapons, including our 107mm rocket launcher, that
Ian put on for the visitors with appropriate gusto. It was impressive
in itself, and because it was staged completely with weapons from
acquired arms caches, it demonstrated our success in keeping firepower out of the hands of the enemy. We were in the eighth month
of our tour. We had been busting our butts throughout that period
to earn the friendship of locals like the Kanday elders, and we had
finally been seen as successful enough that two major U.S. magazines
and a gaggle of generals had seen fit to honor us with their presence.
It had taken a while to get that recognition, and it felt good.

"Life is what happens to you while you're busy making other plans."
Throughout those several weeks of complicated anticipation, I was
thinking that John Lennon's famous line was right on target. Looking back, I see that a consistent theme of that period had been "waiting." At the time, though, there was so much else going on that my
plans for averting an attack or for getting back home were, day to
day, overwhelmed by life itself—by the routine stuff that becomes
so much a part of the everyday grind that it's as invisible and essential as sunlight or air.

I think, for example, of the sitreps I sent Bagram nearly every day
of our deployment in the Pech. Here's an example from April 10:

ASF rotated OPs today and conducted a patrol to Darikar, one
to Guru, and a VCP on the Waygal Valley Road. ASF squad
acted on contact information and recovered a cache in Walo
Tangi village consisting of (1) ZPU 14.5mm anti-aircraft
gun (complete in Cosmoline), (3) PMN AP mines, a Dishka
barrel, (6) boxes of 14.5mm ammo. ODA hosted the district
shura meeting and had all elders sign an agreement that all

CA assistance etc. is dependent on their assistance to the camp and that further aggressions by villages will be on the village elders. 18A and 18F met with the village elders from Shulek and Kalaygal to solicit information and to warn them not to harbor foreigners or ACM. Civil Affairs continued to oversee the construction on clinic and school. Latrine and camp plumbing completed. Camp improvements/construction continued with retaining wall in ODA compound and wire obstacles on the northern perimeter of the camp.

This fairly typical sitrep reveals well the mundane variety of tasks that in the aggregate amounted to a "hearts and minds" initiative. We were always working to improve our positions, both the literal defensive positions of the camp and our positions on the human terrain. This meant that in any given week, on any given day, Hammerhead Six might be called upon to track down an arms cache, visit a school, paint a mosque, talk to a bunch of elders, or supervise indigenous soldiers in the firing of mortars.

Our weapons recovery project continued to thrive. Villagers brought us arms caches almost daily, and we continued to receive tips on additional caches that needed to be retrieved from fields, caves, and compounds. Our ASF soldiers handled many of these retrievals, sometimes on their own and sometimes accompanied by Marines, who were thoroughly enjoying the mission and the autonomy we gave them. Several times a week, an ASF patrol would return to camp with Toyota truckloads of RPGs, rockets, and ammo. We secured so much ordnance that, with limited storage space, we had to spend hours on the range practice firing RPGs just to burn through the inventory.

In late April, the routine continued. On the twenty-first, I distributed awards to the best students in the local girls school—the school we had repaired and expanded. The next day we responded to a volley of three rockets fired at our team house. (This was the same day, incidentally, that Army Ranger Pat Tillman was killed by U.S. friendly fire 145 miles to the south of our camp.) On the twenty-sixth we sent ASF patrols to investigate possible enemy activity on the southern ridge—the direction from which we expected the attack to come. By the end of the month most patrols were being conducted by the Afghans, and I was writing in my journal that I was "proud of what I see around me and how we built it from scratch." We continued to reinforce the OPs for when the attack occurred.

On May 4, we observed armed men at a known RPG launch position, and we received intel that a platoon-sized attack force would hit us that night. What I wrote in my journal that day reveals the mixture of exhilaration and apprehension that many commanders must feel on the eve of battle. "We have worked hard to put together a good defense plan and I feel we are as ready as we can be. I pray that we will be accurate and they will not ... . My goal is still to bring back all my boys and I hope tonight we will give the bad guys the opportunity to return to Allah and my boys to return home to their loved ones."

That night, the long-anticipated attack finally came. It was just after dusk on the fifth of May—the day that Mexicans and Mexican-Americans know as Cinco de Mayo, the anniversary of Mexico's 1862 victory over the French at the Battle of Puebla. But the anticipation, it turned out, was bigger than the event.

In place of the platoon we had prepared for, we got a handful of widely dispersed and seemingly disorganized attackers—none of them getting close enough to us to be recognizable. OP Comanche, manned by Marines, was hit by rockets and small arms, until fellow Marines and ASF soldiers in OP Hammerhead came to their aid.

Listening over my radio to the calls for help and the instant, fierce response from fellow jarheads across the valley, I got a poignant sense of these guys' comradely grit; they did credit that night to themselves, to the ASF, and to the Corps. In the main camp itself, all we got was a flurry of misaimed missiles from the Afghan space program: what I reported as "inaccurate rocket fire with unknown points of origin." Our force suffered only one minor casualty—an ASF soldier wounded in OP Hammerhead.

I gave thanks for our deliverance and with mixed emotions arranged for ODA 935, then at Abad, to set up a VCP near the village of Kandogal to block off the attackers' escape routes out of the valley. They did so but found nothing, and after a few hours we sent them home. So the final entry in my journal for this long-awaited event read, "Last night was a little exciting but mostly disappointing."

We later heard from local sources that the modest attack revealed two things. First, since we had bought up a lot of ordnance that would normally be acquired by the enemy, they were running short of ammo. It didn't mean the supply was gone, just that with a second buyer in the market, there was less inventory and less interest in selling to Ikhlas. Second, they were running short of recruits willing to attack us. Our work with the mullahs was making the charge "Islam haters" seem ridiculous, and so attacking the Americans was not as popular among military-age males as it had been six months earlier. Learning this lessened the "mostly disappointing" factor.

The following day we attended a *shura* in a Waygal Valley village that at one point threatened to erupt into an old men's brawl. Rival elders had been at one another's throats for years over water rights, as part of a blood feud that had already resulted in many homes burned to the ground and several men dead. There was too much anger to get anything accomplished that day. This was more contentious than the *shuras* we had been used to, and it became one of those cases—like the requests for my marital blessings—that I decided was better to let the locals handle for themselves.

Back at camp, we were surprised to see that, for the second time in less than a month, our battalion commander Lieutenant Colonel Custer was paying us a visit. This time, accompanied by Command Sergeant Major Webb and the chaplain, he was holding the proofs of an article he thought we'd like to see. It was Mark Mazzetti's piece for *U.S. News*.[2]

Adorned with photographs of a poppy field, the faces of some of the girls from the school we had built, and a dashing picture of Jason on a weapons raid, the story was entitled "Speak Softly, Carry a Big Gun: Into the Hinterland with the Special Forces." It was a good story. By May 10, when it appeared on the stands, Camp Blessing's location was no longer secret, and the men being interviewed no longer anonymous. There were no last names, but appropriate quotes were attributed to "Ron," "Scott," and "Jim" as well as Colonel Herd. Jimi's ill-chosen reference to our location as "kind of like the Little Big Horn" earned him an appropriate ribbing from Lieutenant Colonel Custer, but overall *U.S. News* presented a sensitive picture of our complex mission: We were there to "develop an intelligence network, earn the trust of the locals, track down terrorists, and build an army of Afghan men who for decades have known nothing but war." A good nutshell description of what we were doing.

Our favorite lines in the story came toward the end. Noting the casual garb that SF soldiers are known for (beards, baseball caps, and sandals), Mazzetti joked that we "might be easily mistaken for heavily-armed ski bums." That was a description that we came to cherish: When any of us meet, even now, it still brings a smile.

The other favorite line had to do with the Kanday *shura* that Scott and I had attended the day the generals visited. Mazzetti took some license with this, depicting us as "nervously checking our watches" while a four-star general was "cooling his heels" back at Blessing. In fact, as I've mentioned, we weren't so disrespectful as to ignore a general's visit to our camp. We left the *shura* in enough time to get back an hour ahead of the royal party (by driving like madmen), so we didn't make him wait—he made us wait. Nonetheless, the point that Mazzetti was making was on target. If it had come to a choice between the general or the *shura*, the general *would* have had to wait until we returned. "The *shura* was more important."

Unconventional warfare isn't a simple concept. Understanding it doesn't come easily to everyone, and certainly not to journalists on the prowl for fireworks. That one line—"The *shura* was more important"—said that Mazzetti had gotten it right.

23

The Unforgivable

There is nothing so subject to the inconstancy of fortune as war.

—Miguel de Cervantes

On May 8, we were still chuckling about the "ski bums" line when Lieutenant Colonel Custer told us that a third team of journalists would be visiting us the following day. This one was from *60 Minutes II*, a spinoff of the CBS news magazine. The team's lead reporter would be Lara Logan, a South African–born journalist who had embedded with U.S. troops shortly after 9/11 and had done incisive interviews with senior commanders, including one of the leaders of the Northern Alliance. Now she wanted a look at the remote Pech Valley and at the Green Berets who had established an "A" Camp there.

We were excited and flattered by the lieutenant colonel's announcement, even as we suspected that there was a domestic political context to the CBS decision. Outside of our AO, the war wasn't going well. The country was roiling with firefights, Pat Tillman had just been killed by his own troops' guns, the Taliban were threatening to kill anyone who voted in the upcoming election, U.S. soldiers were dying at the rate of one a week, and the whereabouts of Osama bin Laden remained unknown. In Iraq, Abu Ghraib had both the Muslim world and the Department of Defense reeling. With Americans hungry for good copy, *60 Minutes II* was interested in covering something positive in the War on Terror. After discussions with military leadership who guided her to our experiment in the Pech Valley, Logan and her CBS bosses figured we might be it.

To be honest, they weren't wrong. Even quiet professionals like to blow their own horns sometimes, and we were unabashedly proud of what our UW approach had accomplished. As we anticipated the arrival of the camera crew, we were cranked at the idea of making it to American TV. We didn't know that, within a couple of hours, a tragic accident would turn this heady feeling into dust.

We had arranged to have lunch just outside of Nangalam that day with the long-bearded *shura* elder we referred to as Brigham. Lieutenant Colonel Custer accepted our invitation to join us, so by late morning six Americans, accompanied by an ASF detail, were driving slowly through the streets of the village, waving to kids and smiling at the adults we recognized. The roads north of Nangalam were narrow, and we were forced to use our Toyotas. We were approaching Brigham's compound when the lead vehicle had a mechanical problem that called for Jason to poke his head under the hood. It turned out to be minor, but while we were standing around waiting for it to be fixed, we were suddenly surrounded by a pack of wild dogs.

They had been a nuisance before, and this day they were more aggressive than usual. As I was waving two of them away, a third came up from behind and sank its jaws into my butt. I felt a searing pain and for a second saw stars. Then, on instinct, I wheeled and put a round from my M4 carbine into the dog's midsection just as it was making another lunge at me.

As he yelped and the pack scattered, I heard a ping and simultaneously saw a spark from a rock fifteen feet away. Then it was weirdly quiet. I forgot about the pain of the bite as I registered what had happened: the bullet had pierced the dog's soft tissue, gone on to the rock, and then ricocheted off it going...where?

Fifty feet from where I stood was a cluster of kids. Although they were at a ninety-degree angle from my line of fire, I knew that ricochets with high velocity, light bullets were unpredictable. My heart was starting to pound as I looked toward them, and I said a silent "Thank God" as I saw that none of them had been hit. For a few seconds it was still as a movie freeze frame.

Then, behind the kids, a middle-aged man standing in a doorway swayed slightly to the right, then the left, and crumpled to the ground.

I was standing over him before I knew I had moved. His eyes were open, looking at nothing. In the center of his forehead, like a third dead eye, was a small dark hole. Randy, standing beside me, reacted faster than I could and directed the ASF to assist.

He was obviously dead, although none of us was willing to accept that fact as we lifted his body into the back of our pickup, reversed direction, and sped back toward the Camp Blessing clinic. I was in a state of shock and I wasn't alone.

I don't remember who passed on the word to Brigham to cancel the lunch, who called Ben to alert him we were coming, who called the Marines to say, "There's been an incident. Be on alert." I do remember myself urging our driver Roger, "Go faster! We've got to go faster!" even though every part of my brain that was still functioning knew that no speed available to mortals would matter a damn.

When we reached the camp, Ben met us at the gate. He checked for a pulse that we all knew wasn't there, then raised his head and shook it no. There was no point in going to the clinic. We left the body in the bed of the pickup, covering it with a blanket out of respect, and waited. Chaplain Eric was there, and his friend Taroon. I hardly heard their words of comfort. I nodded. We waited.

News of the shooting spread quickly through Nangalam. We weren't back at Blessing an hour before a young man approached the front gate and announced himself as the slain man's brother. When he was shown the body, he climbed in the back of the truck and began wailing—that high-pitched, unrestrained shrieking that is the characteristic expression of Afghan grief. It cut through me like a whipsaw, and yet as much as I wished it would stop, I felt obliged to listen, to feel his pain.

"Get Fry out of here. He doesn't need to see this."

Lieutenant Colonel Custer, more alert than me to how this situation might get worse, directed this order to Eric, who saw its wisdom. I wanted to stay, I wanted to feel what the brother was feeling, but the colonel's caution prevailed. As the chaplain walked me back to the team house, we passed an ashen-faced Jason. He put his hand on my shoulder: "I don't know what to say, Ron."

You got that right, I thought. There were no words.

In the team house, Eric did what chaplains do best and provided comfort. He offered prayer with me, Scott, and the sergeant major. This slowed my racing mind, but beyond that my emotional state was chaos. I had passed through the gray gate of shock into a darker world of conflicting sensations. Sadness, anger, disbelief, fear, guilt, apprehension, self-pity, shame, grief: name a negative emotion and I was feeling it.

I had once read a book about the emotional barbs associated with killing, but feeling those barbs directly was a very different thing. I had never felt a thing when ACM were killed by our team, and I had been largely detached when innocents were killed by my ASF at the vehicle checkpoint. In those cases, as commander I had been only technically responsible. This time it was different. Personal.

Into my brain flitted the image of an American soldier standing in a poppy field at high noon. Had that would-be duelist really been me? The contrast with my current situation was shattering. A month ago I had walked into that field open-eyed, brazenly gambling with death to take an enemy's life. Nothing had come of it but a boost in my reputation. Today, on a social call, blind luck had turned my hand against an innocent civilian. Reaching out in friendship, I had done the unforgiveable. The bitter irony made me sick at heart.

I had never before felt anything like this. I couldn't put a name to it. It was only when I looked in a mirror that I realized sorrow must have been a major component of my feelings: My tear-streaked face told me I'd been crying. But not just for the young man my bullet had killed. I knew the instant he dropped in the marketplace that I had possibly sacrificed everything we had built here. My greatest responsibilities were the mission and the lives I had been entrusted with. I had put both at serious risk.

Back in December I had told the team that if we wanted our mission to succeed, there were a couple of things we absolutely could not do. We couldn't disrespect the people's religion and we couldn't kill an innocent person. Those actions would not be forgiven. Yet I had just done exactly that. I had ended the life of a man whose only crime was that he was standing on the same street as a soldier with a loaded M4. I had no doubt there would now be hell to pay.

In the first hours after the incident, it looked like that payment would come soon. A crowd began to form outside our gate. Ten people, twenty, fifty. Many of them were angry members of a group that called itself the youth *shura*. But even older men we had befriended were obviously disturbed. They were shouting, wailing, demanding that the gate be opened and that justice be served. It wasn't clear what they wanted, aside from simply being heard. But it was the most blatant expression of anger we had seen since we had gotten here.

The camp was on full alert. Marines and ODA alike had their M4s ready. The Marines, in full body armor, were supporting the ASF at their security posts. Jimi, visiting an OP that day, remembers watching the seething crowd through the scope of a sniper rifle. Mike, at another OP, remembers calling in to Randy to find out what was happening and being ordered to maintain radio silence.

"Get the hell off the horn," Randy snapped. "We're in trouble here."

Notably, even as their fellow villagers were crying for justice, our ASF soldiers kept their cool. They too were in shock, but they maintained camp security, remained professional, and trusted the ODA to do whatever was needed to restore the peace.

By midafternoon the crowd had swelled to over a hundred strong. Angry but peaceful demonstrations of that size don't always stay peaceful. The Camp Blessing garrison was facing the possibility that it would be forced to defend itself against the very people we had come to Kunar to protect. Unless calmer voices prevailed, there was a tragedy in the making.

Luckily, calmer voices did prevail. While I was in the team house, wondering if I might be going crazy, our three local clerics—Eric, Taroon, and Zawar—were working to keep the crowd's emotions under control. The quick-thinking Taroon had arranged a dozen camp chairs outside the gate so that the less vigorous elders could be comfortable. He and Eric were kneeling in front of these leaders, sharing their sadness about the accident and enlisting their help in keeping the afternoon peaceful. Scott and Randy were also front and center in this process of conciliation, reaching out to the *shura* elders to remind them of the trust we had built up and to ensure them that we would get through this hard time together. At the same time Zawar worked the milling crowd—his congregation—assuring them that, with Allah's aid, a just conclusion would be found to this heart-wrenching event.

Gradually the crowd dispersed. The wailing subsided, and people walked back to Nangalam still angry but consoled by the knowledge that a *shura* would be convened the following day to discuss why the shooting had happened and what should be done about it. In the team house, I felt helpless to affect what was going on, as my presence outside was not going to help the situation.

Late in the afternoon, seeking some solitude on the team house roof, I placed a call to Becky on the sat phone. When her voice came on, I felt some sanctuary. Hearing our boys laughing in the background, I took comfort knowing there was a different world waiting for me once I left this crazy place of violence, intrigue, revenge, hunting humans, and death. My voice nearly cracked every time I tried to speak, but I knew I couldn't burden Becky with what was happening. She could sense I just needed to hear her voice, hear the sounds of my other life, and she didn't ask questions she knew I wouldn't answer. It was an awkward but healing phone call, and it motivated me to do whatever needed to be done to fix the unfixable.

By nightfall I was still shaken but able to look more calmly at what we were facing and to contribute to our discussion about next steps. The ODA was struck by the painful irony that, the following morning, we were going to become the subject of a national news show. *60 Minutes II* had sent a camera crew to report on my team's success as unconventional warriors, and on the eve of their arrival it looked as if the whole thing was about to blow up in our faces.

The timing couldn't be worse. But the facts were that the film crew was now at Camp Vance, that it wouldn't wait forever, and that if there was going to be a story about Hammerhead Six, it would have to be now. I wasn't enthusiastic about the idea but Lieutenant

Colonel Custer, conscious of what we had accomplished and to my mind overly optimistic about us pulling this mess out of the fire, insisted that Logan and her crew should come out as planned.

"She's a seasoned war correspondent," he said. "She's seen worse before."

"Yeah," I said. "But now? Can't this wait a few days?"

"Let her come," he said. "Your team just repelled a frontal assault on the first 'A' Camp in the Afghan war. They can handle a reporter."

It wasn't the reporter I was worried about. It was the mood of a mountain village whose peace I had shattered. I didn't know how long the mullahs' pacification of the crowd would last, and my brain was toggling between pictures of a kumbaya reconciliation and a *60 Minutes II* headline that read GREEN BERET CAMP OVERRUN— MULTIPLE CASUALTIES.

But Custer was confident we would find a bloodless solution. He had been right behind me in the bed of the truck in Nangalam and had witnessed the shooting. He knew the death was an accident and felt strongly that the people would understand. I liked and trusted him, and so I deferred to his judgment. Logan and her crew would arrive in the morning. What would happen then only Allah knew.

Before turning in that night, we held a community meeting with the ODA, the Marines, and the ASF. Taroon started it with a prayer, and then I explained to the company what had happened. Embarrassed and hungry for understanding, I couldn't help but think back to a similar gathering on March 23, when I had publicly "forgiven" the soldiers who had killed the two civilians at the VCP. Now I was the one who was seeking forgiveness. I was thankful that at that previous meeting, I had shown understanding. The faces of our Afghan soldiers told me that they were returning the favor. I prayed that the village of Nangalam would be as generous.

*   *   *

The next day, May 9, started with some unwelcome news. The cameras were expected to arrive around midmorning. Before they did, Lieutenant Colonel Custer regretfully informed us, we were to be dressed in regulation battle dress uniforms and clean-shaven. Good-bye to the SF standard of Tiger Stripes, *pakol* caps, and beards. When Logan arrived, we were to greet her like spic-and-span exemplars of the regular Army.

This was stupid. We weren't regular Army; we were a Special Forces National Guard unit. We hadn't observed sartorial restrictions like these for months; doing so now would give an entirely false impression to the television audience. In addition, if there was ever a time when we—and I particularly—needed to show that we respected Pashtun tradition, this was it. For the Red-Bearded Commander to shave his beard a day after accidently killing a civilian would send a completely off-putting message to the Nangalam community. Our beards were a bridge between us and the Pashtun people. For me to shave would badly undermine my ability to work through the tragedy, because in this culture, a man without a beard commanded no respect. We had seen this on occasions when a clean-shaven senior U.S. officer addressed a local leader and the leader turned to me to offer his response.

The order to shave was a pig-headed example of the military protecting its traditions even when they were clearly counterproductive. This was the Pentagon clinging valiantly to its buggy whips long beyond the point where buggies were useful. I had run into this nonsense before, in Bagram, and had managed to slink around there, bearded but undetected, until a chopper could pick me up and get me back to camp. This time around, I couldn't manage that.

Lieutenant Colonel Custer made me understand the necessity of following the directive. If we didn't shave, he explained, the Army's public affairs folks would withdraw permission for the filming, and the story of our success in the Pech would never be aired. Seeing this bigger picture, we reluctantly obeyed. When the CBS team set down, there were no beards in sight. If you didn't know better, you might have thought that we were a regular Army unit, and that the results we had achieved were representative of the Army's success throughout Afghanistan. That was the not-so-subtle intent behind the "no beards" directive.

But Logan wasn't fooled. She had been around enough to know that in our newly beardless state, we didn't look a lot like Special Forces. When we confirmed that shaving had been a public affairs idea, she was visibly irritated. She had obviously run into the Pentagon image managers before.

The morning before the reporters arrived, we had met with the district leader and key Nangalam elders. When they expressed surprise that my beard was gone, I said that we had shaved in mourning for the loss of the villager. In Pashtun terms that made zero sense, but the white lie had the lucky effect of showing them that we took the killing seriously. We discussed the *shura* set for the next day and how to resolve the incident. As had been the case in the previous two cases of civilian deaths—the VCP shootings and the A-10 gun run—there was a balance to be drawn between justice and mercy. Only this time, I was the one who was caught in that balance.

I had discussed this with Scott and Randy the night before, saying that if we wanted to keep our faith with the people of this valley, if we wanted not to lose everything we built, I would have to offer myself to the elders' justice. I would have to abide by Pashtunwali.

This may sound like a risky and emotional judgment, but I saw it as necessary. If the locals did not feel justice was served, I believed they would wait a few days and then ambush our troops outside the gate or at an OP. Many of the large attacks that cost American blood in Operation Enduring Freedom occurred after civilians had been killed inadvertently and our forces had failed to repair—or even apologize for—the loss of life. In those cases the injured parties sought their own justice. I had no intention of letting anyone kill me, but I had to roll the dice to guarantee that the locals didn't satisfy their sense of balance on other Camp Blessing soldiers.

Randy didn't agree. "That's nuts," he said. "You tell them it's up to them and they're going to kill you."

Maybe. But I believed in my heart that we had built up enough credit that if I came to them honestly penitent, I would be forgiven. I believed, too, that I had to be accountable for what I had done or our mission in the Pech would be lost. Even though it had been an accident, a man's life was gone. I had to show I was willing to pay whatever price this valley demanded. I prayed that it wouldn't be an eye for an eye, but I thought that I had to take the chance, to make it their decision and not mine.

In truth I never believed that they would ask for my life, and I knew that the team would never let it happen. But after all the risks, personal and professional, we had taken up to that point, it seemed appropriate to go all in one more time. We had worked so hard to be accepted as respectful guests that it would seem brash to disrespect their traditions at a moment when respect was suddenly inconvenient.

I knew that failing to handle this matter correctly could have terrible long-term effects. I also figured that submitting myself to Pashtunwali was the best way to keep any vigilantes from taking potshots at my Marines, Green Berets, or ASF guys between now and the following day's *shura*. I would have to live with the accidental death of an innocent Afghan, but I couldn't live with that accident costing a Marine or one of my ODA his life. That was my thinking as I stood before the Pech Valley power brokers.

"We respect your law," I said. "It is for you, the elders, to decide. If it is justice or mercy, we will accept your decision."

It was a gamble, and I can't say I had completely worked out what my response would have been if they had said on the spot, "You must die to settle this." But at the time they said nothing.

I knew two things were going through their minds. They needed justice to be served so their people felt that they were not American lackeys, that their tribal customs were still the law. But on a practical level they also knew that I was an asset to them—a warlord whose respect for them had raised their own status as well as improving the life of their villages. Whatever custom demanded, they knew that asking for my blood made little sense.

Believing this gave me a certain confidence. But I didn't find out right away if it was justified, as the elders took my announcement with the composure I had become accustomed to, nodding slowly, stroking their beards, and uttering a few barely audible "Insh'Allahs." So the die was cast. But I would have to wait a day to discover what it read.

Given the cloud hanging over me, the visit with the reporters went surprisingly well. In the morning, we took them on a patrol to the village of Guru and then up to OP Hammerhead, which proved uneventful but did give them a good idea of the Pech terrain and the difficulty of tracking our adversaries. At the OP, the ASF did a live-fire demonstration with recoilless rifles and RPGs. That night we ran a patrol to the west and then Randy did an interview in the poppy fields. Unfortunately, the night vision on the camera was so good and Randy so easy to identify that for security reasons the footage couldn't be used. Finally, on the morning of May 10, Logan's team accompanied us on an SSE where we were able to secure a cache without busting in doors or arresting anyone.

Logan proved to be an intelligent and charming guest, happy to catch us up on the news from back home. We had some fun at her expense by naming one of our favorite reporters as Bill O'Reilly, the conservative pundit at a rival network, Fox News. She expressed mock indignation, but her questions and educated interest in our mission showed us she bore no hard feelings. Her visit was a refreshing morale booster, and it gave us confidence that she would be able to convey to the American public a fair picture of what we were up to in the Pech Valley.

As interesting as the live firing and cache retrievals seemed to be to the reporters, they were routine for us. What wasn't routine was the *shura* meeting that we had arranged for that afternoon. In most *shura* meetings, I attended as an advisor and sometimes the decider on issues concerning the health or security of a village. In this meeting, I was to be anything but the decider. The issue was my action in the streets of Nangalam, and it was up to the *shura* elders to render a decision.

The meeting was to take place in the district leader's compound— as the seat of local government, an appropriate setting. I was pleased, in spite of the circumstances, that the meeting showed him to be a confident and empowered leader—something that certainly had not been true when we arrived in December. Also in attendance were myself, Mashal, Scott, Randy, Lieutenant Colonel Custer, a Public Affairs official, and Lara Logan's film crew. The PA guy, protective as always of the Army's rep, didn't want the cameras there, but Custer overrode him.

By the time we sat down with the *shura*, I had had a day to think about what I had done and to plan what I might say if I was called to testify in my own defense. I was still shaken by the experience, though, and I never got the chance to prepare my remarks. That turned out to be a lucky break, because in the absence of a canned speech, I was forced to speak from the heart. When the *shura* leader nodded to me, I spoke steadily at first, but had to pause at the end as emotion began showing in my voice.

"We have come to this valley," I said, "to offer our help to you, to build a life that is peaceful for you and your children. We hope you see that we are not just guests in your valley but friends as well. Your happiness is our happiness, too, and your sorrow is our sorrow. When you suffer, we suffer with you. Today I suffer with the family of the man who has died. I come to you as someone who wants to do the right thing and whose heart is breaking because he has done wrong."

I paused. I could have said more but I was afraid I would get choked up. I didn't know what effect my words were having, and I don't think I really considered that very carefully. I wasn't aiming for an effect, only expressing what I truly felt at that moment. In any event, the effect I got was gratifying. The elders murmured to each other for no more than a minute. Then one spoke for the group.

"This was not a crime you intended, but an unfortunate accident. You are like a surgeon. You try to save those who are sick, but you cannot save everyone. You have done so much for us and with us, we cannot let this come between the Americans and the Pashtuns. Sometimes a thing happens that is not in our hands. It is God's will."

He paused and then turned to speak to me as if the other Americans were not present. Placing his hand on his chest, he said, "There will be peace. There will be no blood. This is the will of the family, the *shura*, and our villagers."

He looked me directly in the eyes and nodded to let me know that my offer of the day before had been answered with mercy. To most of the Americans at the meeting, who didn't know about the offer, this probably seemed like a merely cordial acknowledgment.

To Scott and Randy and me—the ones who knew about the gamble—it came as an immense relief and a kind of validation. As other elders spoke, reiterating the same message, it became clear that the villagers valued the progress we had made and were unwilling to place it in jeopardy for the sake of revenge. So I was to live. For pragmatic as well as personal reasons, there would be no *badal*.

The rest of the meeting was arranging for the legal niceties. Negotiations would be made with the slain man's family, and I would be required to pay the blood money that Pashtunwali determined. I would respond to demands of the youth *shura* that such an accident would never happen again. Nangalam would make arrangements to get rid of the dogs. We would renew our faith in each other and we would have lunch.

At the moment when the elder said, "There will be no blood," I was as relieved as I have ever been in my life—relieved that I would be spared, yes, but also that my mistake would not result in my men going home in body bags. Perhaps this relief can be fully understood only by those who have had the responsibility for the lives of others.

Hearing the elder's absolution, I bowed my head, placing my hand on my chest as he had on his, and said, "*Tashakur.*" I could feel the tension draining out of my body. For a second I felt positively light-headed. At the side of the room the CBS camera was rolling. Lara Logan had a smile on her lips and tears in her eyes.

After the meeting broke up, several of the elders came up to me with the same message: We are happy that you are here and that you are our friends. You cannot be held responsible for what is God's will. There was obviously self-interest as well as charity in their showing me mercy. However fully they may or may not have accepted me as their brother, they wanted peace in the valley, they wanted mosques restored, they wanted our help. It's not cynical to say that the spirit of reconciliation was good for us all.

*   *   *

Lara Logan's *60 Minutes II* segment aired on May 19.[1] Becky and friends back home told me they enjoyed it, and even though the team gave me good-natured grief for the screen time devoted to the unnamed "captain," I enjoyed it, too. For what it showed, it was an honest and heartfelt report. It let viewers see that, as Lieutenant Colonel Custer put it, we loved having a mission that went "beyond killing people and breaking things"—that we enjoyed being "part of making a place secure so people have a chance for a normal life." It told how our presence in the Pech had reduced the number of insurgent attacks, how we supported medical care and education, and how we had been successful in securing weapons caches in exchange for assistance. There were nice visuals of the cache retrieval and the *shura* meeting.

What wasn't shown was anything having to do with the shooting incident, with my penitence, or with the *shura*'s decision that there would be no blood. In other words, the most significant events of the days that Logan and her crew spent with us were left completely out of the picture. This wasn't her fault. It was a PA decision that CBS—if it wanted to continue embedding reporters—had to abide by.

This was as ridiculous in its way as showing us without beards, because it put a false, sanitizing gloss over our whole population-centric approach. The public got to keep its image of intrepid warriors, never feeling the gray and never making mistakes. And the Pentagon got to keep its buggy whips.

24

A Shared Struggle

Afghan and American fighting men here continue striving
to accomplish the mission of peace in this land. The struggle in this valley is shared.
—from my remarks at the dedication of Camp Blessing, May 16, 2004

When the elders granted me leniency after the shooting accident,
there was a pragmatic component to their decision. Since we had
been at Camp Blessing, villages up and down the Pech Valley had
seen a decrease in insurgent violence and an increase in prosperity.
We hadn't banished Thomas Hobbes's famous "state of nature"—
poverty and brutishness still stalked these hills—but we had made
significant strides in security, health, education, intercultural understanding, and general welfare. Villagers saw that their lives were
better with the new Afghan government and the Americans in the
valley. Wells had been dug, girls had enrolled in school, arms had
been decommissioned, hundreds had been treated in our clinic, and
numerous mosques were sporting new mortar and paint. Killing
me or driving my team out of the valley would put a stop to these
improvements. It would also risk having us replaced by another
force whose intentions toward the valley's people might not be so
benign. Concern over this possibility surely influenced the population as well as the elders who were their spokesmen.

That May, there was cause for such concern. Although the valley
leadership hadn't been informed of it, our deployment was soon to

end. We had been in-country since September, in the Pech since December, and we were slated to be returned to the States before the end of the month. That was less than three weeks away. Courtney, on an Air Force time line rather than an SF one, had already left. The rest of us had begun to ship back to Bagram what we couldn't fit in our duffels. While I was excited about seeing my family again, I also shared the elders' apprehension about what would happen here when we were gone. Who would follow us? Would they understand what we had accomplished? Would they build on our foundation? Would they even want to?

These questions were very much on my mind as the "A" Camp we had built entered a transition phase. The first signs of the shift came on May 12, as a new Marine contingent arrived by helo and began the Relief in Place of our existing Marines. Slingloads of supplies were dropped by helicopter every couple of days at our three OPs, and the camp was a bustle of activity, with the "old" Marines (the nineteen-year-old veterans) packing up and the new ones receiving orders, supplies, and assignments. On the thirteenth I had a talk with the new kids on the block to be sure they understood the humanitarian as well as the military logic of an "A" Camp— something that doesn't always come easy to these young fire-eaters.

I was wishing I had more time to pound home this message, but you work with what you have, and what I had wasn't long. So I did the same thing I had done with the last platoon. I took all the NCOs and the platoon leader to the girls' school and had them hand out candy and stuffed animals to the girls. I then explained our main role in the valley. "Guys," I said, "we are here to provide security to these people. These are the innocents and the ones we need support from. When we identify our enemies, kill them without mercy, but know that the majority of Afghans here are our friends. We need to treat them as such or they will become the enemy."

Meanwhile, the routine adventures of camp life rock 'n' rolled onward. On the same day that I had my jarhead-recalibration talk, we heard a huge explosion just south of Nangalam. Within twenty minutes a tearful family carried into our clinic the badly mangled body of a small boy. He was gone by the time they arrived. That cut deep into our medics' composure: all three of them had sons about the dead child's age.

The night before the explosion, the Marines had been test-firing their new mortars, and at first we feared that a wayward shell had struck the child. On top of the dog-shooting accident, that would have been a tragedy we couldn't recover from. But the district governor told us that the source of the explosion had been a mine or some other buried ordnance—one of the hundreds of thousands of such hazards left behind by the Russians. One of our ASF patrols confirmed this at the site of the explosion, so we were able to put out the correct story before the rumor mill got rolling and pinned it on us. We took some comfort in knowing that it wasn't our fault.

The following day another victim arrived at the clinic—a young girl whose face had been lacerated when she fell off a roof. Mike worked on her for hours. It's a testament to the grit of the Afghan people—and maybe especially the Afghan women—that this child never uttered a peep as Mike used more than two dozen stitches to close the gashes in her lips and chin. When he gave her a Beanie Baby and a little pink canteen as a reward for her toughness, you would have thought it was her best birthday present ever.

May 16 was a banner day on two fronts. First, villagers completed repairs on the main regional mosque, which stood just outside our front gate serving as the center of worship for a vast mountainous area. Work on this building—as much a community center as a church—had been going on all spring. Its reopening bore witness to a happy irony: we who had entered the valley identified as infidels ended up strengthening the religious community by offering it both respect and material sustenance.

At the same time, I was experiencing a deepening of my own beliefs. On the day that Mike stitched up the little girl, I started by reading scripture before my morning run, and Eric led a Christian service that was spiritually very rewarding. This took place not fifty feet from the mosque we had restored.

The second event of note on May 16 was the formal dedication of Camp Blessing, named in honor of Ranger sergeant Jay Blessing, who had been killed by an IED during Mountain Resolve. As the culmination of our military efforts, this was for us, and for our Afghan soldiers, a very big deal.

The day started for me with a personal surprise. Colonel Herd, after stepping off a CH-53 helicopter with a sizable entourage of VIPs, pulled me aside to tell me two things. One, the preliminary footage for the *60 Minutes II* segment was great. Two, while we would discuss the Report of Survey back at Vance, the decision had been made not to charge me anything for the truck I had destroyed on December 11. I thanked the colonel as I wondered (silently) why it had taken the Army five months to reach that decision. I thought the shift in attitude had something to do with Lara Logan asking embarrassing questions about the incident back at Vance. Some of the team had mentioned the Report of Survey's potential financial stress on me, and she had said she would assist if possible. No matter. I still didn't understand the reasoning behind the Report of Survey in the first place, but the dropping of the matter renewed confidence in my chain of command and somewhat healed a strained relationship between Camp Blessing and the CJSOTF. The news was a perfect start to this momentous day.

Between the Afghan dignitaries and the American brass, there must have been two dozen VIPs gracing our camp that day, including the Combined Joint Task Force 76 commander, Maj. Gen. Eric Olson. With the exception of a Marine squad keeping watch on each of our three OPs, the entire camp contingent formed up for the dedication ceremony. The ASF looked crisp and proud in their Tiger Stripes, and the ODA donned Army uniforms instead of Tiger Stripes to avoid any confusion among the Americans.

The ceremony was held in front of a monument that had been Randy's idea and that had been built up, stone by stone, over the previous few weeks. Facing the monument, on the left were the American VIPs, on the right the local *shura* and district leadership, and in the center the ASF, Marines, and ODA. On this blustery day, an American and an Afghan flag flapped wildly, looking like sentinels of peace against the winds of war.

As the soldiers came to attention, I started by welcoming the assembled bigwigs to "the beautiful Pech Valley" and announcing that we had come together to dedicate the camp "to not only the memory of Sgt. Jay Blessing but to the mission that he gave his life to accomplish." Then I shared some comments that I'll quote in full here because, more than a decade after we left the valley, they still seem to me an honest summary of what we did there.

This camp was begun last year and was manned by American forces working to bring peace to a war-torn area of Afghanistan and drive terrorists out. Since that time the camp has been built, strengthened, and run by an SF and Marine contingent and a company of Afghan patriots. Both Afghan and American fighting men here continue striving to accomplish the mission of peace in this land. The struggle in this valley is shared, and the gratitude for the sacrifice of men like Jay

Blessing is deep and sincere. While the gratitude of American servicemen is based on shared beliefs, a creed that we believe in, and the freedoms that we enjoy, the Afghan patriots are living and willing to die so their families may enjoy the freedoms and opportunities that men like Sgt. Blessing have ensured for the American people. The Afghan soldiers here today would like their gratitude to be felt by the Ranger Regiment and the Blessing family.

The monument behind me, built of rock and mortar, is meant to last as a memorial for American and Afghan soldiers alike to remember Jay and others that have given the ultimate sacrifice; and to cause each of us to rededicate ourselves to the struggle for freedom and liberty.

The theme of this speech—a shared struggle of U.S. and Afghan soldiers—was central to my thinking about our mission, and about our responsibility, as far as it was within our power, to leave the valley in the capable stewardship of its own patriotic fighting men. Although none of the three media reports on Hammerhead Six had emphasized this, I felt then, and I feel now, that the most important thing we did in our time in Afghanistan was to prepare the Afghans to run things when we were gone. As far as I was concerned, that *was* our mission.

After my comments, an officer from the Ranger Regiment gave a short, moving eulogy and a Ranger unit recited (or rather yelled out) the Ranger Creed. There was a particularly emotional moment when a captain from Blessing's unit accepted a folded flag of honor that had flown over our camp, and a particularly impressive few minutes when we offered Jay Blessing and others killed in action a twenty-one-gun salute. Usually such an honor is rendered in cannon or rifle fire at places like Arlington National Cemetery. We did it Pech Valley style, with three rounds each of six mortar firings followed by one rocket. This wasn't Pentagon SOP, but it worked for us, and the VIPs seemed to agree it was an impressive display.

After the gun salute, Major General Olson and Colonel Herd did a ribbon cutting, closing the day's ceremonial agenda. Olson was then pulled in various directions by VIPs who wanted a word or a photo op with him. He accommodated them, but he also took the time to deliver a brief congratulation to our Afghan troops.

The gesture of respect was not lost on them. Earlier in the day, some of them had wondered aloud "Who is that guy?" With his head as well as his face clean-shaven, Olson didn't fit the picture of the Special Forces soldiers they had come to know, so you had to forgive them for asking about his status—and about why the Red-Bearded Commander was paying him such deference. Up to that point many of them seemed to assume that I reported directly to President Bush. When they learned that Olson was not only my superior but in charge of all U.S. military operations in Afghanistan, they were duly impressed. When he stood before them, ramrod tough in his battle dress uniform and flanked by a proud interpreter, it was an important official recognition of what they had achieved. In a brief address, this is what he said:

Today we honor a courageous American soldier and patriot who fought here. But we also honor American soldiers and Afghan soldiers who continue to fight. They fight together, shoulder to shoulder, against the threat to Afghanistan and against the threat to the entire world. You are the front line. You are the defense that the world has against a horrible terrorist threat. You are brave, you are courageous, and you are fighting for a noble cause. It is a great honor for me to fight side by side with you. Thank you very much. We will continue to fight, shoulder to shoulder together, until we win. Thank you for your service to your nation, and thank you for your service to the coalition.

Throughout this accolade, I was lined up with my team facing the men we had trained. I could see the pride and gratitude on their faces as Olson complimented them, and I felt enormous satisfaction myself, for what they and we had managed to accomplish together.

But I knew that our relationship was about to end. That gave a poignant twist to my feelings—a twist that, as Olson spoke, I actually felt physically. Standing behind the ODA at that point was a line of the village elders with whom we had tasted tea and empathy in so many councils. One of them, standing directly behind me, placed a hand on my shoulder and held it there through the general's salute to the troops. This startled me for a second, until I recognized it as a sign of affection that was not out of place in a culture where grown men holding hands was a common practice.

In the few moments that the old man's hand rested on my shoulder, my mind clicked through a litany of possible interpretations. Given the circumstances, with the valley seemingly at peace and ODA 936 on the way out, it could have been a sign of gratitude, such as a petitioner might give a prince; or of approval, such as a father might give his son. It might have indicated the elder's appreciation for our having protected his people, or a reminder that they had also protected us. It might have been a plea for us not to abandon him: Was his touch a request for physical support, a symbolic act of holding us back, a way of saying, "You cannot go"? Or was it simply his way of saying good-bye? Maybe it was all of these things. That was what it felt like.

By the end of that windy spring day, our "A" Camp had received official recognition as Camp Blessing. We had been calling it that for months, so it was nice to have the name solidified in the eyes of command. But there was also, I have to admit, an unstated political purpose to the dedication ceremony. I wanted the military and policymakers to feel connected to Camp Blessing so they would be less likely to break our promises and frustrate the expectations of those in the valley who had, with some risk to themselves, thrown their lot in with us. After we left, I didn't want our nation's indigenous allies to be abandoned as they had been in Vietnam and in other places where Green Berets had died next to local fighters. Making a big deal of the dedication invited U.S. ownership of the "A" Camp model. It meant (I hoped) that support for our "Afghan patriots" wouldn't evaporate when we were gone.

The people of the Pech Valley had risked a lot by partnering with us. I felt strongly that this merited a commitment from our military to insure continued support for the valley's people until they were able to fend off extremists like Abu Ikhlas without our assistance. I was painfully aware that, although we may have made him irrelevant for the time being, he and his AQ followers had not been neutralized. We may have won our private war, but they were still in the game.

By dusk on the sixteenth, the dignitaries were back in their helos and the big day was over. We still had a week or so before our own exfil, though, and an officially surnamed "A" Camp to run in the interim. We got back to business, and things returned to what passed for normal. As the RIP continued and as we met some of the 3rd Special Forces Group Green Berets who were going to be our immediate replacements, there was still the close watch on the hills, and still the routine patrols, camp improvements, school visits, clinic visits—the standard mix.

On May 20, just a few days before we shipped out, we had a more exciting day than usual. In the field, our ASF guys were showing that they had earned their bragging rights as a security force. Two of their squads ran a CONOP in the northern valley, while another, platoon-sized force retrieved two separate arms caches near Kanday village. I wrote in my journal the following day that it was "satisfying to see the ASF receive intel from friends or relatives and then act on it to recover caches. We are sending them to do independent operations more and more." *Satisfying* was an understatement. It felt fantastic to see the local indigs taking charge of their valley.

There was also some excitement back at camp that day. Around noon, Mike was in the clinic when a teenaged boy walked in with a clumsily bandaged hand that had been smashed, he said, by a boulder. This was another one of those cases where *boulder* might have been code for "botched IED," but to our senior medic, that wasn't relevant. He sat the boy down and, unwrapping the bandage, discovered that his middle two fingers had been "degloved," that is, the skin had been peeled completely back to the knuckles, exposing the bone. The ends of the fingers were crushed, leaving only the metacarpals—the sections between the knuckles and the first joints—as salvageable bone.

"When I saw what had happened," Mike recalls, "I knew I would have to amputate what was left of the digits and then try to fold the stripped skin back over the metacarpals. That would have been a tricky job for a Beverly Hills hand surgeon with a cabinet of surgical tools. Unfortunately, we were so near the end of the tour that I had already shipped most of my surgical kit forward to Bagram."

What he hadn't yet shipped forward was his Leatherman tool—that multiblade pocket device that is like a Swiss Army knife on steroids. So, assisted by his fellow medic Randy, our CA guy James Trusty, and a Navy corpsman, Mike got the kid sedated, sterilized the Leatherman tool, and began to do what Special Forces soldiers do best: improvise in unrehearsed situations.

Luckily, our pharmacy still had plenty of drugs. With the boy in dreamland thanks to a mixture of atropine, ketamine, valium, lidocaine, and morphine, Mike used the Leatherman to saw the shattered digits off and file the metacarpals down, then folded the flaps of skin over the stumps and sutured them closed. With James watching the patient's airway and Randy monitoring painkiller and antibiotic levels, the operation lasted almost four hours. The kid woke up that evening groggy and a bit bewildered. He wouldn't be making a living as a concert violinist, but thanks to Mike's resourcefulness and surgical skills, he would have the use of a hand that might easily have been lost.

This was just days before our time in the Pech would end. We were short-timers for sure. But as Yogi Berra liked to say, "It ain't over till it's over." Mike made us all proud that day, just as the ASF was making us proud. I wrote in my journal that night, "We have gotten good at conducting multiple operations, and we do it fairly well." I was thinking of recon patrols as well as finger surgery, and I was hoping that after we were gone, whoever took our place would be half as good at improvising as Mike Montoya.

25

Nanawatay

Nanawatay means repentance over past hostility or inimical attitudes and the granting of asylum. Walking down to someone under Nanawatay means having an expression or attitude of submission—a combination of humility, sorrow, and apology—and giving space to the other person to respond with "grace."

—S. Fida Yunas, *Character Traits: Customs/Traditions/Practices of the Pashtuns*

Take heed to yourselves. If thy brother trespass against thee, rebuke him; and if he repent, forgive him.

—Luke 17:3

The dedication of Camp Blessing provided a formal, celebratory ending to our Pech Valley experience. But for my team, and especially for me personally, there was another, informal ceremony to be performed before we could leave the valley with our minds at ease. We had to compensate the family of the shopkeeper whose life had been ended by a ricochet from my M4. His name, we learned, was Ahmed. Even though the Nangalam elders had ruled that the law of exchange (*badal*) would not require my blood, Pashtunwali still demanded that Ahmed's family receive a symbolic "blood payment" partly in money and partly in goods. In this valley, that meant goats and rice.

The money part of this reckoning was settled in a meeting with Ahmed's brother. This was the man who, on the day of the tragedy, had leaped into the truck with the victim's body and inflamed the soft spring air with the sounds of his wailing. When he came to the camp again, a couple of days later, he was composed, even respectful. He knew, he told me, that I had not intended harm to his brother and that, as it was Allah's will that he died, he would honor the elders' decision not to seek revenge. But he was now the sole guardian of Ahmed's children—Ahmed's wife had died some time ago—and he would need monetary help to care properly for these two young ones. This was the first time I heard that I had orphaned two children.

After some debate and consultation with Mashal, the brother and I agreed on a cash payment of $2,500. This was on the high end of the scale for accidental shooting victims, but as the fee was to cover the care of the children, and as I was not in a good position to split hairs, I agreed to the sum. The brother and I parted amiably, our hands resting on our chests in acknowledgment of our shared sadness.

For the noncash part of the compensation payment, I had to go to the home of the man I had killed to make a peace offering to his other relatives and ask for their forgiveness. In Pashtun tradition, I was to learn later, this is known as seeking "asylum" or "doing *nanawatay*." I undertook this final obligation the following day.

Accompanied by Scott, Randy, Mashal, and an ASF squad, I walked through Nangalam, past the spot where the shooting had happened, and then continued a few hundred yards up a dirt trail to the hamlet that Ahmed had called home. Behind us we led, on rope leashes, two young goats; in each ASF soldier's rucksack was a twenty-five-pound bag of rice. It was a short walk on a beautiful day, but I was conscious that it was also a penitential journey, and I hoped that at the end I would find absolution.

In the hamlet—so small that no mapmaker had labeled it—we met a handful of village elders in a humble adobe house. We sat around a rug in a small room, drinking tea and eating candied pecans, while with Mashal's help I explained again how much I regretted this terrible accident, and how much I felt that the sorrow I had brought here was my sorrow, too. Since no one introduced himself as a member of Ahmed's family, I thought perhaps that the elders were acting on their behalf—or that, aside from his brother and children, Ahmed had no other survivors. I would have welcomed that information; it would have limited the circle of people my action had harmed.

In any event, like the *shura* that had pronounced "no blood," these elders too accepted my penitence, and with one exception they seemed to appreciate the effort we were making to honor their customs.

The exception was a short, white-bearded man who sat darkly off to the side. In appearance he reminded me of the proud, irascible dwarves in *Lord of the Rings*. Throughout the meeting, he kept to himself, every so often glancing at us—at me, I thought—with unregenerate hostility. He didn't participate in the conversation, gave no indication of approval, and seemed throughout the encounter a wraith sent to put our cordiality to the test. Even when he wasn't looking directly at me, I had the sense that he was silently condemning me.

After half an hour, the elders acknowledged the goats and rice and proclaimed that, on behalf of the family, they accepted them, along with the money to the brother, as payment of my obligation. I was puzzled about the whereabouts of the family itself—who they were, and why these elders were their spokesmen—but I let that pass, thankful that the peace offering had been found acceptable. The meeting had gone as well as could be expected.

"Is that it?" I asked Mashal. "Is the debt now paid?"

"Yes," he replied. "There is nothing further that you need to do."

But there was. Something wasn't right. I felt it bone-deep, like something that went beyond protocol, beyond obligation.

As we got up to make our farewells, as we shook hands with the elders and thanked them for their understanding, I caught the eye again of the man in the corner. He hadn't budged. He regarded me now with the same baleful pain that had shadowed this hour of détente from the beginning. I felt that if I didn't confront his darkness before leaving this place, I would never be free of it.

"Who is that man?" I asked Mashal.

The answer hit me hard.

"He is Ahmed's father. This is his house."

Instantly the old man's dark stare became understandable. In looking at me across a small room of his own home, he was seeing not the Red-Bearded Commander, not an American soldier, not the latest of the countless foreigners who had occupied his country. He was seeing only the man who killed his son.

I thought immediately of my own two little boys, safe at home with Becky, and I ached to think what I would feel if a soldier from halfway around the world took one of them away. I thought of what my own father—a seasoned soldier himself—would feel if someone killed me. And I was overwhelmed with pity and shame and sorrow for the agony that I had brought, unwittingly but undeniably, to this black-eyed, smoldering Afghan. And then, in an instant, I knew what I had to do. This was the man I had to beg for asylum.

I walked across the room and stood before him. The anger in his face was unremitting. I dropped to one knee and, as I had witnessed others doing to me, reached up and gently grasped his beard.

For what was probably thirty seconds but seemed like hours, the old man held my gaze, his eyes hard-edged and implacable. I felt for that long moment that if he could have cut me down on the spot, he would have done so. Then suddenly, without transition, he began to cry. The blackness washed away, and his face shivered with tenderness. He reached an arm around my head and pulled me to him in a tight embrace.

I came to my feet and returned the embrace. For a long time—so long that I lost track of where I was, of anything in the room but him and me—we held each other close, silently sobbing.

Rarely have I felt so connected to another human being. For a few extraordinary moments, there was no politics or religion, no East or West, no competition or judgment or even awareness of the things that set the planet's peoples against each other. It was just two human beings, two fathers, sharing a deep sorrow that had become, in the alchemy of mercy, a somber acceptance.

As we finally parted from each other and nodded good-bye, I could see that everyone who had witnessed what happened had felt it too. In a room full of young soldiers and aging mujahideen, there was an eerie hush as tear-streaked faces turned to each other in wonder and thanksgiving. I had walked down in *nanawatay* and found forgiveness.

On the way back to camp, I felt almost light-headedly peaceful, and when we arrived there, it was clear that news of what happened had preceded us. It seemed that everybody at Camp Blessing—Afghans, the ODA, the Marines—wanted to shake my hand or give me a hug. They knew something small but spectacular had happened up the trail.

I knew it too. I don't use the word *magic* lightly, but there was something magical about that encounter with poor Ahmed's father. On a very personal level, it stretched me, enriched my faith in humanity, made me searingly aware of how similarly fragile and connected all of us are.

I saw this recognition, too, as a fittingly elevated climax to our sojourn here. The fact that a Special Forces A-Team could share with Afghan villagers such a profoundly emotional experience made me see, with a quiet pride, that our mission in the Pech had been a success in a way that neither the media nor our senior commanders ever fully understood.

They saw that we had made some headway in reducing the influence of insurgents, had improved the valley's living conditions, and had brought a semblance of stability to a war-weary region. They might have hoped that we had captured one of our two main quarries, Abu Ikhlas or Gulbuddin Hekmatyar, but they were pleased to see that we had made them far less relevant.

I saw something different—something that was even more evanescent than an Al Qaeda ghost, and that the embrace of Ahmed's father had shown me was real. I saw that for a moment he and I had gone beyond friend, enemy, Afghan, American, Christian, Muslim, villager, soldier. I saw that he was just a man like me. A father like me. I saw that, as we strove to be good guests—guests worthy of hospitality and of respect—we had captured something more precious than a high-value target. Working with the Afghan people, breaching ancient walls of pitiless scorn, we had managed for a time to look into each other's hearts.

Afterword

Lessons Learned

We were looking generations down the line, trying to affect kids who didn't yet have an anti-American paradigm. When the new guys came in, all of that got washed down the stream.

—Randy Derr

When we left Kunar Province in the spring of 2004, we were feeling exhilarated about what we had accomplished. In our time at Camp Blessing, we had improved the Pech Valley's health, education, and welfare; trained a defense force capable of providing security for thousands of villagers; won friends among the *shuras*, district leaders, mullahs, and general population; and created an atmosphere where the locals were far less hospitable to insurgent influence.

There were still troublemakers in the shadows. But because of our focus on winning hearts and minds, their ability to recruit new fighters and to mobilize neutrals to their cause had been rendered nearly impotent. U.S.–Afghan relations in our AO were at an all-time high, and many of the refugees who had fled to Pakistan during the Taliban period were returning to their homes in an uncharacteristically calm Pech Valley.

The valley's people saw this change gratefully, and on the day we left, they showed their appreciation in a warm send-off. For security reasons we had not told any Afghans the exact day of our departure, but they knew it was coming. On the morning of May 25, we shaved our beards, donned U.S. Army uniforms, and left our "A" Camp for the last time. Hearing the sound of helo rotors west up the valley, the ASF knew the end of the Hammerhead Six deployment had arrived. On the way to the landing zone, we passed through a gauntlet of emotional ASF soldiers. There were few words exchanged, but the bittersweet feeling was palpable in handshakes and embraces, in the glint of half-suppressed tears in the soldiers' eyes.

Also seeing us off were kids from the primary school, the district leader, elders, and a large crowd of villagers. Like the ASF—and like us—they were visibly moved at this moment of departure. As we approached the LZ and got ready to board, we could see, pushing to the front of the crowd, the teenager whose smashed fingers Mike had labored over five days before. He was waving with his neatly bandaged hand and smiling sadly.

And then it was over. One moment Randy and I were standing on the LZ as the rest of the team boarded the helicopter. Another and we were on the loading ramp ourselves, looking out one last time at our mountain home. Once we were airborne, the pilot left the ramp of the Chinook down for several minutes, allowing us to see the poppy fields, the Pech River, the villages of Manogay and Nangalam, and Camp Blessing fade into indistinctness.

With my "kingdom" disappearing in the distance, I reflected on our war in the Pech. We had come to secure the area, deny the enemy a sanctuary, and make the area friendly to American troops and the new Afghan government. I thought we had done well on all those counts. My team thought so, too, even as we realized that there was still much to be done. As Randy later put it poignantly, "Think of what we could have done if we stayed another year."

As I thought about the connection we had made with the people and the relative peace that our efforts had brought to this land, I dared to ask myself, Did we win? I thought, at that moment, that the answer was yes. Whatever was happening in Kabul, elsewhere in Afghanistan, or Washington, I believed that in this one small valley, as unconventional forces in a small, almost private war, we had emerged victorious. With guns and sweat, respect and conviction, we had made a difference.

I wasn't alone in this belief. When we arrived at Camp Vance an hour later, we were swamped with people offering us congratulations. The *60 Minutes II* piece had just come out, so we were viewed, here and at home, as the celebrities of the hour. At lunch Colonel Herd called me "the most famous ODA commander in the Army," and said that if CBS had hired professional actors, they couldn't have been more impressive on-screen than my Green Berets. Later, we met in his office where he asked me a question.

"What your guys did at Camp Blessing ought to become the model for all of Afghanistan. Do you think that's possible, Captain? Can it be replicated?"

To me the answer was obvious. "Yes, sir," I said. "But it takes work. If a team involves itself in the local community like we did, if it really wants to protect the people and make them prosper, then yes. It can be done."

That, apparently, was the answer he was hoping to hear. On his laptop he pulled up a PowerPoint presentation that he was giving that afternoon to a cluster of generals. One of the slides had a map of the Pech Valley with Camp Blessing circled as the focus of the show. He told me enthusiastically how, if we could place "A" Camps like ours in dozens of Afghan valleys, their spheres of influence would spread so that the entire country would be changed. If our small private victory could be replicated by dozens of other "A" Camps, the enemy would have no place to stand.

It was the "ink spot" theory of counterinsurgency: start small and spread outward, like a drop of ink spreads throughout a napkin. It sounded great to me. I was convinced that it could happen. If.

Over the next few days, as we prepared for the final hop home, we received similar expressions of confidence from a long stream of officers and NCOs, including the CENTCOM chief of staff, a Marine major general, and even Gen. Bryan Brown, overall commander of U.S. Special Operations Command. The White House, it seemed, was impressed with the contribution we had made to the War on Terror by rolling up our sleeves and thinking beyond our guns. I received these plaudits gratefully on behalf of my team. They had worked their butts off for months, and the sweat had paid off. I was immensely proud of their efforts.

Given all this public recognition, you might have thought that the "Camp Blessing model" would quickly become a new normal. Everyone from DOD on down was saying that our version of counterinsurgency should be replicated. Logically, this insight would have a major impact on policy.

It didn't. The forces replacing us viewed our population-centric strategy as too "passive." They preferred a more conventional, enemy-centric approach that would send troops aggressively into the Korengal Valley to stamp out hornets' nests. Almost immediately, they mounted search-and-destroy missions that increased the Taliban body count but that also increased collateral damage. This quickly eroded the goodwill we had built up, turned formerly neutral villagers against the Americans, and created whole new legions of revenge-seeking jihadists: cadres of "accidental guerrillas."[1]

In a vicious circle, U.S. planners added yet more troops, and the coalition became a new player in the "eye for an eye" blood economy. Instead of bearded Special Forces leading a counterinsurgency effort, with Marines serving as security and additional muscle, conventional forces took over the counterinsurgency responsibilities themselves. The "A" Camp model, designed to protect the local population, was replaced by a series of combat outposts (COPs) whose function seemed to be to protect their own occupants. Instead of our local Afghan troops patrolling the hills, the Afghan National Army deployed a couple of battalions with limited tribal and ethnic ties to the local villages.

Given the history of the region, it should have been easy to predict how the locals would react. Marines were targeted and killed. The enemy rallied the locals to expel the foreign invaders. As casualties mounted, the Americans added still more troops. In 2008, at the height of greater Pech Valley operations, there were 800 American troops and 2,000 Afghan troops in the area that in 2004 we had managed with 60 Americans (Green Berets and Marines) and a company of 110 Afghans. A force of 170 had been replaced by a force of 2,800, with little but additional casualties to show for the increase.

A year after our departure, in the Korengal Valley five miles southeast of Camp Blessing, as portrayed in the 2007 book and the 2014 film *Lone Survivor*, nineteen Americans lost their lives in the tragic mission known as Operation Red Wings. Shortly thereafter, a soldier depicted in the documentary film *Restrepo* called the Korengal "the deadliest place on earth"; it eventually claimed the lives of forty-two Americans. In the summer of 2008, in the Waygal Valley five miles north of Camp Blessing, nine Americans were killed and twenty-seven wounded in the village of Wanat in the bloodiest single battle of the Afghan war. Intel reports showed that the attack force, numbering two hundred, was composed largely of locals rejecting the American presence there. In 2011, the U.S. military pulled out of the Pech Valley in the first real retreat of the war. By that time, more than a hundred Americans had lost their lives there.

I do not pretend that I understand all the factors through which a relatively pacified Pech slipped back into carnage. I do know that, by working peacefully by, with, and through its local population, the soldiers of ODA 936 created a spirit of cooperation that facilitated our success and that, if only for a moment, helped to keep violence at bay. I firmly believe that if the lessons we learned there had been studied by those in charge of the war—if the generals, Pentagon staffers, and policymakers had truly sought to replicate our mission—the American chapter of the Pech Valley story might have turned out differently.

All of which raises a disturbing question.

If a Special Forces experiment—the population-centric "A" Camp model—had such success in pacifying the congenitally turbulent Pech Valley, why was it replaced with a conventional enemy-centric strategy that had already proved the undoing of the British and the Russians, and that with awful rapidity once again made the region a graveyard for Americans? Or, to ask the question from a strategic perspective, why were conventional forces put in charge of an unconventional war? The military logic escapes me. It escapes my battalion commander, Lt. Col. Marcus Custer, too. In a recent conversation, he said ruefully, "We would never put an Army general in charge of a naval blockade, an Air Force general in charge of an amphibious assault, or a Marine general in charge of an air campaign. So why do we put conventional generals, leading conventional troops, in charge of fighting an unconventional war?"

I have yet to hear a satisfactory explanation. But I believe it's important to ask the question—and to question the answer. Doing so may help us understand how defeat was seemingly snatched from the jaws of victory.

There are other questions that might also be asked—questions about how, for a while, terrorists were marginalized and the beleaguered people of the Pech saw Americans as friends. I've said that my team won its small, private war, and I believe I've given sufficient evidence in this book to support that claim. It's worth asking, therefore, why we were successful. What did we do that was different in the local folks' eyes? Why did they weep rather than cheer when we flew away?

Was part of it appearances? We looked like them, more than any military force had done before or after. Was it our beards and our *pakol* caps that made them take to us? Did they see that this wasn't just dress-up, but respect for their culture?

Was it that, in building them a security force, we hired local men—the elders' own sons—rather than importing national army soldiers from distant Kabul?

Was it that we worked hard to limit collateral damage? Or that, when it happened, we owned our mistakes and agreed to make amends? Was our respect for the local tribal code a factor in our success?

Was the fact that ODA 936 was made up of National Guardsmen instead of active duty personnel a factor? Did being outside the Big Army tent give us greater flexibility and less worry about decisions that might have impacted our careers? And did our maturity as husbands and fathers with civilian experience positively impact how we interacted with Afghan husbands and fathers?

Did the experience some of us had as Mormon missionaries affect how we viewed the "cultural immersion" experience? And what did it mean to the locals that we respected their religion?

Or did our small footprint—a complement of less than two hundred—make it easier for locals to see us as guests rather than an occupying army?

Probably all of these things played some role in making the ODA 936 deployment a break in the pattern. But what does that say about the Afghan war, about the role of unconventional warfare in such a conflict, about other small wars in the twenty-first century? What does the Hammerhead Six experience tell us about where we go from here?

In the past decade, I've thought a lot about that question. I've considered the lessons my team learned in the Pech Valley and thought about how they might bring clarity to the use of unconventional warfare and counterinsurgency. I've written this book partly to share those principles with other Special Forces commanders and NCOs who might, in other valleys at other times, be facing challenges similar to the ones we faced.

For the Special Forces of the future, then, I'll end this book by laying out seven general principles about unconventional warfare and counterinsurgency that the Hammerhead Six tour of duty showed me were true. I believe that when you find yourself in a foreign land simmering with unknown unknowns, these known knowns may help you find your way. They may mitigate culture shock by helping you see the locals—the people you are there to liberate—as fellow human beings. They may help you to accomplish your mission. They may even help you save lives—including your own.

Lessons Learned

One Green Beret equals one hundred rifles. All Special Operations forces are capable of executing Direct Action missions. The Green Beret is the only asset in the Defense Department's arsenal with the proven legacy and skill set to inspire, train, and lead irregular forces. That is what is meant by the expression that one Green Beret equals one hundred rifles. A Green Beret turns indig villagers into soldiers fighting on our side and prepared to take over the fight when we are gone.

In our ODA, it was a common joke that if a SEAL and a Green Beret were dropped off in an enemy-infested jungle for six months, the SEAL would come out with longer hair and a memoir and the Green Beret would come out with an army. As a Green Beret, conducting missions by, with, or through indigenous forces is what makes you an exponential commando, a true force multiplier. Nobody else even tries to do this. So build on this strength. Embrace what makes you unique.

Master your craft. Educate yourself. Don't assume you know everything when you complete your training. Before you deploy, spend as much time as you can studying the people, culture, economy, and history of whatever area your Special Forces Group is responsible for. I learned more about the Pashtuns and the enemy we were sent to fight from reading Ahmed Rashid's book *Taliban* than I did in any intelligence brief the Army provided. Do not expect the Army to bring you up to speed. You need to be a self-taught expert about your own Area of Operations and to take to heart any lessons you can glean from other units who have served in the area where you will deploy.

Maturity matters. Every day, the military takes high school graduates and turns them into Marines, Rangers, paratroopers, and SEALs. This is not feasible for Green Berets. Unconventional warfare requires the Green Beret to be older, wiser, and more experienced than conventional forces or other Special Ops units. In the Pech Valley, we had to establish rapport with Pashtun males who had wives and kids and who were making a living on an acre of poppies and a small herd of goats. That was tough enough for us, with our own families and varied work experiences. To expect an eighteen-year-old Marine or Army infantryman to do it is unrealistic. To understand older people's struggles, it helps to be a little gray in the beard yourself.

"Thinking like a Green Beret" means being able to think out of the box and take calculated risks. Developing those abilities takes some life experience. In our case, we were all trained soldiers, but we also had on board a former train engineer, an ICU nurse, a gem dealer, former missionaries with overseas experience, a police officer, and several entrepreneurs. This gave us a wide repertoire of problem-solving ideas and experiences to draw upon when unconventional solutions were required.

It is my strong feeling that SF should be the mature brain trust of Special Operations and should not be diluted with young, inexperienced soldiers. If the SF community needs to be expanded beyond what the Army can provide, it would be best to allow select Marines, SEALs, and Air Force personnel, with significant experience and a desire to learn unconventional warfare, to try out and be selected for a temporary or permanent branch transfer to Army Special Forces.

Embrace the gray. Throughout our history, Special Forces have applied risk, bravery, brashness, and unconventional thinking to achieve great things. Often these things have been accomplished in gray zones of uncertainty. But as a Green Beret, the guidelines that conventional soldiers live by are a luxury that you may not always have. The Army does not understand or trust your unconventional skills, tactics, and thinking, but it wants the results that only you can achieve. You may risk your career by making decisions that only you know are right. Make them anyway.

You must learn to be comfortable making moral, legal, ethical, political, and economic decisions in cultures that do not share all your values. You may be asked to make assurances that your government may not uphold. Promise only what you are confident you can deliver. You will be forced to balance the goals and motivations of the indigs and the goals of the American people and the U.S. government. They will not always align. To negotiate effectively in this gray zone, you must remember that at all times, the mission and the welfare of your team must trump all other factors.

Think beyond your guns. As frustrating as it sometimes is for soldiers trained in the art of warfare, our best weapons in counterinsurgency and UW are not always our guns. As Sun Tzu said, "To subdue the enemy without fighting is the acme of skill." In counterinsurgency we are not just fighting the enemy, we are trying to undermine his cause by reducing its attraction to the local people. We are selling our vision of the future versus that of our enemy. Civil Affairs, information operations, and breaking bread with local leaders will sometimes accomplish this more effectively than Direct Action.

The funding for such outreach must be managed carefully. All conflicts have a budget in treasure and blood that, if squandered, will lead to defeat, retreat, or "tactical redeployment" prior to mission accomplishment. When money is thrown around haphazardly, with little accountability, the focus shifts from exchanging value to prying as much money as possible from the "sucker" Americans. That does not engender partnership or respect.

In the Pech Valley, we found that community outreach, or civic action programs—clinics, schools, mosque restoration—had a significant impact on the populace and gave a great return on investment. They worked best when we observed two principles: (a) Spread the wealth. A small project done twenty times in various villages will have more impact than a single huge endeavor that never gets completed or affects only one part of the population or one contractor. (b) Make your aid conditional on local support.

Build the bridge not as a bribe for the uncommitted, but as a reward for friendship already demonstrated.

Mistakes are opportunities. Be assured that you will make mistakes. The test of a true Green Beret is to own those mistakes, to take responsibility for them, and to work with the injured parties to fix the unfixable. All too often, when an outside force causes unintentional damage to a local population, the unspoken reaction is to minimize the tragedy ("That's just the way war is") or, worse, to disclaim responsibility. In addition to being insensitive, this can have disastrous outcomes for your entire operation.

So when you screw up, admit it and ask for understanding. Be willing to work with local authorities and customs to resolve tensions. In UW, you don't have the luxury of walking away from tragedies. You must resolve them in honest dialogue with those you have harmed. Because we did this in all three of our collateral damage incidents, we not only survived but deepened the sense of trust we had established. A little humility will go a long way in winning the human terrain.

Give a damn. To earn the trust of a local population, you have to care about them—and show that you care. Showing local people that you respect them and are concerned for their welfare is neither passive nor irrelevant. It's how you win hearts and minds, and is therefore highly productive. It's also less expensive than Direct Action. As our commo sergeant Roger Wilcox liked to say, "Bullets cost money. Kindness is free."

Giving a damn isn't easily faked. The indigs you meet may be uneducated by American standards, but they will know when you really care, when you really respect them and their culture, and when you are just trying to manipulate or coerce them to do your will. Fake it and they will sense your condescension, will turn and run in the face of fire, and may just slit your throat as you sleep (it's happened before). Give a damn for real and you will find loyal men who will walk miles and miles in the hills looking for a common enemy, taste your food to check for poison, and risk their own lives in a firefight to keep you from harm.

Giving a damn also means respecting the local culture and religion as you would your own. This may not require you to wear a beard or local garb in all locations. It does require that you be neither disrespectful nor patronizing. Our intel sergeant Scott Jennings puts it well: "Attitude counts. If you go in feeling superior to the Afghans, you're going to fail." In the Pech Valley we succeeded partly because we weren't there to turn Islam into Christianity or Nangalam into Peoria. We did not personally agree with a lot of the Afghan culture or religion, but we accepted that their culture and religion were important *to them*, and we acted accordingly. If you want to be seen as guests rather than occupiers, you cannot do otherwise.

As Hammerhead Six, ODA 936 lived in a region of northeastern Afghanistan that after our departure became known to coalition forces as the Valley of Death. Yet we served there for six months with no one killed in action, and managed in that time to forge friendships that overcame ancient barriers of culture and religion. I do not believe that we were simply lucky.

What I believe is that in merging our goals and in sincerely attempting to serve and protect the local people, we ended up being protected by them. Entering the valley as guests, we were treated as guests. That did not make us invulnerable to enemy bullets, but it reduced the number of bullets available to the enemy and the number of locals willing to join their ranks. Maybe that was why we made progress. It might have been the ultimate reason we came out alive.

Many who came after us were not so lucky. In Afghanistan, as in so many other places throughout our history, brave men and women have laid down their lives for the ideals that make this nation great. They deserve the utmost gratitude and respect from this nation and from the citizens of Afghanistan who benefitted from their sacrifice. As the United States faces engagements in other asymmetrical conflicts, it is important to learn what we can from what sometimes goes right so that in future engagements, we can optimize our progress and minimize bloodshed. I hope this work has contributed to that end. May the next generation of Green Berets be the smartest and best-prepared unconventional warriors the world has ever seen, so that the citizens of this nation may retain their liberties and our oppressed allies of the future may attain theirs.

"De Oppresso Liber"

Acknowledgments

My first and deepest thanks go to my family for their unwavering support of my military service and this project. My parents, Larry and Christine Fry, and siblings, Rich, Tom, and Cindy, were literally there from the beginning and were incredible influences on who I became as a man. Growing up in a house where faith, patriotism, and core values were taught is something I am grateful for and try to replicate in my own home. My wife, Becky, is a beautiful, caring woman who has more confidence in me than I deserve. I love her more than she knows. The joys of my life—Tanner, Owen, Bailey, Reagan, and Russell—inspire me to be the best I can be and remind me every day why this nation and our ideals are worth defending.

Tad Tuleja deserves more than just having his name on the cover for his contribution to this project. His efforts to take my journal, recollections, and interviews of ODA 936 members and to organize them in a way that is readable have been impressive. His ability to convert "milspeak" into civilian script contributed greatly to this work. He is a true professional who has become a great friend.

Tad and I are both grateful to Eric A. Eliason, Tad's academic colleague and our chaplain, for serving as the initial liaison for this project. In addition, Paul Whitlatch and Mauro DiPreta at Hachette, and our agent Jim Hornfischer deserve significant thanks for turning the idea into reality. Working with professionals in this arena made what felt like a daunting task an enjoyable experience. Their belief in the story and its potential impact is very much appreciated.

Mentors. I had the ability to observe some great leadership in my time in the military that forged what type of leader I became when the guidon was passed to my hands. Thanks especially to the cadre at BYU ROTC; those officers in the 504th Parachute Infantry Regiment (Ulrich, Pratt, McBride, Snukis, and Ellerbe, to name a few) that helped forge me into an infantry leader; the cadre of JFK Special Warfare Center; and the officers of 1/19th SFG (Hewitt, Stewart, Custer, Wood) who taught me the nuances of an unconventional warrior. Your influence and mentorship have not been forgotten.

The U.S. Army. The U.S. military has done more to liberate peoples on this globe than any institution of man that has ever existed in the history of the world. This in and of itself deserves acknowledgment. Although at times this work points out the bureaucratic disconnect between senior army leadership and ground commanders, the fact that Camp Blessing happened underscores the agility (or potential agility) of this organization to adapt to what makes sense in solving the "unsolvable." To establish an "A" Camp with a Special Forces team commanding Afghan and American conventional forces, responsible for a huge swath of Afghan land and people, truly represents thinking out of the box. I appreciate their willingness to innovate and the confidence senior leadership had in me and ODA 936 to attempt such an endeavor.

Camp Blessing Marines and 10th Mountain Infantry. Having led infantry before joining Special Forces, I have an appreciation for the hard and thankless work that grunts put in for their country. The infantry and Marines, their lieutenants, NCOs, and men deserve great credit for what they contributed to make Camp Blessing happen. Their willingness to act as examples to the ASF soldiers we trained and led, and to subordinate and adapt their vision of winning in Afghanistan to that of the Special Forces they were assigned to, was a credit to their commands, the Army, and the Corps. I hope that this work assists in forging partnerships like this in the future.

ODA 936. I cannot say thanks enough to the men of ODA 936—Randy Derr, Scott Jennings, Dave Moon, Ian Waters, Jimi Rymut, Jason Mackay, Mike Montoya, Ben Guile, and Roger Wilcox—for their loyalty, commitment, friendship, and desire to magnify and deliver on the mission we were given. They proved that when a small group of men fully commit themselves to a righteous and worthy endeavor, incredible things can happen. I include in this group our Air Force attachment Courtney Hinson, Chaplain Eliason, our PSYOP attachments Chris Aguirre and Justin Jones, and Civil Affairs attachments Brent Watson and James Trusty. Sadly, James Trusty is no longer with us, but his contributions and dedication have hopefully been covered in a way that grants him the respect he deserves. Working with these men of such personal character and professional caliber was inspiring and fulfilling. Their contributions to this work and support in writing this memoir from the commander's perspective are greatly appreciated.

Finally, I must honor the memory of the Americans and Afghan soldiers who fell in the Pech. It was their dedication and willingness to sacrifice for a cause they believed in that really inspired this book. The Americans served and gave all for a nation that they love; the Afghans served and gave all for the hope of a nation. Their sacrifices deserve to be remembered, respected, and learned from.

Notes

Chapter 1. Into the Gray

1. For a vivid insider's picture of Special Forces training, see Tony Schwalm, *The Guerrilla Factory: The Making of Special Forces Officers, the Green Berets.* New York: Simon & Schuster, 2012.

Chapter 2. The Fort

1. We heard this story from an Afghan soldier who, he claimed, had been one of the victorious mujahideen.
2. Excellent accounts of two of these early-arriving ODAs appear in Doug Stanton, *Horse Soldiers.* New York: Scribner, 2010; and Eric Blehm, *The Only Thing Worth Dying For.* New York: Harper, 2010.
3. Sebastian Junger, *War.* New York: Twelve, 2011: 75.

Chapter 3. A War of All Against All

1. A good brief history of Afghanistan, on which we've drawn for this section, is John C. Griffiths, *Afghanistan: Land of Conflict and Beauty.* London: Andre Deutsch, 2009. For the Taliban period, see Ahmed Rashid, *Taliban: Militant Islam, Oil, and Fundamentalism in Central Asia.* New Haven, CT: Yale University Press, 2001. For the American experience since 9/11, see Carlotta Gall, *The Wrong Enemy: America in Afghanistan, 2001–2014.* Boston: Houghton Mifflin Harcourt, 2014.
2. Griffiths, 182.
3. CIA support for the mujahideen is covered colorfully in George Crile, *Charlie Wilson's War.* New York: Grove, 2003.
4. See "The Kerala Massacre," *Christian Science Monitor*, February 4, 1980. Available online at http://www.csmonitor.com/1980/0204/020416.html.

5. Carlotta Gall argues that in focusing on the Taliban rather than its chief supporter, Pakistan, America was fighting "the wrong enemy."
6. Rashid, 134.
7. Dexter Filkins, *The Forever War.* New York: Knopf, 2008: 30.

Chapter 4. Hunter's Moon

1. Jake Tapper, *The Outpost: An Untold Story of American Valor.* New York: Little, Brown, 2012.

Chapter 5. A Baited Ambush

1. This is one of the standing orders that Maj. Robert Rogers, founder of today's Army Rangers, issued to his guerrilla troops in 1759. The orders, which still appear in today's Ranger Handbook, begin with the blunt injunction "Don't forget nothing."
2. See, for example, Rashid, 5. A particularly grisly example occurred on January 19, 1999, when Taliban "judges" hung the severed limbs of six robbers from trees in downtown Kabul. Ibid., 232.
3. Liddell Hart was an influential British war theorist. The mosquito analogy appeared in his *Strategy: The Indirect Approach.* London: Faber and Faber, 1954.

Chapter 6. Hammer and Anvil

1. This mantra is invoked frequently in Walter M. Herd, *Unconventional Warrior: Memoir of a Special Operations Commander in Afghanistan.* Jefferson, NC: McFarland, 2013.

Chapter 7. Odysseus Redux

1. Fuller's famous eight principles were those of the objective, the offensive, security, concentration, economy of force, movement, surprise, and cooperation. See Col. J. F. C. Fuller, *The Reformation of War.* London: Hutchinson, 1923: 28ff.
2. For an American perspective on "jinglefication," see Eric A. Eliason, "'Folk Folkloristics': Reflections on American Soldiers' Responses to

Afghan Traditional Culture," in *Warrior Ways: Explorations in Modern Military Folklore*, ed. Eric A. Eliason and Tad Tuleja. Logan, UT: Utah State University Press, 2012.

3. The company commander is quoted in Greg Heath, "10th Mtn. Div. Shows Its Mettle in Operation Mountain Resolve," posted Nov. 17, 2003, on website Defend America: U.S. Department of Defense News About the War on Terror.

Chapter 8. The Experiment

1. *Special Forces "A" Camp Manual.* Boulder, CO: Paladin Press, 1994: 4. The volume has no byline, but the Preface credits its contents to Special Forces veterans Pappy Jones, Ron Girelli, and Scott Snyder.

2. A good overview of the Vietnam "A" Camps is Gordon Rottman, *Special Forces Camps in Vietnam 1961–70*. Oxford and New York: Osprey, 2005. See also John A. Nagl, *Learning to Eat Soup with a Knife: Counterinsurgency Lessons from Malaya and Vietnam*. Westport, CT: Praeger, 2002.

3. Several articles on the CIDG program and a current equivalent, Village Stability Operations, can be found in the archives of *Small Wars Journal*, available online at http://www.smallwarsjournal.com.

Chapter 9. The Neighborhood

1. The Hesco company produces defensive containers that are widely used by the U.S. and other militaries. The ones we used resembled large, collapsible chicken-wire baskets; when filled with rocks and positioned side by side, they formed sturdy and inexpensive protective barriers.

2. Robin Moore, *The Green Berets*. New York: Crown, 1965. In preparation for writing the book, Moore had undergone SF training himself. In 1966, he helped Staff Sgt. Barry Sadler write his Top 40 hit "Ballad of the Green Berets," which is the theme song of the John Wayne movie.

3. The stripling warriors appear in the Book of Mormon, Alma 53:10–22.

Chapter 10. A Captain's First Duty

1. Bing West, *The Wrong War: Grit, Strategy, and the Way Out of Afghanistan*. New York: Random House, 2011: 6.

2. Omar N. Bradley, *A Soldier's Story*. New York: Henry Holt, 1951: 310.
3. The quote is Barker's invention, but Rivers was a real person, famous for treating shell-shocked soldiers during World War I. See *Regeneration*. New York: Viking, 1991.

Chapter 11. Commander's Intent

1. Eugene Burdick and William Lederer, *The Ugly American*. New York, Norton: 1958. The book was filmed in 1963, with Marlon Brando in the starring role.

Chapter 12. Culture Clashes

1. David Kilcullen, *Counterinsurgency*. New York: Oxford University Press, 2010: 36.
2. Marine sergeant Dakota Meyer, a Medal of Honor winner, noted this attitude among Afghans he trained in 2009. In his memoir he writes, "When an Afghan soldier went home without permission—what I would call deserting the unit—the others weren't upset. We were advising an army with no established standards of group behavior." Dakota Meyer and Bing West. *Into the Fire*. New York: Random House, 2012: 55.

Chapter 14. The Decider

1. *Osama*, directed by Siddiq Barmak, was released in 2003. It is available, subtitled in English, on an MGM Home Entertainment DVD. Thanks to Mickey Weems for bringing the beard-touching scene to our attention.
2. See S. Fida Yunas, *Character Traits: Customs/Traditions/Practices of the Pashtuns*. Hayatabad, Pakistan: privately printed, 2011: 56–58.
3. Cited in Rashid, *Taliban*, 118. We draw in this section on the excellent overview of the Taliban drug economy that Rashid provides in Chapter 9, "High on Heroin," 117–127.

Chapter 18. Fireworks

1. The Human Rights Watch report "Enduring Freedom," dated March 7, 2004, is available at http://www.hrw.org/reports/2004/03/07/enduring-freedom-0.

2. From the Joint Chiefs of Staff publication *Joint Targeting* (JP3-60), Appendix A: Legal Considerations in Targeting. January 2013: A2.

Chapter 19. A Tale of Two Mullahs

1. Eric A. Eliason and Ron Fry, "I Destroy My Enemies by Making Them My Friends: A Battle-Proven Cost-Effective Model for Winning the Symbolic War for Mosques." Unpublished paper.
2. Eric describes his course of instruction in "Training Afghan and Iraqi Military Chaplaincies: A Battle-Proven Model from an Experiment in Afghan Indigenous Chaplain Training." *Small Wars Journal*, May 2008. http://smallwarsjournal.com/mag/docs-temp/64-eliason.pdf.

Chapter 21. High Noon

1. Luttrell describes his ordeal in the memoir *Lone Survivor: The Eyewitness Account of Operation Redwing and the Lost Heroes of SEAL Team 10*, written with Patrick Robinson. New York: Little, Brown, 2007.

Chapter 22. The Waiting Game

1. Michael Ware, "Where's Bin Laden?: U.S. Special Forces in Afghanistan Are Going Native in Their Hunt for Al-Qaeda's No. 1." *Time*, March 29, 2004: 30–31.
2. Mark Mazzetti, "Speak Softly, Carry a Big Gun: Into the Hinterland with the Special Forces." *U.S. News & World Report*, May 10, 2004: 40–42.

Chapter 23. The Unforgivable

1. The transcript of Lara Logan's *60 Minutes II* report is available online at http://www.groups.sfahq.com/19th/afghanistan.htm.

Afterword. Lessons Learned

1. David Kilcullen, *The Accidental Guerrilla: Fighting Small Wars in the Midst of a Big One*. New York: Oxford University Press, 2009.

Glossary

ahsalam alaikum: "Peace be upon you." The standard Afghan greeting.

aimal: friend.

Al Qaeda: "The Base." Jihadist group founded by Osama bin Laden.

Allahu akbar: "God is great." A common jihadi battle cry, although Muslims also use it reverently and nonaggressively.

badal: revenge. Literally "exchange," that is, the response which must be exchanged for an insult or attack.

burka: female full body covering required by Taliban law.

chai: tea, the universal Afghan beverage, served as a sign of friendship.

commandon: commander. Often abbreviated to "don."

hafiz: term of respect for someone who has memorized the Koran.

hajji: one who has completed the haj, a pilgrimage to Mecca required of devout Muslims. In Western slang, a disparaging term for a Middle Eastern man.

Insh'Allah: "God willing." An acknowledgment of submission to the divine.

jamas: loose-fitting men's trousers.

jihad: struggle. The good Muslim's struggle for spiritual perfection (the greater jihad) or war against nonbelievers (the lesser jihad).

jihadi: one who wages jihad.

jirga: council of tribal elders.

kafir: nonbeliever, infidel.

loya jirga: grand council. A national assembly held to make major decisions.

madrassa: religious school devoted to training boys in the ways of Islam.

mujahideen: armed jihadis, specifically those who fought against the Soviet invasion of the 1980s. The singular is mujahid.

mullah: religious leader.

naan: unleavened Afghan bread.

nanawatay: forgiveness, asylum, protection, submission.

pakol: woolen cap worn by Afghan males.

Pashto: principal language of eastern Afghanistan.

Pashtunwali: tribal code of the Pashtun region.

shura: council of elders, responsible for much village governance.

Taliban: "The Students." An insurgent group founded by Mullah Mohammed Omar; the singular is talib.

tashakur: thank you.

tor: raw opium; literally "black."

Wahabi: fundamentalist Islamic movement based in Saudi Arabia.

zakat: tax that good Muslims pay for the support of the poor.

Index